Praise for
Keepers of the Earth

"Keepers of the Earth is a fascinating way to learn about our environment. The combination of Native American stories and related activities will spark children's imaginations and help them to explore their environment."
    —Augusto Medina, Ph.D., education specialist, World Wildlife Fund

"This wonderful balance of scientific and indigenous people's outlooks empowers children to touch the continuum of nature pulsating within and around them. The reconnection makes possible their creation of vital new stories to cope with today's misguided beliefs about the natural world."
    —Dr. Michael J. Cohen, director, National Audubon Society Expedition Institute; author, *How Nature Works: Regenerating Kinship with Planet Earth*

"By combining the Native American flair for storytelling with modern western understandings of science and education, Caduto and Bruchac reacquaint youngsters with the natural world and our relationships with it. *Keepers of the Earth* is a unique approach to guiding our youth to a sustainable future. School, club and camp youth leaders will find this book a treasure."
    —Charles E. Roth, director of Educational Services, Massachusetts Audubon Society

"Keepers of the Earth should be in every library. Social studies, science, environmental responsibility can be greatly enriched by using this book. The 25 legends from 20 different cultures selected by Abenaki Joseph Bruchac, and interpreted by easily understood scientific information and hands-on activities by Michael Caduto makes this a gold mine for teaching important concepts."
    —Dr. Helen Ross Russell, author of *Ten Minute Field Trips: Using the Schoolground to Teach*

KEEPERS OF THE EARTH

BIRDFOOT'S GRAMPA

The old man
must have stopped our car
two dozen times to climb out
and gather into his hands
the small toads blinded
by our lights and leaping,
live drops of rain.

The rain was falling,
a mist about his white hair
and I kept saying
you can't save them all,
accept it, get back in
we've got places to go.

But, leathery hands full
of wet brown life,
knee deep in the summer
roadside grass,
he just smiled and said
they have places to go to
too.

—Joseph Bruchac
Entering Onondaga

KEEPERS OF THE EARTH

Native American Stories and Environmental Activities for Children

Michael J. Caduto and Joseph Bruchac

Foreword by N. Scott Momaday

Illustrations by John Kahionhes Fadden and Carol Wood

FULCRUM, INC.
GOLDEN, COLORADO

Library of Congress Cataloging-in-Publication Data

Caduto, Michael J.
        Keepers of the Earth.

        Includes index.
        1. Indians of North America—Legends.
        2. Indians of North America—Religion and mythology—Juvenile literature.
        3. Creative activities and seat work.
                [1. Indians of North America—Legends. 2. Indians of North America—Religion and mythology.
                3. Nature craft]
        I. Bruchac, Joseph, 1942–   .   II. Fadden, John Kahionhes.   III. Wood, Carol.   IV. Title

E98.F6C12   1988   398.2'08997   88-3620
ISBN 1-55591-027-0

           9 0

Printed in the United States

Fulcrum, Inc.
Golden, Colorado

Permissions

Permission to reprint the following is gratefully acknowledged:

The poem "Birdfoot's Grampa" on page vi by Joseph Bruchac is from Joseph Bruchac's *Entering Onondaga* (1978) published by Cold Mountain Press and reprinted here with permission of the author.

The map on pages xx–xxi, showing the culture regions of the Native American groups discussed in this book and in the teacher's guide, is adapted from *Indians of North America*, courtesy National Geographic Society. Cartography by Stacy Morin, Country Roads, Inc., Orrington, Maine. © 1989 Michael J. Caduto.

The illustration on page 5 by Carol Wood is used here with permission of Michael J. Caduto (© 1985).

The photographs on pages 10, 14, 35, 50, 86, 132 and 140 taken by Peter Hope for the Vermont Institute of Natural Science are reprinted with their permission.

The list of problem-solving skills on page 11 was adapted from William B. Stapp's and Dorothy A. Cox's *Environmental Education Activities Manual* (1979) and is reprinted with permission of the authors.

The quote describing a life ethic on page 11 from Michael J. Caduto's *A Guide on Environmental Values Education* (1985) is reprinted with permission of the United Nations Educational, Scientific, and Cultural Organization (UNESCO).

The photographs on pages 11, 85 and 105 by Michael J. Caduto are reprinted with his permission.

The photographs on pages 13, 22, 98 and 152 taken by Cecil B. Hoisington for the Vermont Institute of Natural Science are reprinted with their permission.

The story on page 21 is from Joseph Bruchac's *The Wind Eagle and Other Abenaki Stories* (1985) and is reprinted with permission of the author and Bowman Books.

The illustration on page 60 was adapted from "Geosynclines, Mountains, and Continent Building," by R.S. Dietz, *Scientific American*, 1972 (March), vol. 226, no. 3, pp. 30-38, and is reprinted with permission of Scientific American, Inc.

The illustrations on pages 104, 114 and 131 were adapted from Anthony Smith's *The Seasons* (1970) and are reprinted here with permission of Weidenfeld and Nicolson Publishing Company, Ltd., London.

The photograph on page 112 is reprinted with the permission of the National Aeronautics and Space Administration (NASA).

The photograph on page 121 is used with permission of Mount Wilson and Las Campanas Observatories, Carnegie Institution of Washington.

The photographs on pages 139 and 183 by Ann Day Heinzerling are reprinted with her permission.

The photograph on page 140 by Peter Stettenheim is reprinted with his permission.

The paraphrased version of the information describing tree parts and their functions on page 146 from the "Trees are Terrific" issue of *Ranger Rick's NatureScope*, 1985, vol. 2, no.1, pp. 6-7, is reprinted with permission of the National Wildlife Federation.

The photograph on page 147 by Lewis E. Carpenter is reprinted with his permission, courtesy of the Audubon Society of Rhode Island.

The illustration on page 153 was adapted from Friedrich G. Barth's *Insects and Flowers: The Biology of a Partnership* (1985) and is reprinted with permission of both Princeton University Press and Allen & Unwin, Ltd., London (British Commonwealth).

The photograph on page 159 by Don Blades is reprinted with his permission, courtesy the Vermont Institute of Natural Science.

Excerpts from "Nature in Native American Myths: A Program in Environmental Ethics" on pages 169–170 by Michael J. Caduto are reprinted with permission of the Vermont Institute of Natural Science. This article also appeared in *Nature Study*, 1984 (September), vol. 38, no. 1, pp. 3-5, and is reprinted here with permission of the American Nature Study Society.

The illustration on page 170 by Michael J. Caduto is reprinted here with his permission.

The photograph on page 174 is reprinted with permission of the Vermont Institute of Natural Science.

The photograph on page 175 by Michael Warren is reprinted with his permission.

The table of birdhouse specifications and the illustrations of nesting boxes on page 176 were adapted from Verne E. Davison's *Attracting Birds: From the Great Plains to the Atlantic* (© 1966 by Verne E. Davison) and is reprinted with permission of Harper & Row Publishers, Inc.

The illustration on page 191 by Joseph Bruchac is reprinted here with his permission.

The story illustrations by John Kahionhes Fadden throughout this book are reprinted with his permission.

The stories by Joseph Bruchac throughout this book are reprinted with his permission.

The illustrations by Carol Wood that accompany the activities throughout this book are reprinted with her permission.

The activities by Michael J. Caduto throughout this book are reprinted with his permission.

For the children of yesterday,
today
and tomorrow.

✧ Contents ✧

EARTH

WIND AND WEATHER

WATER

SKY

LIFE, DEATH, SPIRIT

UNITY OF EARTH

⬦ Foreword ⬦

"Who are you?" someone asks.

"I am the story of myself," comes the answer.

It is true that man invests himself in story. And it is true, as someone has said, that God made man because He loves stories.

In his traditional world the Native American lives in the presence of stories. The storyteller is one whose spirit is indispensable to the people. He is magician, artist and creator. And, above all, he is a holy man. His is a sacred business.

How are we to come to an understanding of the storyteller and his art? It will be useful, perhaps, to consider the following tenets.

Stories are made of words and of such implications as the storyteller places upon words. The story lies at the center of language, and language is composed of words. Words, then, are the primary tools of the storyteller. It is to his purpose to use words well.

There are many kinds of stories. The basic story is one which centers upon an event, and the words proceed toward the formulation of meaning. This is the narrative process. The storyteller sets words in procession; his object is most often the establishment of meaning.

In general, stories are true to human experience. Indeed, the truth of human experience is their principal information. This is to say that stories tend to support and confirm our perceptions of the world and of the creatures within it. Even the most fantastic story is rooted in our common experience; otherwise it would have no meaning for us. Strictly speaking, it would not be a story.

Stories are formed. The formation of the story is particular and perceptible. The storyteller proceeds according to a plan, a design, a sense of proportion and order. Stories are begun, they proceed and they come to an end.

Stories are predicated upon belief. Belief is more essential to the story than is understanding.

The storyteller creates his listener. In effect the storyteller says to his listener, "In my story I determine you; for a moment—the duration of the story—your reason for being is the story itself; for the sake of the story, you are. In my story I create a state of being in which you are immediately involved."

The primary object of the story is the realization of wonder and delight.

For nearly twenty years I have taught the subject of Native American oral tradition, and I have been a student of that subject for a longer time than that. I have found these several tenets especially relevant to the whole matter of storytelling. The stories in the present collection center upon one of the most important of all considerations in human experience: the relationship between man and nature. In the Native American world this relationship is so crucial as to be definitive of the way in which man formulates his own best idea of himself. In the presence of these stories we have an affirmation of the human spirit. It is a just and wondrous celebration.

—N. Scott Momaday

⋄ Acknowledgments ⋄

We are grateful to those people who have made this book possible: Betsy Armstrong, Bob Baron, Chris Bierwirth, Pat Frederick, Darby Junkin and the rest of the staff at Fulcrum, Inc. who patiently and creatively brought the book from draft to finished copy; the many people whose beautiful photographs appear on these pages; the illustrators John Kahionhes Fadden and Carol Wood, whose illustrations can be distinguished by Kahionhes' signature; and the people who reviewed the overall manuscript: Odds Bodkin, Talesman, The Wisdom Tree, Inc., Henniker, New Hampshire; Dr. Clifford Knapp, Northern Illinois University; and Charles E. Roth, Director, Office of Education and Interpretation, Massachusetts Audubon Society.

The following people checked the manuscript for accuracy in their respective areas of expertise: Mark Breen, Meteorologist, Fairbanks Museum and Planetarium, St. Johnsbury, Vermont; Dr. James H. Brown, Jr. and Dr. Thomas P. Husband, Department of Natural Resources Science, University of Rhode Island; Eliot Coleman, Farm Manager and Teacher, The Mountain School, Vershire Center, Vermont; Alan C. Graham, Entomologist; Dr. Beatrice Medicine, Director, The Native Centre, University of Calgary, Alberta, Canada; Dr. W. S. Penhallow, Physics Department, University of Rhode Island; Dr. Robert Reynolds, Department of Geology, Dartmouth College; and Dr. Prentice Stout, Marine Education Specialist, University of Rhode Island.

These parents, teachers, naturalists, environmental educators and youth leaders donated large amounts of their time as they field-tested and evaluated the activities newly designed for this book: Janet Altobell; Linda Coolidge; Kathy Fitzgerald; Cris Fleming, Education Program Director, Audubon Naturalist Society of the Central Atlantic States, Inc.; Sam Francis; Diane Girard; Joan Holzwarth; Lori Jean Kinsey; Roger F. Klinger, Coordinator of Natural History, Historic Saint Mary's City, Maryland; Kevin Kopp; Lynn Leighton; Elaine Levenson; Betsy Rybeck Lynd; Linda M. Orlando; Peggy Pickett; Mary Margaret Powden; Emily Preston, Massachusetts Audubon Society; Vicky Price; Dawn E. Rashid; Donna Rogler; Theresa Symancyk; Beverly Tsonos; Meredith Wade; Kathryn Whitehorne; Millie Wintz; Andrew and Sandra Wood; and Mike Zetteck.

Thank you to the following people and organizations for the help, inspiration and friendship they have given as a foundation for the book: Carolyn Cyr, Dewasentah, Swift Eagle, Paul Feeney, E. Barrie Kavasch, Steve Matthews, Mdawelasis, John Moody, Dr. William B. Stapp, Alan Tate, Tehanetorens, Suzanne Weinmann, the friends and families of the authors and the staff of the Vermont Institute of Natural Science[1] for generously providing many of the photographs and assistance with bibliographies.

Finally, our gratitude to the native people of North America for their generosity and cultural richness, which is revealed through the gift of their stories. Thanks to the stories themselves, and the Earth, our Mother, from whom we and all our stories come, and to the parents, teachers and youth leaders of all kinds who will bring these stories and experiences to life for the children to whom this book is dedicated. Oleohneh.

Notes
1. Vermont Institute of Natural Science, Church Hill Road, Woodstock, Vermont 05091

ARCTIC
OCEAN

BERING
SEA

NORTH
ALASKAN
INUIT (ESKIMO)

BERING
STRAIT
INUIT
(ESKIMO)
KOTZEBUE
INUIT (ESK.)
NORTHERN
INTERIOR
INUIT (ESK.)

Koyukon

Ingalik

Kutchin

MACKENZIE
INUIT (ESKIMO)

COPPER
INUIT
(ESKIMO)

CENTRA

Tanaina
Tanana
Han
Chugach
Ahtna

Hare
Yellowknife

Tutchone

S
U
B
A

Dogrib

CARIBO
(ES

Kaska
Slavey

Chipewyan

Tahltan

Sekani

Beaver

Western Woods
Cree

SIMSHIAN

Carrier

Sarcee

Chilcotin

Plains Cree

Bella
Bella
Bella
Coola

HAIDA

KWAKIUTL

COLVILLE

SIKSIKA
(BLACKFOOT)

KALISPEL

Gros
Ventre
(Atsina)
Assiniboin
(Stoney)

LUMMI

KLICKITAT

Flathead
(Salish)

MULTNOMAH
NEZ
PERCE

CROW
(ABSAROKE)

Mandan
LAKOTA (SIOUX)

Klamath
Modoc

Shoshone-
Bannock

NORTHERN
CHEYENNE

DAKOTA (S

YUROK

Northern
Paiute
(Paviotso)

Wind
River
Shoshone

Ponca

YANA

Gosiute

O

PAWNEE

GREAT
BASIN

Ute

Arapaho

Ka

YOKUTS

Panamint Paiute

SOUTHERN CHEYE

Canyon
de Chelly
HAVASUPAI

WALAPAI

HOPI
DINE
(NAVAJO)

JICARILLA
APACHE

KIOWA

ZUNI PUEBLO
IPAI

YAVAPAI

WESTERN
APACHE

APACHE

KIOWA
APACH

COMANCHE

PAPAGO
UPPER PIMA

CHIRICAHUA
APACHE

MESCALERO
APACHE

Wich

SOUTHWEST

Lipan

PACIFIC
OCEAN

PACIFIC NORTHWEST WEST COAST

PLATEAU

TLINGIT

NIS
QUALLY

SCALE

0   100   200   400 STATUTE
                          MILES

Cultural areas and tribal locations of Native North Americans. This map shows tribal locations as they appeared around 1600, except for the Seminole Indians in the southeast and the Tuscaroras in the northeast. The Seminoles formed from a group which withdrew from the Muskogee (Creek) Indians and joined with several other groups on the Georgia/Florida border to form the

BAFFIN
BAY

Iglulik

C   T   I   C

(ESKIMO)
Iglulingmiut

BAFFINLAND
INUIT (ESKIMO)

DAVIS STRAIT

miut

SATLIRMIUT
(SOUTHAMPTON INUIT)
(ESKIMO)

LABRADOR
SEA

HUDSON

BAY

LABRADOR INUIT
(ESKIMO)

Montagnais

*West
Main
Cree*

Naskapi

*East
Cree*

C   T   I

GULF OF
ST. LAWRENCE

MICMAC

ANISHINABE
JIBWAY or CHIPPEWA)

Algonquin

MALISEET
PASSAMAQUODDY

Nipissing

HAUDENAUSAUNEE
(IROQUOIS)

ABENAKI
PENOBSCOT   WABANAKI PEOPLES

ASTERN

Menominee

*Huron
(Wyandot)*

MOHAWK   PENNACOOK

ONEIDA

ONONDAGA   *Massachuset*

Mississquoi
Nipmuck

Mahican

CAYUGA   WAMPANOAG
SENECA
TUSCARORA   *Narragansett*
Mohegan, Pequot

ATLANTIC

OCEAN

ESQUAKIE
Winnebago   *Potawatomi*
Sauk   *Neutral*
Fox   Erie
Kickapoo   *Munsee*

*Delaware (Lenni
Lenape)*

WOOD-
Miami

Shawnee

Illinois

LAND

Nanticoke

Powhatan

Susquehanna

CHEROKEE   TUSCARORA

East Coast Algonquians

apaw CHICKASAW   *Catawba*

MUSKOGEE (CREEK)

SOUTHEAST

CHOCTAW

Natchez

LF OF MEXICO   SEMINOLE

⟶ ◁▢▷ **NATIVE** ◁▢▷ ⟵

NORTH AMERICA

⟶ ◁▢▷ ⟵

Seminoles, a name which has been used since about 1775. In the eastern woodlands the Haudenausaunee (Iroquois) consist of six nations, the Mohawk, Oneida, Onondaga, Cayuga, Seneca and Tuscarora. The Tuscaroras were admitted to the Iroquois League in 1722 after many refugees from the Tuscarora Wars (1711–1713) in the southeast fled northward. The Wabanaki Peoples include the MicMac, Maliseet, Passamaquoddy, Abenaki, Penobscot and Pennacook.

✤ Introduction ✤

If this book were an animal, the stories would be its skeleton and the related activities would be the flesh and sinew on those bones. And you—parent, teacher, naturalist or storyteller—provide the skin, fur and movement, the touches of imagination, magic and mystery that bring the stories and lessons to life. This is a book about living, learning and caring: a collection of carefully chosen North American Indian stories and hands-on activities that promote understanding and appreciation of, empathy for, and responsible action toward the Earth,[1] including its people. These are valuable tools for those who want to inspire children and help them to feel a part of their surroundings. When the stories and activities in this book and its companion teacher's guide are followed carefully as children progress from kindergarten through the primary grades, roughly ages five through twelve years, they provide a complete program of study in the important concepts and topics of ecology and natural history.

Tell children a story and they listen with their whole beings. Lead children to touch and understand a grasshopper, a rock, a flower, a ray of sunlight and you begin to establish connections between children and their surroundings. Have them look at a tree—feel it, smell it, taste its sap, study its many parts and how they work. Help them to understand how it is part of a forest community of plants, animals, rocks, soil and water. Visit places where people have affected the forest to help children appreciate their stewardship role in the world; how all things are intertwined. Keep the children at the center of their learning encounters. Build on these experiences with activities that help them to care for, and take care of, the Earth and other people—to develop a conservation ethic. Dine (Navajo) tradition tells us that this Earth is destined to be destroyed unless people live in the right way.

As the stories unfold and you help the children to bring the activities to life, a holistic, interdisciplinary approach to teaching about the Earth and Native American cultures begins. With their close ties to the land, American Indian cultures are a vital link between human society and nature. The story characters are voices through which the wisdom of American Indians speaks in today's language, fostering listening and reading skills and enhancing understanding of how the native people live close to the land. Each story is a natural teaching tool which becomes a springboard as you dive into the activities designed to provoke curiosity among children and which facilitate discovery of their environments and

the influence they have on those surroundings. These activities are pedagogically sound and extensively field-tested. They involve the students in creative arts, theater, reading, writing, science, social studies, mathematics, sensory awareness and more. The activities engage a child's whole self: emotions, senses, thoughts and actions. They emphasize creative thinking and synthesis of knowledge and experiences. Because of the active and involving nature of the experiences found in this book, children who have special needs physically, mentally and emotionally respond well with proper care and skilled instruction.

These stories and activities have been enjoyed by families and in camp settings, nature centers, environmental education programs, public and private schools, library story hours, and in both rural and urban settings. Churches and other spiritual groups have found American Indian traditions to be an inspiration for developing environmental stewardship and deeper ties with the Earth as part of creation. While the stories and activities arise from North America, with some adaptations for local conditions they are relevant and useful to people and places in other lands as well.

Because Indians see themselves as *part* of nature, and not apart from it, their stories use natural images to teach both about relationships between people, and between people and the Earth. To the Indians, what was done to a tree or rock was done to a brother or sister. This outlook has important implications throughout this book where it deals with environmental problems and solutions.

Native Americans emphasize a close relationship with nature versus control over the natural world. In many stories the lessons are taught both directly and through metaphors. A good example of this is the story, "The Coming of Corn" in Chapter 16. The relationship between the Boy and his Grandmother personifies the relationship between the planter and the crop.

Steps for Using This Book Effectively

The book is divided into two parts plus a separate teacher's guide. Part I offers thoughts and suggestions for facilitating the use of stories and activities. If you would like to further round out your background in certain areas before beginning Part II, the teacher's guide discusses the nature of Indian myths and the cultures from which these particular stories come. It also considers the important educational philosophies and approaches upon which this book is based.

Part II is the heart of the book. In this section we use stories as an introduction to the subjects explored in the activities. In some cases the activities follow directly from the story, while in others the story is a stepping-stone that leads into the activities in a more general way. Stories and activities are arranged under broad topical headings in the contents. The "Index of Activities Arranged by Subject" (page 202) describes the specific lessons taught by the activities and their locations throughout the book.

Each story is followed by a section that summarizes the story and a "Discussion" section that provides background information on the topics it introduces. These discussion sections in themselves are a unique collection of essays covering a broad range of topics in natural history. Relevant questions bridge the stories and activities. Chapters end with suggestions for extending the experience.

Since they grow out from the stories, the activities focus on one or more of the following four areas and are keyed in the text with the corresponding symbol(s):

 • sensory awareness of Earth

 • understanding of Earth

 • caring for Earth

 • caring for people

Additional symbols identify activities that occur

 • outdoors, or

• indoors (Many of these activities can also be done outdoors, although it is not necessary to do so.)

When an activity is marked with both the indoor *and* outdoor symbols, it means that parts of the activity are better conducted outdoors while other parts are better when conducted indoors.

Begin by sharing a story and illustrations with the children or by having them present the story. Lead a discussion using the background information and the "Questions" at the end of the story. Another approach is to conduct some or all of the activities before sharing the story, in order to give the children some prior background in that subject.

Each "Activity" begins with a title and a brief description of what the children will do during the activity. Broad "Goals" are also included. Conduct the activities that are at the appropriate "Age" as marked in the text. Activities are marked as being appropriate for

younger children (roughly ages 5 to 8 years) and older children (roughly ages 9 to 12 years). Some activities are appropriate for both age groups. Many of the activities can be adapted to work well with different ages.

A detailed "Procedure" is provided for each activity. "Materials" are listed at the end of the activity. Virtually all of the materials needed for the stories and activities can be found outdoors, in the learning center and at home: they are simple, common and inexpensive. Use the activities described under "Extending the Experience" at the end of each chapter to extend and reinforce the lessons of the stories and activities. Another valuable tool is the Glossary and Pronunciation Key to Native American Words and Names appearing in this book.

Explore, with the children, the Indian group from which the story comes. The map on pages xx–xxi shows the cultural areas and tribal locations of the Native American groups discussed in this book and in the teacher's guide. These specific cultures, and their larger cultural groupings, are described in detail in the teacher's guide.

We encourage you to be creative and to use this book as a complement to your family experiences or your educational program for elementary age children. The "Further Resources on North American Indians and Environmental Studies" in the teacher's guide provides lists of books for learning and teaching about North American Indians and the Earth, as well as guides to values education and to facilitating storytelling, puppet shows and interdisciplinary studies.

Author's Note

• The use of gender varies among individuals and cultures. In order to maintain the accuracy and spirit of word usage and meaning among the writings contributed to this book by other authors, we have included them in their unedited form. The balance of the text has been written so as to avoid any gender bias.

• Although, by convention, we use the terms "Native American" and "American Indian" interchangeably throughout this book, not all native North Americans are American Indians. The Inuit (Eskimo) peoples of the far north (see Chapter 11) comprise a culture that is distinct from the North American Indians who inhabit this continent.

Hunting as a Subject of Environmental Education

Chapters 20 and 21 address, among other subjects, the topic of hunting. We have included hunting for several reasons. First, hunting is, and has been, an integral part of the lives and cultures of Native North Americans. For the Indians hunting was, and in some cases still is, a matter of survival. For animals hunting is always a matter of survival.

The same kind of skills that enable hunters to stalk and capture their prey can help children to become more aware and sensitive in their relationship with the Earth, such as when they try to get close to an animal in the wild to observe it and learn about it.

Further, hunting needs to be taught about because it is a reality in our world and we believe that education should be inclusive and not gloss over controversial subjects. The description of the deer kill in "A Journey with the Abenakis" in Chapter 20 is quite graphic because we want the children to know what the animal goes through as well as the hunter's experience.

And last, we want to show in Chapter 21 that, since hunting is commonplace, there are ways it can be managed to assure that animal populations are being kept healthy.

Hunting is one part of the relationship between people and animals. Here we do not advocate or condemn hunting and we encourage users of this book to study the methods given in Chapter 2, pages 11–12, for approaching values and controversial issues in education.

Notes

1. As used here, *Earth* refers to all of our surroundings: plants, animals and the physical environment, which includes water, air, rocks and sky. Although, by convention, people are often referred to separately in the text, here they are considered to be a *part* of the Earth, as Native Americans believe them to be.

PART I

A GUIDE FOR USING AND ENJOYING THIS BOOK

"I shall now tell a story," said Great Stone. "Then tell it," said the boy.

CHAPTER 1

⋄ Of Science and Indian Myths ⋄

Long ago, there were no stories in the world. Life was not easy for the people, especially during the long winters when the wind blew hard and the snow piled high about the longhouse.

One winter day a boy went hunting. He was a good hunter and managed to shoot several partridge. As he made his way back home through the snow, he grew tired and rested near a great rock which was shaped almost like the head of a person. No sooner had he sat down than he heard a deep voice speak.

"I shall now tell a story," said the voice.

The boy jumped up and looked around. No one was to be seen.

"Who are you?" said the boy.

"I am Great Stone," said the rumbling voice which seemed to come from within the Earth. Then the boy realized it was the big standing rock which spoke. "I shall now tell a story."

"Then tell it," said the boy.

"First you must give me something," said the stone. So the boy took one of the partridge and placed it on the rock.

"Now tell your story, Grandfather," said the boy.

Then the great stone began to speak. It told a wonderful story of how the Earth was created. As the boy listened he did not feel the cold wind and the snow seemed to go away. When the stone had finished the boy stood up.

"Thank you, Grandfather," said the boy. "I shall go now and share this story with my family. I will come back tomorrow."

The boy hurried home to the longhouse. When he got there he told everyone something wonderful had happened. Everyone gathered around the fire and he told them the story he heard from the great stone. The story seemed to drive away the cold and the people were happy as they listened and they slept peacefully that night, dreaming good dreams. The next day, the boy went back again to the stone and gave it another bird which he had shot.

"I shall now tell a story," said the big stone and the boy listened.

It went on this way for a long time. Throughout the winter the boy came each day with a present of game. Then Great Stone told him a story of the old times. The boy heard the stories of talking animals and monsters, tales of what things were like when the Earth was new. They were good stories and they taught important lessons. The boy remembered each tale and retold it to the people who gathered at night around the fire to listen. One day, though, when the winter was ending and the spring about to come, the great stone did not speak when the boy placed his gift of wild game.

"Grandfather," said the boy, "Tell me a story."

Then the great stone spoke for the last time. "I have told you all of my stories," said Great Stone. "Now the stories are yours to keep for the people. You will pass these stories on to your children and other stories will be added to them as years pass. Where there are stories, there will be more stories. I have spoken. Naho."

Thus it was that stories came into this world. To this day, they are told by the people of the longhouse during the winter season to warm the people. Whenever a storyteller finishes a tale, the people always give thanks, just as the boy thanked the storytelling stone long ago.

This Seneca story begins a journey through the world of Native American beliefs. It is a landscape lit by the life-giving rays of the sun, threatened by the tremors of a volcano enraged because people do not treat the land with more respect. Rivers flow and ragged wings cause the wind to blow. Whales and seals are created beneath rolling ocean swells of frigid Arctic waters. A hump-backed flute player brings the seasons and plants seeds as a gift to the Earth and people. Life and death come to the Earth. The moon brings light to dark of night and a fisher takes its place among the stars as the Big Dipper. An impetuous young man is turned to bones by the spirit of White Buffalo Calf Woman, who brings the sacred pipe to remind the People that all things are connected as one.

Science takes us on another journey, a different way of seeing than through the eyes of American Indians. Through intellectual and systematic study, science reveals the natures of the Earth and humankind in intricate and intriguing detail. Slowly, through the centuries, a sense of order has emerged. Although the knowledge of science, in chronological age, is a child compared to the antiquity of American Indians, the wisdom from both has led us to some of the same lessons about the oneness of people and the environment.

At times, science and Indian beliefs have clashed, usually to the detriment of Indian life and ways. People's use of science brought a greater ability to control the physical environment and this has had a powerful impact on human societies. Students of science at first dismissed Indian spiritual beliefs as entertaining but archaic stories. An early encounter between William James, a noted scientist and philosopher of the nineteenth century, and an elderly woman is revealing.

James once traveled widely to speak on evolution and the origins of the solar system, among other important scientific subjects of the time. On one occasion, after listening patiently to James' summary of the views of the scientific community, an aging Indian woman approached him from the audience and shared the story of creation from her tradition, which ended with the Earth riding on the back of an enormous turtle. When she was finished, James was determined to convince her that it was a fallacy to believe the Earth rested forever on the labored shell of a turtle.

"Ma'am, I find your story very interesting, but one point is hard for me to reconcile," James said. "If the Earth is supported by the turtle, then what is it that holds the turtle up?"

"Why, another turtle Mr. James."

"But don't you see that there would be nothing to hold up the second turtle, or the one beneath it?" he asked.

To which she replied, "I'm sorry Mr. James, but it's turtles all the way down."

So it is with these enduring stories and the evolving knowledge of science. Everyone's view of the world is molded by experience: a mix of fantasy, feeling, fact and faith. Each new event and experience affects our ideas concerning the nature of life and our surroundings, shifting the way we see ourselves, other people and our environments.

Every shining pine needle, every sandy shore, every mist in the dark woods, every clearing and humming insect is holy in the memory and experience of my people. Teach your children what we have taught our children, that the Earth is our mother. The rivers are our brothers, they quench our thirst and feed our children. The air is precious to the red man, for all things share the same breath — the beast, the tree, the man, they all share the same breath. And what is man without the beasts? If all the beasts were gone, men would die from a great loneliness of spirit.

This we know. The Earth does not belong to man; man belongs to the Earth. Man did not weave the web of life, he is merely a strand in it. Whatever he does to the web, he does to himself. All things are connected like the blood which unites one family. All things are connected.

—Sealth (Chief Seattle)
Spoken as an admonition to all at the tribal assembly of 1854, prior to signing the Indian Treaties.

The science of *ecology*, the study of the interactions between living things and their environments, circles back to the ancient wisdom found in the rich oral traditions of American Indian stories. Time and again the stories have said that all of the living and nonliving parts of the Earth are *one* and that people are a part of that wholeness. Today, ecological science agrees.

Every one of us is ecologically significant. Our thoughts, feelings and physical sensations, which give us a sense of identity, are all based on our interactions with the Earth and other people. If our social, physical, environmental and spiritual interactions are seen as circles radiating out from each individual, they all intersect at the point that we call the *self*. And since these circles reach out to touch the people and the Earth around us, our own personal environment is part of all those things. Each affects the other.

Because of human intelligence and our ability to alter the Earth and reproduce in great numbers, we are unique among living things in being powerful determin-

ers of the global environment. Our living planet is a closed system with finite resources that are all we have to support life on Earth. In our hands rests the responsibility to preserve the life-sustaining power of the Earth—our home that gives us everything from drinking water to the ephemeral beauty of a dew-covered flower petal glistening quicksilver in the morning rays of sunlight. And the environment is of value in itself just because it exists; simply because it *is*.

The ecological lessons of science and North American Indian stories show us how to care for the Earth. Through their combined knowledge we can help children to discover their own roles in maintaining this fragile balance for themselves and all living things in the generations to come.

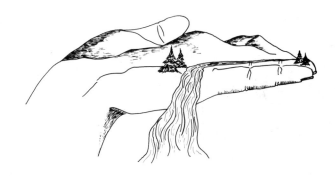

CHAPTER 2

Tips and Techniques for Bringing This Book to Life

Telling the Stories

Stories form a link between our imagination and our surroundings. They are a way of reaching deep into a child's inner world, to the places where dreams and fantasies are constantly sculpting an ever-growing world view. The emotional identification a child forms with a story character, such as Gluscabi in Chapters 3, 9 and 20, Loo-Wit the Fire-Keeper in Chapter 6 or Turtle in Chapter 19, leads that child to actually *become* that character, to experience the sounds, sights, smells, sensations and emotions that character lives through. Stories build a bridge between a child's life and the lessons the stories teach.

Each chapter in Part II of *Keepers of the Earth* begins with an Indian story that is the key to unlocking a child's imagination while evoking useful images and exciting interest in the subjects that are then explored in the activities. The natural curiosity with which children regard American Indians is a window to educational opportunities. Several chapters contain supplemental stories that introduce or enhance the lessons of the activities. Guided fantasies are also used to create firsthand learning experiences that would not otherwise be possible. Some examples are "Rock to Rock" (Chapter 8), 'Birth of a Raindrop' in "Rain Making" (Chapter 10) and "Winter is Coming" (Chapter 19). In all cases the supplemental stories and guided fantasies build upon the subjects introduced by the Indian stories that open each chapter.

While reading the fantasies, have the children close their eyes, relax and clear their minds to make them more receptive to the images conjured up. Use sounds such as music, a drumbeat or the sound effects of events in the fantasy to enhance your effectiveness. Don't be afraid to use different voices and be dramatic!

Although none of the Indian stories appears in the original native language in which it was first told, we have tried in our retellings to capture the motion and the imagery of the original tales and to make sure that the central message of each story is kept intact, for stories are powerful tools used for teaching and discipline in Native American cultures. If you decide to retell your own versions of these stories, to memorize them rather than read them from the book, or to develop them into puppet shows, plays or skits, we urge you to pay close attention to the way these stories work. They are, however, meant to be *told*, rather than read silently.

Among North American Indian cultures there were certain stories that were usually told at specific times of the year, especially the winter. Northeastern Indians told stories during the long cold season between the first and last frosts. Although you may not be able to restrict your use of these stories to this period of time, it is good to point out to children the traditional storytelling seasons. With this in mind, we'd like to suggest some ways to approach the oral use of these stories.

Seeing the Story

To begin with, you should read each story aloud to yourself several times before you try to read it to children or tell it from memory. Let the story become a part of you. This was the method of the old-time American Indian storytellers, who listened again and again to each tale, rehearsing the story alone before trying to share it with an audience. After a story has become part of you, you may find yourself "seeing" the story as you tell it. At that point you may wish to bring your telling to life with descriptions of those things you see as you tell the tales aloud. When the story is a part of you and you are sharing it effectively with the listeners—creating the "reality" of that story—the characters and events will live and move in their mind's eye. But be careful as you do this and do not try changing the endings or combining these stories together. When you "see" a story it is like seeing an animal after having only heard about it before. It comes alive for you. But one animal is different from another and so, too, is each story. Some stories may be wolves. Some may be turtles. But to combine the two does not work.

Once you "see" a story and feel comfortable with its telling, you may find it helpful to have a way of recalling the story at the proper time. The Iroquois storyteller or *Hage'ota* carried a bag full of items which acted as mnemonic devices—each item represented a story. The Hageota, or perhaps a child in the audience, would pull an item out of the bag, the item would be shown to the people and the story would begin. This process also transforms the storytelling into a shared experience by bringing the children into the act of choosing the stories to be told.

Making a storyteller's bag is an easy project. You and your children can gather things from the natural world or make things to add to the bag. Feathers, stones, small carvings, animal teeth, anything which can be jostled around in a bag without breaking can be part of your collection. Read the stories in this book carefully and then use your imagination.

The Setting of the Story

In American Indian culture, everyone was allowed to have their say and people listened with patience. People would sit in a circle during the time of storytelling because in a circle no person is at the head. All are "the same height." Remembering this may help you and it is good to remind your listeners—who are not just an audience but part of the story—of that.

Pay close attention to the setting in which you read or tell a story. If it is in a quiet place where people can sit comfortably in a circle—whether in chairs or on the floor, you are already one step ahead. But if other things are going on around you, if some people are seated outside the group or where they cannot hear well, your story will lose some of its power. We have often waited until we have brought a child into the circle before beginning a story. It is amazing how quiet and involved someone who was standing outside a group and acting uninterested or hostile can become when they are "brought in." Be sure that you are comfortable as you do your storytelling. Pay attention to how you feel as you speak from a standing position or while seated in a chair. There is no *one* right way for everyone. Some people do best while sitting in a chair or on the floor, others feel more assured while standing or even walking around. Find *your* way.

Speaking the Story

One of the greatest of the orators of the Iroquois was a man named Red Jacket. He credited his deep sonorous voice to his habit of standing next to the great falls at Niagara and speaking over their roar. While this may have been part of Red Jacket's secret, another part which has not been spoken of so often is that Red Jacket knew the right way to breathe when he spoke. In his youth he was one of the greatest runners among his people and no one can run great distances without knowing the secrets of deep and even breathing. Breathing is one of the most important things for a storyteller. Too many people try to speak while breathing from high in their chest. This tightens your chest and can strain your voice. Your breath—and your voice—should come from your diaphragm, that part of your body which is just below your ribs and above your stomach. Place the tips of your fingers there and breathe in. If your diaphragm does not move out, then your breathing is wrong. American Indian people see that area as the center of power for your body and it is certainly the source of power for oral presentations. Your voice will be stronger, project farther and sound better when it comes from the diaphragm.

When Red Jacket spoke above the roar of the great falls, he was also learning that resonance is a vital part of a good speaking voice. Try humming as an exercise to develop that natural resonance. One common method of voice training is to hum the vowel sounds, first with the letter "M" before them and then with the letter "B." Clarity is as important as resonance, so when you read or tell your stories, be sure not to let your voice trail away, especially on significant words. Remember that you are the *carrier* of the story. You must bring it to everyone in the room with you. Lift your chin up as you speak and look to the very back of the room. Imagine your voice as beginning in front of your mouth and reaching to the farthest wall. You do not have to shout to be heard.

Pace is also important in telling a story. Many people tend to either speak too fast or too slow. If the story has truly become a part of you, then you should be able to sense its pace and follow it in your reading or telling. But you may wish to check yourself by tape-recording a story as you read or retell it from memory. See if there are places where you speak too quickly, if there are words which are not well enunciated, if you have placed emphasis on the points in the story which should be emphasized.

Involving the Listeners

A good story cannot exist without a good listener. There are certain things which you, as a reader or teller, can do to help your listeners be more effective and more involved. We have already mentioned the setting in which the story is told, but there are other ways to bring the listeners into the tale. One device is the use of "response words." Tell the listeners that whenever you say "Ho?" they are to respond with "Hey!" That will let you know that they are still awake and listening. The "Ho?" and "Hey!" can also be used as pacing elements in the story or to make the listeners feel themselves entering the tale. For example:

"Then he started to climb . . ."

"Ho?"

"HEY!"
"He climbed higher and higher . . ."
"Ho?"
"HEY!"
"He climbed so high . . ."
"Ho?"
"HEY!"
"That the people looked like ants . . ."
"Ho?"
"HEY!"

As you tell your story, do not always look at the same person in your audience. If you are telling stories to a large group of children, make eye contact with different people and see them as individuals, not just a faceless mass. Ask questions which can be answered by someone who has been listening to the story. For example:

"And so that bright red suit of feathers went to who?"
"Cardinal!"
"Yes! Then Buzzard tried on another suit of feathers. It was blue with a black streaked crest. But that suit was not fine enough, either, for the messenger of all the birds. So that blue suit went to who?"
"Bluejay!"

If there is singing, chanting, movement or hand clapping in your story, teach it to the children before the story begins. Then, at the appropriate time in the story, have everyone join in.

As you tell a story, you should also be aware of how you use your hands, your facial expressions, the motions of your body. Some storytellers or readers prefer to sit quite still and to let their voices do all of the work. Others become theatrical. Again, you should find the way you are most comfortable. Flailing your arms about aimlessly can be distracting or overly dramatic. One way to make your hand gestures more meaningful and to give the eyes of your listeners something really significant to focus upon is to incorporate American Indian sign language in your tellings. Many of the signs are the same as those used by the deaf, and the *lingua franca* sign language that Native Americans developed because of the widespread trade across pre-Columbian America is both effective and beautiful to watch. Two inexpensive and easy-to-use books which teach American Indian sign language through photos and simple drawings are *Indian Sign Language* by William Tomkins and *Indian Talk: Hand Signals of the North American Indians* by Iron Eyes Cody.

In addition to the response words "Ho?" and "Hey!" you may want to make use of any one of a number of formulaic beginnings and endings which were used traditionally by Native American people when telling stories. One way which the Abenaki people begin a story is with the words, "Here my story camps." They then close the story with such phrases as "that is the end" or "Then I left." The Iroquois often begin by saying, "Would you like to hear a story?" as do many other American Indian people. They then end with the words, "Da neho!" which mean, "That is all." Such simple beginnings and endings may be of help to you as a storyteller because they give you a clear way into and out of the tale.

Conducting the Activities

The following checklist provides specific ideas for creating experiences that are meaningful, informative and fun.

Plan Wisely and in Detail

Consider the time available. List your activities and the time needed for each one. Plan a few extra activities to be sure there is always something to do if the activities move along quickly. If some children or groups finish a project earlier than others, you can provide meaningful tasks or projects for them to work on while waiting for others to finish. Prioritize the last few activities. This way, in case you begin to run out of time, you can be sure to include those activities that are most important and allow enough time to lead the final activity without rushing through it.

Choose and Adapt Activities for the Children's Levels

Young children need concrete experience and are not yet as adept at the second-order, abstract thought used to build concepts. They may understand that rain falls from a cloud because they can see it coming down, but it may be hard for them to visualize how a cloud forms from invisible water vapor that evaporates from ponds, lakes, rivers, oceans and leaves. Older children understand concepts more readily, such as the water cycle, and they are challenged by longer activities which probe a subject in greater depth.

With younger children, the activities need to be brief and active with hands-on exercises throughout. Allow plenty of time for facilitating social interaction and answering questions, questions and more questions! As anyone who works with children knows, two of the most frequently spoken words are, "But why?"

Set the Stage

Prepare the children with one or two preactivities to help them focus on the intended theme. Use a story, puppet show, slide show, filmstrip, movie or an activity.

Link the Activities in a Meaningful Way

Provide connections between activities. Discussion and leading questions help the children to discover these links themselves. Keep tying the meaning of each activity in with the overall theme. A focused summary at the end of each activity is a good way to do this. Ask the children, "What happened?" "What does it mean?"

Put the Children into the Center of the Experience

Use and design activities that have the children exploring and asking questions. Facilitating and sharing the experience is more effective and exciting than a show-and-tell approach. Establish your goals and let the children participate in the planning to reach those goals. Early involvement increases motivation later on. Let the children take turns leading or co-leading the group.

Figure 2-1. A good activity focuses on interaction between children and the environment.

Teach by Example

Children love to imitate adults as they grow and search for their own identity. Consistency between your actions and words is crucial. Being a role model is among the most powerful teaching tools.

Use Firsthand, Sensory Experiences Whenever Possible

Help the children to experience the subject first-hand. If the lesson is about trees then take them to a tree in the back yard, or to a forest, a park or a grove of trees on the school grounds. If you are studying water, visit a pond. Avoid prolonged discussion. To see it, smell it, hear it, touch it or taste it is to know it better. This is true for all ages, especially young children. The active approach also aids in motor skill development.

Use Creative Questions and Answers

Emphasize the children's own discoveries.

Questions can be used to direct their attention to important objects or subjects of inquiry. Avoid giving the answers away. Here is an example:

Child: "Why do leaves have veins?"
Leader: "Why do you have veins in your body? What flows through those veins?"
Child: "Blood flows through my veins."
Leader: "Do plants have any fluids in them?"
Child: "Yes, sap. I get it, sap flows through the veins of plants!"
Leader: "Right! Good thinking!"

If you do not know the answer to a question it is fine to say so. Children and adults alike can usually tell if you are using questions or other devices as a smokescreen to mask a lack of knowledge. Use an unanswered question as a shared learning experience while you probe the possible solutions together.

Emphasize Positive Feelings as Well as Knowledge

A child who empathizes with someone or something is more likely to want to learn about that person or thing. You can *say* that a spider carries an egg sac, has eight legs and eyes and traps insects in a web. But watch what happens when you read *Charlotte's Web* by E. B. White, and then create a giant web of yarn on the ceiling and play a catch-the-fly-in-the-web game. Instead of squishing the spider living in a corner of the ceiling, adopt it as a pet and care for it. Catch some flies and put them in the web to feed the spider. This leads into a discussion of how some things die to provide food for other living things. With these activities children become excited and motivated: they laugh at times, and some even cry if the spider gets swatted by someone else. They care.

Provide a supportive atmosphere—a trusting and respectful experience throughout—as a compassionate means to a compassionate end. This approach reinforces efforts to establish positive self-esteem, behavior and environmental attitudes. A child who values and cares for herself or himself is more likely to value the Earth and trust other people.

Foster Aesthetic Appreciation

Allow quiet time for observing a flower and drawing its many parts. Share your poetry, photographs or memories with the children. Have them share theirs with you. Allow them slow, quiet moments by building these times into the rhythms of each day. Late afternoons are good times for this, when energy starts to wane. You could also set a contemplative tone for the day by beginning it with a story.

Emphasize Group Work and Positive Social Interaction

Use teams and small groups to practice positive communication, cooperation and conflict resolution skills. This approach fosters self-knowledge and a sense of connection with others—of feeling safe, open and confident in social interaction. Involve everyone. No matter how great or small one child's contribution may seem to you, it is that child's whole world and the basis for his or her self-esteem.

Foster Problem-Solving/Research Skills

Here is a process to facilitate decision-making and problem-solving for environmental concerns:
- recognize the problem(s)
- define the problem(s)
- listen with comprehension
- collect information about the problem(s)
- organize the information
- analyze the information
- generate alternatives for possible solutions to the problem(s)
- develop a plan of action
- implement the plan of action[1]

These are also valuable skills for researching and solving personal problems.

Use Long-term Projects

Plant a tree and care for it. Establish a garden and cultivate it. Keep a pet and teach responsible caring. If, through your activities at home or your teaching at an environmental or nature center, you have contact with lots of children, have them work on long-term projects. A garden hoed by many children over time still gives each child a feeling of nurturing something alive and green.

Include a Connection with Other Communities and Countries

We are all part of the global environment. Children can be taught to understand their relationship with other cultures and distant lands. How does our heavy reliance in North America on the natural resources imported from other countries affect those societies and their environments? What are the ecological problems associated with acid rain, nuclear energy and other environmental issues that so clearly transcend cultural and political boundaries? These are among the many environmental issues that link North Americans to the lives of other peoples around the world.

Include Moral Issues: Environmental and Social Ethics

Indian stories and Earth activities involve values and moral issues as well as knowledge because they teach about life—human relationships and interactions between people and our environments. Moral issues include our thoughts, feelings and actions toward our selves, other people and the environment. Value can be defined as a strong and enduring preference, by an individual or groups of people, for a specific object, behavior or way of life.[2]

> We are one in relationship with the Earth and other people. Doing good supports this relationship. Love and moral goodness are inseparable, they are the elemental components of a life ethic.[3]

It is important to foster caring, nurturing and compassion in children's lives. Empathy is the tangible sense of our interconnectedness. When we feel what another person feels and understand that the Earth is a living organism whose parts also have an awareness, even though different from our own, we want to help because we share that emotional experience.

A child's level of moral development is another important consideration when planning values activities. (See the teacher's guide for a more detailed discussion of values education, moral development and related teaching methods.)

Face Problems and Controversy and Deal with Them Constructively and Positively

Accept problems as part of reality when studying the environment and other cultures. Emphasize positive approaches to problems.

Figure 2-2. The strip mining of coal is an important controversial issue to explore. The trees provide a scale for visualizing the size of this strip mining operation.

Controversial issues need to be approached cautiously. One way to avoid biased teaching of controversial issues is to analyze the subjects of bias, prejudice and ideology. Children who are fluent in the ideas of controversy are better able to approach moral issues objectively. Experience involving controversial issues motivates and involves children in seeking solutions to problems such as water pollution, acid rain and world hunger.

Respect Spiritual and Religious Beliefs

Spiritual beliefs and religious practices are major factors in determining a child's orientation toward the Earth and other people. Each individual's form of spiritual expression needs to be acknowledged and respected when the children's inevitable concerns arise, such as, "This story says that the Earth was created on the back of a giant turtle, but that's not what I was taught to believe." We have found a good response to be, "Yes, people believe in different accounts of creation, and this story tells us about the beliefs of certain Native American cultures." Spirituality can be a part of environmental activities in appropriate settings.

Respect the Privacy of Personal Beliefs and Feelings

When asking questions of other people's children, give them the right not to answer if the response will reveal sensitive personal beliefs or self-knowledge. One example is Study Question 5 in Chapter 4, which asks the children how they believe the world was created.

Discipline Compassionately and Decisively

If there are children in your group who insist on diverting attention away from the center of learning, try to involve them in the activity or discussion by asking them for help in solving a problem or completing a task. You may need to stand near an overly active child or even put your arm around her or his shoulders. These techniques help to comfort or give attention to the attention seekers in a positive way while avoiding a confrontation. If a rule is questioned, explain the meaning behind it and turn the experience into a constructive dialogue. This approach also fosters the development of positive personal moral standards.

Avoid using power plays or demeaning methods of punishment. A child who is a severe problem and continual distraction may have to leave the group so the learning can continue. This can be a positive experience if the child is asked to sit and reflect on what has happened, why, and how he or she could learn from the experience.

Don't send mixed messages. Establish the rules and the consequences of excessively disruptive behavior early in the lesson and be consistent in applying both.

Keep a Sense of Humor, Joy and Appreciation

A light touch opens hearts and minds. Be watchful for "teachable moments" in nature that can captivate and enthrall—a butterfly emerging from its chrysalis; a snake shedding its skin. You may want to build up a repertoire of nature puns for the older children. For example:
Question: "What did the wild grape say when the deer stepped on it?"
Answer: "Nothing much, it just let out a little 'wine.'"
Some children will laugh and some groan (just like adults), but they love it!

Be Yourself

Use whatever works best for your personality. Some adults take a high energy approach to leading activities, while others use a more low-keyed style. There are many ways of leading as long as you are well prepared and promoting a positive relationship with the children.

Provide a Culminating Activity or Experience

Wrap up, synthesize and summarize a lesson with an activity that brings it all together. A good example is the "Earth Circle of Life" in Chapter 23.

Taking Your Children Outdoors

Waves tumble over sands; wind rushes through pine boughs; flowers scent the breeze over a field; a pungent smell wafts from the pavement near a vacant lot after a rain—these and more are waiting to be experienced outdoors. There is adventure in the unknown, and even the familiar looks different when it is visited with the intent of discovering what has been looked at and not yet seen, heard yet never listened to. Whether in the backyard, on the school grounds, a vacant lot, nature-center lands, a wilderness area or a vest-pocket park in the city, there are discoveries awaiting.

A trip into natural surroundings or the local community is a chance to study the environment firsthand. It is a time to visit plants and animals in their homes, to learn wilderness survival skills. It may be a visit to a local market to study the food that feeds our bodies, the most personal environment of all. Of course, not every child's experience will be filled with wonder and aesthetic beauty; fear is also a natural part of discovering the new. Some fears are well-founded, such as being afraid to disturb a bee's nest. Other fears are irrational.

We once led a group of children from a very large urban neighborhood on an excursion to a pond. There were the usual shrieks when a frog jumped in and swam for its life. But the toughest looking young boy became pale when a frog we were looking at jumped out of our

Figure 2-3. Watch for the unexpected pleasures outdoors. Here, a dew-covered spider's web is a gossamer work of art.

hands and touched him. This streetwise child recoiled from a harmless amphibian. With a little help from his friends, we coaxed him into touching the frog's skin. By the end of our pond study he understood frogs better and would even hold one at arm's length. He didn't like them, but he accepted them. It was a start.

Planning the Outdoor Excursion

Once you have chosen your activities, scout out the area you intend to take your children to and become familiar with the site. Note the plants, animals and physical aspects of that place and include them in your activities. If there is a nature trail present, you may want to use it for access. If not, plan a route that will do minimal damage to the plant and animal communities along the way. When multiple trips are planned into a wild area, you can establish a path to reduce widespread trampling of the plants, or vary the route in and out to spread the traffic and control wear on the habitat. Consider the access carefully if your group includes children in wheelchairs or with other special needs: No one wants to be left behind.

Choose activities that fulfill your goals and objec-

tives. Think of a theme for the entire program; something broad like "survival" allows for focus and flexibility. Children love to play games en route to a site. You can use the "deer walk" to create suspense and interest. First have them cup their hands behind their ears to create "deer ears." Listen carefully and compare the intensity of sounds heard with and without the deer ears. Ask the children why deer can usually hear people coming before the people notice the deer.

"Because they listen quietly?"

"Right, and that's how we'll walk, with our deer ears alert and as quiet as can be," you reply. "Deer will signal danger by raising their tails and showing the white patch underneath. Whenever you see a white flag [hold up a sample flag], quietly gather around and we'll look at whatever our fellow deer thinks is interesting to see." (Pass out white flags to everyone.) In this way the walk becomes part of the experience. Puppets, stuffed animals, stories or other fun props keep the children's interest. Some leaders find it useful to carry an index card with a general outline of the program written on it, along with a list of intended activities.

Conduct the whole program in your mind's eye

beforehand and plan for all contingencies that you can anticipate: transportation, proper attire for seasonal weather conditions (especially rain, snow, cold and extreme heat), materials you will need for each activity and name tags. If you are planning a program at a nature center, a letter sent home beforehand to parents, or to the visiting classroom, will help to assure that the children come prepared with proper clothing. Parents, teachers, seniors, older students or other community volunteers are all excellent resources for helping with the excursion. Try to keep the ratio of adults to children in each group at around one to five or six.

Above all, be prepared! A complete first aid kit is a must, including anti-bee sting serum in case someone in your group is allergic. Your trail kit should also include these items:

- small knife
- compass
- insect repellant
- trash bags
- water, especially during hot days and on long walks

Since most kinds of weather can be enjoyed if you are prepared for them, it is a good policy to go outside under all but the worst conditions. Be ready with a full complement of "rainy day" activities just in case. Heavy rains, winds, lightning or other severe weather can come unexpectedly depending upon the weather patterns in your region.

Conducting the Field Trip
(with Special Tips for Larger Groups)

It's time to go! The children are anxious to begin and energy is high.

Figure 2-4. Remind children that they are visiting the homes of plants and animals, like this curious young raccoon.

"There are a few things that I want to say before we go outside," you begin. "We're visiting the plants and animals in *their* homes, so how do you think we should act?"

"On our good behavior," someone says.

"Right, if you take a rock off the path or turn a log over, you're removing the roof of an animal's home. When a leaf gets pulled off a plant it's part of a living thing.* Do you think you'd like it if someone visited your home and carried the roof away or pulled a piece off of *you?*"

"No!" they respond, laughing.

"O.K., then what should you do if you look under a log or rock?"

"Put it back the way we found it!"

You continue, "Since there are so many of us, we need to respect each other when someone's talking. Please raise your hand if you want to say something and listen whenever someone is talking. If you see me raise my hand, that is the signal to raise your hand and listen because there's something to see, do or discuss."

The tone of empathy and caring is set for the whole walk during the crucial first few minutes. This is also a good time to orient the children, in a general way, to the theme of the field trip and to what they can expect. But don't forget to keep plenty of surprises up your sleeve!

You are on the trail now and there is something you want to point out. Walk past that spot far enough so that roughly one half of the group has passed it. Then backtrack to the spot and you will be standing in the middle of the group to make it easier for the children to hear. Always try to stand facing the sun so that it falls on their backs and does not glare in their eyes. Ask questions to

*Suggested Ground Rules for Collecting Plants and Animals: Emphasize that this is a visit to the homes of plants and animals. If the children want to collect animals (insects, frogs, snakes, turtles), they should look at the animals and return them to their homes unless the children know how to properly care for them at home or in the classroom or nature center. Even animals that are kept for observation should be returned to their home after a week or so. Wild animals are not pets. Be especially careful not to collect mammals, birds or other animals that may carry diseases. Special permits are often required for collecting these animals.

If plants are collected, they should only be picked where there is a healthy population of that kind of plant. (This is also a sound practice when collecting animals.) Always have the children give thanks for what they have collected and be mindful of leaving plants and animals to create new ones for the future. We do not usually have the children pick plants unless the picking is necessary for a certain activity. In these cases, we emphasize that this is a special occasion and that we need to respect what the plants are giving to us and not pick them indiscriminately. A good approach is to do the collecting ahead of time for the children so they are not actually picking large volumes of plants or plant parts.

help them discover what you want them to see. Draw the children in and include everyone. These are great times to tell stories or to listen to one of the children's stories. But be careful! You may need to limit their storytelling. Children love to share stories and some children can talk so long that the flower you are looking at will have gone to seed by the end of the story. You can handle this tricky issue by allowing special times for their stories toward the end of the field trip.

Approach the excursion with "structured flexibility," being open to the special encounter—the unexpected find or event. One of our favorite activities along the trail is the camouflage game. First hold a brief discussion and answer period about what camouflage is and how animals use it, such as cryptic coloration, hiding behind things and under leaves or being shaped like a natural object. Be sure to have pictures of some well-camouflaged animals to hold up as you talk. Tell the children you want them to camouflage themselves whenever you yell "Camouflage!" Give them 10 seconds to hide and tell them not to go more than 20 feet (6.1 meters) away. Close your eyes as you count. Call out the names or locations of children that you can see when you open your eyes.

After you have played the game once, tell the children that the counting time will be shortened by one second during each round of the game, which can come at any time along the trail when you suddenly yell "Camouflage!" This adds an undertone of anticipation to the excursion.

When children are quiet and listening, they often see special things. Suppose a child comes up to you after the camouflage game and says, "I saw a spider with a moth caught in its web! It's over behind that big rock." Postpone the next planned activity and use the occasion as a time to marvel at the event while letting the children generate their own questions. Or, use some creative questioning to tie the sighting in with your lesson and quell some fears about spiders at the same time.

Snack breaks are good times to share special moments. They are also opportune for reading or telling one of the stories in this book that relates to the theme of your walk.

Don't forget to include quiet time during the outdoor excursion. Children can enjoy keeping a journal in which they write, draw pictures, make bark rubbings or practice other creative forms of expression. Their sketches and writings range from humorous stories and comic-strip variety pictures, to beautiful drawings and sensitive poetic verse.

> "Waterfall"
> It is sometimes very noisy
> It is beautiful
> water rushing down,
> down to a lake or
> stream.
> Peaceful now.
> —Stephanie (eleven years old)

Projects also get the children involved. You could pile brush for small mammal homes, pick up trash or build a wood duck nesting box for a pond if it is a long-term study with multiple visits. (See the activities in Chapters 5 and 21 for more ideas.) Projects, along with team activities, provide the means for small group cooperation and social development.

When you are ready to wrap up the visit, it is more effective to conduct a summarizing activity on site or on the way back *before* coming within sight of the house, school bus, learning center or other final destination. While the children are in the midst of the excitement and involvement at the site, their attention is still focused there. If you try to wrap up away from the site, the element of concentration on that place and the day's events is weakened and the children's thoughts are already turning to their next experience.

This chapter has provided both ideas and practical suggestions for effectively using and integrating the Native American stories and environmental activities found in Part II. Now it's time to begin! We hope that you and your children enjoy these stories and activities as much as we enjoy sharing them.

Notes

1. William B. Stapp and Dorothy A. Cox, *Environmental Education Activities Manual* (Dexter, Michigan: Thomson-Shore, Inc., 1979), p. 16. Available from the authors at 32493 Shady Ridge Drive, Farmington Hills, Michigan 48018.

2. An adaptation of definitions of value by Milton Rokeach, from: *Beliefs, Attitudes and Values: A Theory of Organization and Change* (San Francisco, California: Jossey Bass, Publishers, 1976), p. 125, and *The Nature of Human Values* (New York: MacMillan Publishing Co., Inc., 1973), p. 5.

3. Michael J. Caduto, *A Guide on Environmental Values Education* (Paris, France: United Nations Educational, Scientific and Cultural Organization [UNESCO], 1985), p. 34.

PART II

NATIVE AMERICAN STORIES AND ENVIRONMENTAL ACTIVITIES

✦ CREATION ✦

From dust Gluscabi formed himself. He sat up from the Earth and said, "Here I am."

CHAPTER 3

✦ The Coming of Gluscabi ✦

(Abenaki—Northeast Woodlands)

After Tabaldak had finished making human beings, he dusted his hands off and some of that dust sprinkled on the Earth. From that dust Gluscabi formed himself. He sat up from the Earth and said, "Here I am." So it is that some of the Abenaki people call Gluscabi by another name, "Odzihozo," which means, "the man who made himself from something." He was not as powerful as Tabaldak, The Owner, but like his grandchildren, the human beings, he had the power to change things, sometimes for the worse.

When Gluscabi sat up from the Earth, The Owner was astonished. "How did it happen now that you came to be?" he said.

Then Gluscabi said, "Well, it is because I formed myself from this dust left over from the first humans that you made."

"You are very wonderful," The Owner told him.

"I am wonderful because you sprinkled me," Gluscabi answered.

"Let us roam around now," said The Owner. So they left that place and went uphill to the top of a mountain. There they gazed about, open-eyed, so far around they could see. They could see the lakes, the rivers, the trees, how all the land lay, the Earth.

Then The Owner said, "Behold here how wonderful is my work. By the wish of my mind I created all this existing world, oceans, rivers, lakes." And he and Gluscabi gazed open-eyed.

Gluscabi, "The Man Who Made Himself," springs up from the dust left over after Tabaldak had finished making human beings. When Tabaldak and Gluscabi meet, they go to a special place where the beauty of the Earth lies before them.

(Gluscabi also appears in Chapter 9, "Gluscabi and the Wind Eagle," Chapter 20, "Gluscabi and the Game Animals" and as Koluscap in Chapter 10, "Koluscap and the Water Monster.")

Discussion

At the end of the story there is a strong sense of appreciation felt by Gluscabi and Tabaldak for the wonders of the Earth. Indian peoples share this strong connection with the land and the places where they live. "Home" is not just a location, but *the place* with which they share a close relationship. It is a part of their own identity. This way of being connected with the Earth is revealed in their stories.

The following questions and activities help children to have meaningful experiences with special places in their surroundings and to develop a sense of identity with the Earth.

Questions

1. What has Tabaldak just finished doing when he dusts his hands off?
2. Where does Gluscabi come from in this story? How can someone create himself or herself from something like dust?
3. How do Gluscabi and Tabaldak feel when they meet?
4. How do Tabaldak and Gluscabi feel when they climb to the top of the mountain and look out over the Earth? How would you feel?
5. Have you ever been to a natural place that was beautiful to look at? Describe it. Is there a special place that you go to when you want to be out in nature? Where is that place? What is it like?

Activities
Once Upon a Place

ACTIVITY: Visit a special place in a natural area several times, using activities to increase sensory and intellectual awareness of those surroundings. Keep a record of these visits, using a journal or other medium, and share the experience with others.

GOALS: Appreciate that stories are an important way for us to enjoy and understand the world around us. Develop a sense of place, a relationship with a natural

Figure 3-1. A meaningful relationship with the Earth begins with the positive experiences associated with a special place outdoors.

area. Enhance sensory awareness skills. Understand the importance of giving and receiving.

AGE: Younger Children and Older Children

PROCEDURE: Find a natural area that the children can visit periodically, such as a woodland, field, pond or park. Ponds, lakes, streams and wetlands work especially well because they often teem with life. During the first visit the children will each pick a special spot in that environment. It should be a place in which they enjoy sitting and exploring and one which makes them feel safe. Have the children go to their spots and sit quietly for about five to ten minutes the first time. A short visit is recommended initially because it takes time for them to get used to sitting quietly, and it often takes a few trips before their places take on special meaning. Gather the

group together and have each child share one experience from her or his place.

For each subsequent visit have the children bring a gift to their places. This gift should be something simple from nature, such as a leaf, acorn or some soil. Also, have them record their discoveries with words or pictures in a journal, or by making models out of clay or other media. Here are some activities for them to do at their places:

• Become an ant. Lie on your stomach with your eyes close to the ground and imagine you are an ant walking along the soil. What does it look like? Feel like? Smell like? Do you hear any strange sounds? Use your hand lens to look more closely to get an ant's-eye view. Draw a picture or write a short description to say what it is like being an ant.

• Sit upright and do not move. Pretend that you are part of the nature around you. If you must move, do so very slowly. You may find that insects or other animals come close to you.

• Choose one plant growing at your place and look at it carefully. You could choose a large tree or a blade of grass. Get to know it by using your senses.

• Write a poem or draw a picture on a rock. Then place the rock with the poem or picture face down as a gift to the Earth. Or do the same thing on a leaf, stick or piece of bark. Put the leaf, stick or bark poem under a rock or log and, during the course of your return visits, watch your gift slowly decay over time as it is received by the Earth.

• Lie on your back and close your eyes for the entire visit to your place. Live in the world of sound without using your sight.

• Walk around your place and look for litter from people's visits; clean it up if necessary.

After several visits, when the children have become familiar with their places, direct the older children in more challenging activities such as learning the names of some of the plants that grow there and their natural history—for instance, how and why the plants grow where they do, set seeds and form spores.

Have the children share their highlights with each other after each visit. Reinforce the idea that the gifts they receive from their places are the experiences and memories that they bring away from those spots and the things they have collected. These gifts can be included in their journals. Have them visit at different times of the day and under varying weather conditions to provide a variety of experiences. Take a picture of each child in her or his place at least once during these visits.

If safety allows, visit the site on a starry night. The birds of daytime will be replaced by the less-known creatures of the night world: bats, owls, nighthawks and more. Everything will sound, smell and appear different than during the day.

When the outdoor visits are over, have the children create stories from their "Once Upon a Place" collections and memories. Young children may have pictures and objects that can be shared with others. Encourage older children to write a story, puppet show, play, song or report about their place. Be sure they tell what they brought to the place and what they received from it.

MATERIALS: Natural area (preferably where it is quiet); pencils; paper; clay; paints and brushes; water; crayons; field guides to plants, animals, rocks, etc.; hand lenses; one collecting box for each child (shoe-box size will do); camera and film; cardboard backing to write against; bags for litter cleanup; journals.

Extending the Experience

• Return to the places periodically to renew a sense of belonging there.

• Encourage the children to find special places on their own and to visit them, care for them and learn about the plants, animals and the rest of nature there.

• Set up a spot where the children can display their journals, collections and illustrations of their places.

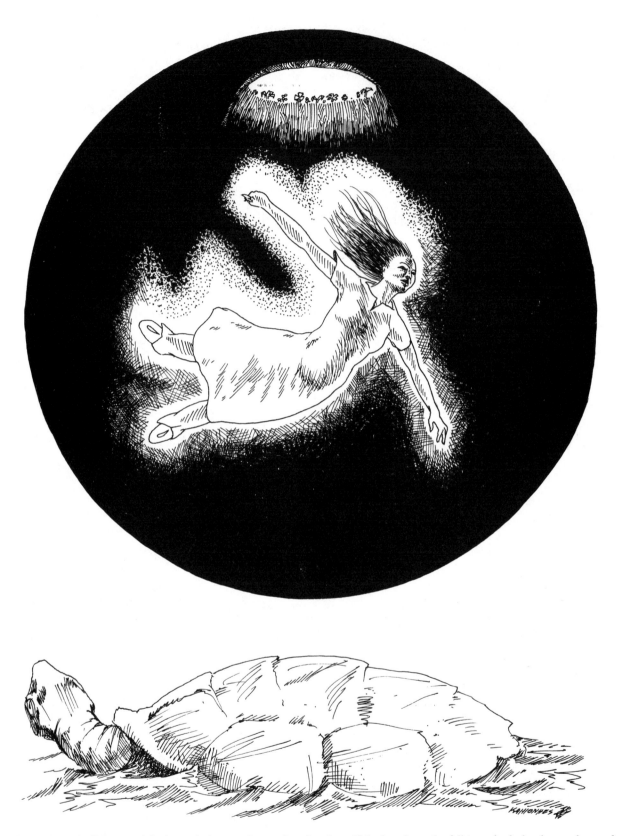

Her grasp slipped off the tip of the branch, leaving her with only a handful of seeds as she fell into the hole, down, down, down.

CHAPTER 4

✦ The Earth on Turtle's Back ✦

(Onondaga—Northeast Woodlands)

Before this Earth existed, there was only water. It stretched as far as one could see, and in that water there were birds and animals swimming around. Far above, in the clouds, there was a Skyland. In that Skyland there was a great and beautiful tree. It had four white roots which stretched to each of the sacred directions, and from its branches all kinds of fruits and flowers grew.

There was an ancient chief in the Skyland. His young wife was expecting a child, and one night she dreamed that she saw the Great Tree uprooted. The next morning she told her husband the story.

He nodded as she finished telling her dream. "My wife," he said, "I am sad that you had this dream. It is clearly a dream of great power and, as is our way, when one has such a powerful dream we must do all that we can to make it true. The Great Tree must be uprooted."

Then the Ancient Chief called the young men together and told them that they must pull up the tree. But the roots of the tree were so deep, so strong, that they could not budge it. At last the Ancient Chief himself came to the tree. He wrapped his arms around it, bent his knees and strained. At last, with one great effort, he uprooted the tree and placed it on its side. Where the tree's roots had gone deep into the Skyland there was now a big hole. The wife of the chief came close and leaned over to look down, grasping the tip of one of the Great Tree's branches to steady her. It seemed as if she saw something down there, far below, glittering like water. She leaned out further to look and, as she leaned, she lost her balance and fell into the hole. Her grasp slipped off the tip of the branch, leaving her with only a handful of seeds as she fell, down, down, down, down.

Far below, in the waters, some of the birds and animals looked up.

"Someone is falling toward us from the sky," said one of the birds.

"We must do something to help her," said another. Then two Swans flew up. They caught the Woman From The Sky between their wide wings. Slowly, they began to bring her down toward the water, where the birds and animals were watching.

"She is not like us," said one of the animals. "Look, she doesn't have webbed feet. I don't think she can live in the water."

"What shall we do, then?" said another of the water animals.

"I know," said one of the water birds. "I have heard that there is Earth far below the waters. If we dive down and bring up Earth, then she will have a place to stand."

So the birds and animals decided that someone would have to bring up Earth. One by one they tried.

The Duck dove down first, some say. He swam down and down, far beneath the surface, but could not reach the bottom and floated back up. Then the Beaver tried. He went even deeper, so deep that it was all dark, but he could not reach the bottom, either. The Loon tried, swimming with his strong wings. He was gone a long long time, but he, too, failed to bring up Earth. Soon it seemed that all had tried and all had failed. Then a small voice spoke.

"I will bring up Earth or die trying."

They looked to see who it was. It was the tiny Muskrat. She dove down and swam and swam. She was not as strong or as swift as the others, but she was determined. She went so deep that it was all dark, and still she swam deeper. She went so deep that her lungs felt ready to burst, but she swam deeper still. At last, just as she was becoming unconscious, she reached out one small paw and grasped at the bottom, barely touching it before she floated up, almost dead.

When the other animals saw her break the surface they thought she had failed. Then they saw her right paw was held tightly shut.

"She has the Earth," they said. "Now where can we put it?"

"Place it on my back," said a deep voice. It was the Great Turtle, who had come up from the depths.

They brought the Muskrat over to the Great Turtle and placed her paw against his back. To this day there are marks at the back of the Turtle's shell which were made by Muskrat's paw. The tiny bit of Earth fell on the back of the Turtle. Almost immediately, it began to grow larger and larger and larger until it became the whole world.

Then the two Swans brought the Sky Woman down. She stepped onto the new Earth and opened her hand, letting the seeds fall onto the bare soil. From those seeds the trees and the grass sprang up. Life on Earth had begun.

From the young wife's dream to the events that follow, this is a story of sacrifices that bring new life. The Great Tree is uprooted, yet its seeds become the source of plants on the Earth. Muskrat tries so hard to reach the bottom of the waters that she nearly dies. Her determination helps her to succeed in bringing up the Earth, where others who are stronger and faster have failed. The Great Turtle gives his shell to hold the Earth and the seeds brought by the Great Chief's wife bring life to the new Earth.

Discussion

When the woman is caught by the swans and they are bringing her down slowly, one of the animals realizes that she cannot live in the water. The woman needs a different home than the ocean—a home on dry land. This chapter explores the Earth as our home, and how it provides the things we need to live: food, air, water and shelter.

Questions

1. Why does the Chief think his wife's dream is so important? Are your dreams important? What do you do when you remember your dreams?
2. Why does the Ancient Chief pull up the Great Tree?
3. In what ways do the animals help the Chief's wife once she falls through the hole in Skyland? Why is the Earth brought up from beneath the waters?
4. Why does Muskrat succeed in bringing the Earth up when the other animals fail, even though they are stronger and swifter than she is? What lesson does Muskrat bring to the people who hear this story? Can you think of a time when you were working on a hard task and you succeeded because you kept on trying?
5. This is one Indian story of creation, of how the Earth was made. What are some other ways that people believe the Earth was created? Are these other beliefs any more true or less true than the Indian's beliefs? What do you believe?
6. What are the things that the Chief's wife will need to survive on the Earth on Turtle's back? Where do these things come from in the story? Where do all of our survival needs come from?

Activities
Nature: Who Needs It? The Turtle's Gifts to People

ACTIVITY: Trace the supplies of food, air, water and shelter back to their origins in nature using (A) a simulation of gas exchange between people and plants, (B) a water flow maze, (C) a food source bingo game and (D) models of children's homes and samples of raw materials used to build those homes. Discuss the North American origins of some common foods that are now used around the world.

GOALS: Understand that the air, water, food and shelter we need each day all come from the Earth, like the one created on Turtle's back. Understand that many important foods originated in North America and are now used worldwide.

AGE: Younger Children and Older Children

PROCEDURE A: *Air Supply.* Explain how plants use sunlight in the process of *photosynthesis* ("made from light"), during which water and carbon dioxide are converted in the green chlorophyll of the leaf into glucose, protein, starch, other nutrients and water. Oxygen, too, is released. (See Chapter 7, page 50 for a more detailed look at photosynthesis and further activities around this theme.) Animals use this oxygen for *respiration*, the process during which food is metabolized to get energy for growth and maintenance. People and animals in turn give off carbon dioxide when they respire, a gas which plants need for photosynthesis.[1]

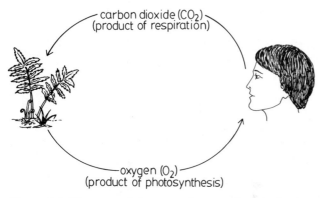

Figure 4-1. The gas cycle between plants and animals. During respiration animals use oxygen and produce carbon dioxide, while during photosynthesis plants give off more oxygen than they use during respiration.

Use a large plant as an example to reinforce this idea. Tie the end of the flexible rubber hose in among the plant's leaves. Whenever a child passes by she or he

can pick up the hose to exhale some carbon dioxide for the plant and to inhale some oxygen from the plant. This action symbolizes the life-giving *gas cycle* between plants and animals (Figure 4-1).

PROCEDURE B: *A-Maze-Ing Water.* Study the water supply to your house, school or nature center, and draw a map tracing the water from its source (river, well, reservoir, etc.) to the nearest water faucets and bathrooms. Adapt this map to create a maze in which the only correct route is to trace the path of a drop of water from its source to the nearest sink or other water supply. Make one copy of the maze for each child and have the children follow a drop of water from source to sink.

PROCEDURE C: *Bread and Burger Bingo.* Make the children their favorite lunch and with it, a list of their foods and drinks. Help them to think of the source of each kind of food and drink (e.g., milk→cow→grass; bread→wheat, rye, corn; chicken→grain; etc.) and write these sources next to the appropriate items on the list. The main ingredients in each of the foods will be traced back to a plant (or plants) grown in the soil. Have the children assign each of the foods to one of the four basic food groups: (1) milk and dairy products; (2) meat, poultry, fish, eggs, legumes, nuts; (3) fruits and vegetables; (4) breads and cereals.

Use the favorite foods and their sources to create the bingo game. Make the bingo cards four squares across and four squares down for a total of sixteen squares. Each of the sixteen squares will contain a food source and the bingo caller will call out the names of the foods. Whenever a food name is called, the appropriate source is named by someone in the group and everyone covers the space where that source is marked on their card. Here are some examples:

bread→wheat, rye, corn
ice cream→milk→cow→grain + grass
cheese→milk→cow→grain + grass
apples→apple trees
hamburger→cattle→grain + grass
carrot→root of carrot plant
egg→chicken→grain
cola→nut from cola tree plus a sweetener such as sugar or corn syrup
french fries→potatoes
sugar→sugar cane or beet
popcorn→corn plant

Point out that many food plants now eaten worldwide first originated in North and South America, such as corn, all squash (including pumpkins), potatoes, peppers, tomatoes, sunflower seeds, Jerusalem artichokes, almost all kinds of beans and chocolate.

Begin calling out the foods and have the children name sources and mark them on their cards until someone gets four in a row in any direction. Then that person will become the caller until someone else gets another row of four. Continue until someone has filled the whole card. Then discuss the foods and sources not called. You will need to jumble the order of food sources as you write them on the bingo cards to assure that cards have food sources marked in different orders.

PROCEDURE D: *Making Shelter.* Have your children make drawings or models of their home out of cardboard and paper. Then tell them to think of all the materials that the home is made of, such as wood, glass, brick, plastic, cement and stone. Help them to figure out which natural resources are used to make the different parts of the home: brick→clay; glass→sand; cement→minerals from rocks; plastic→oil; and so on. Have the children gather samples of these natural resources, and the materials that they create, and match them up. (See Chapter 21 for similar activities which explore the needs of animals.)

MATERIALS: (A) large plant, string, flexible rubber hose, chalk, chalkboard. (B) paper, water mazes tracing water from its natural source to the home or learning center, pencils. (C) lunches, chalkboard and chalk or large paper and felt-tipped marker for making list of foods and their sources, bingo cards and markers, box with bingo pieces marked with the names of the kinds of foods to be called out. (D) construction paper, cardboard, scissors, clay, glue, crayons, pencils, rulers, paste, string for arrows, other materials and resource samples as needed.

Extending the Experience
•   Use a flour mill to grind wheat and bake fresh bread.
•   Make butter. Put cream into baby food jars (one jar for each child) and have the children shake the jars until the cream churns into butter.
•   Gather wild edibles and prepare them for a meal.
•   Introduce the children to other stories of creation—from Greek mythology, for example—and compare them to this story and the stories from Chapters 3 and 5.
• Find and share examples of people who, like Muskrat in this story, overcame great odds to succeed because of their tremendous determination.

Notes
1.   Plants also respire, but during the day they create more oxygen than they use. At night, when sunlight is unavailable for photosynthesis, plants are still respiring, so they produce more carbon dioxide than oxygen.

The Big Reed grew up and up. It left the First World behind and it carried the First Beings into the Second World.

CHAPTER 5

Four Woﾟrlds:
The Dine Story of Creation

(Dine [Navajo]—Southwest)

Before this world existed, there was a First World far below the world where we are now. In that world everything was black. There was darkness everywhere, and in that darkness there were six beings. Those beings were First Man, the son of Night and the Blue Sky over the sunset; First Woman, the daughter of Day Break and the Yellow Sky of sunset; Salt Woman; Fire God; Coyote and Begochiddy. Begochiddy, who was the child of the Sun, was both man and woman, and had blue eyes and golden hair.

There were no mountains or plants in that first world, so Begochiddy began to make them. Begochiddy made four mountains. To the east Begochiddy made a white mountain. To the south Begochiddy made a blue mountain. To the west Begochiddy made a yellow mountain. To the north Begochiddy made a black mountain. Then Begochiddy created the ants and other insects and made the first plants. But things were not right in that First World. One story is that Fire God became jealous and started to burn everything up. According to another story, the First Beings were just not happy in that dark world. Whatever the reason was, they decided to leave the First World.

"Gather together the plants and the other things I have made," said Begochiddy to First Man.

First Man did as Begochiddy said. Then he and the other beings came to the red mountain which Begochiddy created in the center of the First World. There Begochiddy planted the Big Reed. As the Big Reed began to grow, the First Beings climbed into it. Up and up it grew, leaving the First World behind. It grew up and up until it came to the Second World.

In the Second World Begochiddy created even more things. Begochiddy created the clouds. Begochiddy created more plants and mountains. The color of the Second World was blue, and there were other beings in it—Swallow People and Cat People. The Cat People tried to fight Begochiddy and the others, but First Man used his magic and overcame them. For a time, everyone was happy. Then things began to go wrong. Once more Begochiddy planted Big Reed. Once more Begochiddy told First Man and the others to put all the things created into Big Reed. Big Reed began to grow. Up and up it went and carried them all to the Third World.

The Third World was yellow. Though there was no sun and no moon, the mountains gave light. It was the most beautiful of the worlds they had seen. In this world Begochiddy created rivers and springs. Begochiddy made water animals and trees, birds and lightning. Then Begochiddy created all kinds of human beings. In this beautiful Third World everything spoke one language. All of the things and beings in creation understood each other. But everything was not perfect in the Third World. Yellow and red streaks appeared across the eastern sky. They were placed there by First Man and represented the diseases about to come to the people through evil magic. Before long, the men and women began to quarrel with each other. The men said that the women were causing trouble. The women said that it was the men. Coyote came to Begochiddy and told him that men and women were always quarreling. Begochiddy decided to put a stop to it.

"All of the men," Begochiddy said, "must stay on the right bank of the river. All of the women must stay on the left bank. Neither may cross the river to be with the other."

So it was done. The men and women lived apart for some time, but they were not happy without each other. Finally they went to Begochiddy. Some say it was the women who came first, but others say it was the men.

"We are not happy by ourselves," they said. "We wish to be reunited."

So Begochiddy brought men and women back together.

"If there is more trouble," he warned them, "this Third World will be destroyed by a flood."

All of this time, Coyote was roaming around. Wherever he went he was curious about everything, including things he should have left well enough alone. One day, Salt Woman went walking by the two big rivers Begochiddy had made in this Third World. When she came to the place where the rivers crossed, she saw something strange in the water. It looked like a baby with long black hair. She went back and told the others about it. Coyote decided to go and see for himself. Sure enough, there where the rivers crossed was a baby with long black hair in the water. Coyote lifted it out of the water and hid it under his blanket. He told no one what he had done.

Four days passed and then a great noise was heard all around the Third World. Begochiddy knew what it was, knew what was going to happen. Someone had done wrong. Now this Third World was about to be destroyed by flood. From the east a black storm came. From the south a blue storm approached. From the west came a yellow storm. From the north a white storm swept. Once again Begochiddy gathered all the beings and things created. Once again Big Reed grew up and up. It lifted up all the beings and things as storm waters rose beneath them.

This time, though, was not as easy as before. Big Reed stopped growing before it entered the next world. The Spider People wove a web to bring them closer, but they could not break through into the new world. The Ant People tried to dig through, but they could not do it. Finally Begochiddy told the Locust to try. Using his hard head, the Locust broke through into the Fourth World. Now Begochiddy climbed up through the hole the Locust made. He found himself on an island with only water to be seen in all directions. Begochiddy saw right away that there were others in this Fourth World who had great power. To the east was Talking God. To the south was First Bringer of Seeds. To the west was House God. To the north was Second Bringer of Seeds. Begochiddy waved to each of them. Then the four powerful beings made the waters recede, leaving a world covered with mud. Begochiddy went back down Big Reed to the others.

"Grandparent," said the others, "how is it in the new world?"

Coyote lifted the baby out of the water and hid it under his blanket. He told no one what he had done.

"The new world is good," Begochiddy said, "but it has not yet dried. Someone must try to walk up there. Who will try?"

"I will go," said Badger. Then he went up through the hole and tried to walk on the new Fourth World. His feet broke through the surface, though, and became covered with mud. To this day all badgers have black feet.

"This will not do," Begochiddy said. "How can we dry this new world?"

"We shall dry it," said the winds. Then the winds went up to the Fourth World. The cyclones and the whirlwinds and the small dust devils went up to the Fourth World. They swirled about and dried the surface well so the people could walk. Then the Ant People went up and walked on the dried surface of the Fourth World, and all the other people and created things followed.

Begochiddy, though, looked back down through the hole to the Third World. The water there was still rising.

"Who is the one who angered the Water Monster?" Begochiddy said.

No one answered, but Coyote pulled his blanket tighter around himself.

"Open your blanket," Begochiddy said.

Then Coyote opened his blanket and Begochiddy saw the water baby.

"You must give the Water Monster back its child," said Begochiddy.

Coyote did as Begochiddy said. He dropped the water baby back down to the Third World, and the waters receded.

Now Begochiddy went around the Fourth World and placed things in order. The mountains were put in their places. The Sun and Moon and Stars were put into the sky. Fire God tried to keep all the fire to himself, even though the people needed it to keep warm and cook their food. One night, though, as Fire God slept, Coyote stole fire from him and gave it to all the people. Then Begochiddy told the human beings the right way to live, how to give thanks, how to care for the plants such as corn and squash and beans. Begochiddy gave them many different languages, then, and sent them to live throughout the world. It was now, in this Fourth World, that Changing Woman came to be. She became the greatest friend of the human beings, helping them in many ways. It was Changing Woman who gave birth to the Hero Twins, who traveled throughout the world doing great deeds, destroying the monsters that threatened the people.

So the Fourth World came to be. However, just as the worlds before it were destroyed when wrong was done, so too this Fourth World was destined to be destroyed when the people do not live the right way. That is what the Dine say to this day.

Begochiddy designs the First World. The discontent and misdeeds of the other beings bring flight from the First World into the Second, Third and finally the Fourth World. Begochiddy plants the Big Reed each time to carry everything from each world to the next. When Coyote, the human beings and the others reach the Fourth World, Begochiddy tells the human beings how to live right, to care for the plants and to give thanks—for the Fourth World, our world of today, can also be destroyed by human beings.

(Coyote also appears in Chapter 8, "Old Man Coyote and the Rock," and in Chapter 13, "How Coyote Was the Moon." The Hero Twins also appear in Chapter 10, "The Hero Twins and the Swallower of Clouds.")

Discussion

The Earth is home for all of its creatures. It is our *habitat*, the place where people, plants and animals live and meet our survival needs. As *stewards* of the Earth, people have the responsibility to care for the well-being of the living and nonliving things found here. Every action we take affects our habitat and those with whom we share it. This is the basis of *ecology*, the study of the interactions between living things and their environments. In the past we have sometimes succeeded, and sometimes failed, to be good stewards. Giving thanks and taking care of the Earth are two ways we can help to sustain life—to keep the Earth well for the children to come.

Figure 5-1. Earth is home for all living things and people are stewards of the fragile life on Earth.

This chapter focuses on conservation, especially the care of trees and forests. The following questions and activities explore the values of trees for people and wildlife. There are many ways that people can "give back" to the trees by being good Earth stewards, by taking responsibility to wisely manage our forests and care for individual trees.

Questions

1. How do First Man, First Woman, Coyote, Salt Woman and Fire God cause Begochiddy to move everyone out of each of the first three worlds and finally into the Fourth World?
2. What does Coyote do to anger the Water Monster and cause him to flood the Third World?
3. Which lessons does Begochiddy teach the human beings regarding how to live the right way in the Fourth World?

Activities
Brother Soil, Sister Tree

ACTIVITY: Discuss the values of trees and how we can take care of them. Adopt a tree, care for it and plant a tree seed or seedling.

GOALS: Understand that trees give us food, oxygen, beauty and wood, among other things, and that they also provide food and shelter for animals. Realize that by nurturing the soil and planting tree seeds and seedlings, we can complete the circle of giving and receiving between trees and people.

AGE: Younger Children

PROCEDURE: Read *The Giving Tree* to the children and discuss the story: Was the tree good to the boy? Was the boy good to the tree? Did the boy care for the tree? What happened to the tree as the boy grew older and kept demanding from it? How could the boy have acted differently?

Facilitate a discussion of the values and uses of trees and make a list of all those things: wood for building and for heat; beauty; shade; noise reduction; oxygen from the leaves (see Chapter 7, page 50); clean air (leaves filter out particulate pollution); pleasant sounds from the wind through the leaves; apples, almonds and other foods for people and animals; homes for animals; erosion protection where roots hold the soil in place; and more.

Visit a park, forest or even your backyard and have each child adopt a tree as his or her own. During the first visits the children can become acquainted with their tree.

• Hug your tree! Make friends with it.
• Make bark rubbings using crayons or charcoal and blank newsprint.
• Create a leaf print by painting one side of a leaf with tempera paint and then pressing it down gently and thoroughly onto paper to form the leaf pattern.
• Spend some time blindfolded with your tree. Feel the bark, branches, leaves and roots, and listen to the birds and wind overhead. Imagine you are a bird in your tree's branches. What is it like? Find out about the birds and animals living in your tree.

During each visit for this activity, the children can care for the tree by bringing leaves to feed the soil near its roots, by watering the tree, or by cleaning up litter discarded by people in the area around the tree. Have them greet the tree each time they arrive and thank it before leaving.

Have each child find a suitable place nearby where there is room for planting a seed or young tree away from the roots of other trees. He or she can dig a hole, plant a seed or tree, and water it. Seeds will require that you put a shallow layer of soil over them.[1] If you are planting young trees the roots should be buried several inches deeper than they were where the tree was originally growing. Early spring is a good time to do the planting because soil water is usually more abundant and there is a long growing season ahead for the young tree to get established. The tree should be transplanted before the vigorous spring growth begins in order to avoid the stress caused by disrupting the tree's annual growth cycle.

MATERIALS: Copy of *The Giving Tree* by Shel Silverstein, felt-tipped marking pens, leaves or grass to feed the soil, sheets of blank newsprint, crayons or charcoal, leaves, containers of water for paints, tempera paints and brushes, construction paper, blindfolds, buckets of water for tree planting, trash bags, tree seeds or seedlings from local trees, containers of soil, shovels.

Tree People

ACTIVITY: Read about how one young person started a conservation movement and got involved with a local habitat management project. Research the needs locally for help with forest management and become involved with a specific project. Establish an ongoing conservation group to continue community conservation projects.

GOALS: Understand that we each affect the habitats of plants, animals and people by the things we do. Appreciate that good stewardship toward the environment means taking an active role.

AGE: Older Children

PROCEDURE: Have children take turns reading sections of "TreePeople" until it is completed. Lead a discussion about what trees give to us and ask for suggestions on how the children can become involved with local habitat management. For instance, there may be an eroded streambank, railroad bed or vacant lot that needs trees and grass planted on it; a reforestation project going on in a tree farm or national forest nearby whose directors may grant permission to have the children come and help plant trees; or a portion of a city park that needs trees planted and/or cared for.

Coordinate the research effort among the children as they find out what projects are available locally and what they need to do to help out. If seedlings are needed, have the children hold a bake sale or other event to raise funds to buy them. Contact the local office of the federal Soil Conservation Service or Forest Service to get some seedlings. If nursery-grown trees are needed, have the children raise enough money to buy one tree and plant it as a group project. Divide the children into small groups of three or four and assign each group some responsibility in the overall project.

As a follow-up, encourage the children to form a local group or club that would seek out and participate in conservation projects in their community.

TreePeople

In the summer of 1970, 15-year-old Andrew Lipkis was at camp in the San Bernardino Mountains near Los Angeles, California. A naturalist told the campers that smog was killing the trees and that the forest would one day soon be gone. Air pollution decreases the level of green chlorophyll in leaves. Chlorophyll is the substance that enables plants to form food from sunlight. The reduced chlorophyll decreases plants' ability to produce food and can cause them to become weakened and prone to disease and insect attack. Soon Andy had organized fellow campers, who planted a camp parking lot and baseball field with Coulter pines, incense cedar, grass and shrubs, thus converting it to a meadow.

Andy never lost his enthusiasm for what could be done with a little money and cooperation from many kinds of people. In 1973 he saved 8,000 seedlings from being plowed under by the California State Division of Forestry, and he organized area campers, scouts and other volunteers to pot and plant these trees. To accomplish this, money had to be raised and topsoil donated; a dairy contributed 8,000 milk cartons in which to pot the trees, and volunteers rallied to pot and plant 8,000 seedlings. The California Conservation Project, now called TreePeople, was born.

Trees help the city by filtering particulate pollution (such as soot and dust) from the air, by shading buildings to save energy, preventing erosion, beautifying the neighborhoods and countryside, decreasing noise, raising property values and creating green areas for recreation.

Then it was learned that the City of Los Angeles wanted to plant one million trees which, when mature, would filter out 200 tons (181.4 metric tons) of particulate pollutants from the air each day. But it would cost the city $200 million and would take twenty years to accomplish. TreePeople organized volunteers and got support from the mayor, celebrities and an advertising firm. On July 24, 1984, TreePeople met its goal. Three years after the city released its findings on trees and air pollution, and four days before the 1984 Summer Olympics opened in Los Angeles, the one millionth tree was planted.

MATERIALS: Copies of " Tree People" (found at the end of the description of this activity), other resources as needed depending upon the conservation project adopted (for instance, seeds, a tree, etc.).

Extending the Experience

• Study habitat management in other regions and countries and some current environmental problems such as the strip mining of coal and the need for land reclamation, deforestation in the Amazonian rainforest or *desertification* (the spreading of the desert) in African nations such as those in the Sahara desert region.

• Read Dr. Seuss' *The Lorax*. Children love this story and it gives them a sense of empathy for the animals, trees, air, water and the rest of Earth. *The Lorax* can also be produced as a play.

• Establish a terrarium as a mini-habitat that can be cared for in your child's own room.

• Encourage the children to learn about, care for and keep records of the life in their own backyards: trees, grass, animals, etc.

Notes

1. The seeds of many species of trees require special treatment in order to germinate, such as exposure to prolonged cold temperatures and weathering of the seed coat. Consult your local Soil Conservation Service or Forest Service office for sources of seeds and advice on how to germinate them. The larger seeds taken from citrus fruits are good to use. They need only to be planted and watered for young trees to sprout.

✦ FIRE ✦

Each brother gathered together a group of men to support his claim. Soon it appeared there would be war.

CHAPTER 6

⋆ Loo-Wit, The Fire-Keeper ⋆

(Nisqually—Pacific Northwest)

When the world was young, the Creator gave everyone all that was needed to be happy. The weather was always pleasant. There was food for everyone and room for all the people. Despite this, though, two brothers began to quarrel over the land. Each wanted to control it. It reached the point where each brother gathered together a group of men to support his claim. Soon it appeared there would be war.

The Creator saw this and was not pleased. He waited until the two brothers were asleep one night and then carried them to a new country. There a beautiful river flowed through and tall mountains rose into the clouds. He woke them just as the sun rose and they looked out from the mountaintop to the land below. They saw what a good place it was. It made their hearts good.

"Now," the Creator said, "this will be your land." Then he gave each of the brothers a bow and a single arrow. "Shoot your arrow into the air," the Creator said. "Where your arrow falls will be the land of you and your people, and you shall be a great chief there."

The brothers did as they were told. The older brother shot his arrow. It arched over the river and landed to the south in the valley of the Willamette River. There is where he and his people went, and they became the Multnomahs. The younger brother shot his arrow. It flew to the north of the great river. He and his people went there and became the Klickitats.

Then the Creator made a great stone bridge across the river. "This bridge," the Creator said, "is a sign of peace. You and your peoples can visit each other by crossing over this bridge. As long as you remain at peace, as long as your hearts are good, this bridge will stand."

For many seasons the two peoples remained at peace. They passed freely back and forth across the great stone bridge. One day, though, the people to the north looked south toward the Willamette and said, "Their lands are better than ours." One day, though, the people to the south looked north toward the Klickitat and said, "Their lands are more beautiful than ours." Then, once again, the people began to quarrel.

The Creator saw this and was not pleased. The people were becoming greedy again. Their hearts were becoming bad. The Creator darkened the skies and took fire away. Now the people grew cold. The rains of autumn began and the people suffered greatly.

"Give us back fire," they begged. "We wish to live again with each other in peace."

Their prayers reached the Creator's heart. There was only one place on Earth where fire still remained. An old woman named Loo-Wit had stayed out of the quarreling and was not greedy. It was in her lodge only that fire still burned. So the Creator went to Loo-Wit.

"If you will share your fire with all the people," The Creator said, "I will give you

The people saw a young woman as beautiful as the sunshine itself. Before her, there on the stone bridge, burned a fire.

whatever you wish. Tell me what you want."

"I want to be young and beautiful," Loo-Wit said.

"That is the way it will be," said the Creator. "Now take your fire to the Great Stone Bridge above the river. Let all the people come to you and get fire. You must keep the fire burning there to remind people that their hearts must stay good."

The next morning, the skies grew clear and the people saw the sun rise for the first time in many days. The sun shone on the Great Stone Bridge and there the people saw a young woman as beautiful as the sunshine itself. Before her, there on the bridge, burned a fire. The people came to the fire and made up their quarrels. Loo-Wit gave each of them fire. Now their homes again became warm and peace was everywhere.

One day, though, the chief of the people to the north came to Loo-Wit's fire. He saw how beautiful she was and wanted her to be his wife. At the same time, the chief of the people to the south also saw Loo-Wit's beauty. He, too, wanted to marry her. Loo-Wit could not decide which of the two she liked better. Then the chiefs began to quarrel. Their peoples took up the quarrel and fighting began.

When The Creator saw the fighting he became angry. He broke down the Great Stone Bridge. He took each of the two chiefs and changed them into mountains. The chief of the Klickitat became the mountain we now know as Mount Adams. The chief of the Multnomahs became the mountain we now know as Mount Hood. Even as mountains, they continued to quarrel, throwing flames and stones at each other. In some places, the stones they threw almost blocked the river between them. That is why the Columbia River is so narrow in the place called the Dalles today.

Loo-Wit was heartbroken over the pain caused by her beauty. She no longer wanted to a beautiful young woman. She could no longer find peace as a human being. The Creator took pity on her and changed her into a mountain also, the most beautiful of the mountains. She was placed so that she stood between Mount Adams and Mount Hood, and she was allowed to keep the fire within herself which she had once shared on the Great Stone Bridge. Eventually she became known as Mount St. Helens and she slept peacefully.

Though she was asleep, Loo-Wit was still aware, the people said. The Creator had placed her between the two quarreling mountains to keep the peace, and it was intended that humans, too, should look at her beauty and remember to keep their hearts good, to share the land and treat it well. If we human beings do not treat the land with respect, the people said, Loo-Wit will wake up and let us know how unhappy she and the Creator have become again. So they said long before the day in the 1980s when Mount St. Helens woke again.

This story is about the generosity of the Creator, the foolishness of the two brothers and the importance of energy in the form of the sun and fire. Every time the Creator gives the people the things they need to live, they become greedy and begin to quarrel. First the brothers quarrel over controlling the land. Then, because the Klickitats and Multnomahs quarrel over whose land is "better" or "more beautiful," the Creator takes away the sun and leaves only one person with fire, an old woman named Loo-Wit. Eventually the Creator gives back the sun and Loo-Wit shares the fire. Then the chief of the Klickitats and the chief of the Multnomahs fight over the beautiful Loo-Wit. In his anger the Creator turns them into what we know as Mount Adams and Mount Hood respectively. Yet still they fight. Loo-Wit, who is turned into our Mount St. Helens, wants the people to share the land and treat it with respect. In recent years she has shown her anger because the people have not been respectful. To the Indians, the violent eruption of Mount St. Helens in 1980 shows how unhappy she is over the ways people are misbehaving.

Discussion

There are important lessons here: of the need for energy from the sun and fire, of the fickleness of human nature, of our tendency toward greed and fighting and of the potential for people to live as a peaceful community sharing the Earth.

This chapter defines energy, explores some values and ways of conserving it and looks at its many forms and properties. Renewable and nonrenewable sources of energy are studied. Additional activities are designed to foster a positive, empathic relationship among people and between people and the Earth.

Energy is the ability to do work. *Heat, light* (radiant energy) and *motion* (mechanical energy) are three important forms of energy.

Radiant energy from the sun is trapped by photosynthesis in the form of *chemical energy* (food). (See Chapter 7 page 50 for a discussion of photosynthesis.) As chemical energy is used by plants and animals during respiration, it can produce new growth, be converted to mechanical energy or be dispersed as heat. This heat may be used or lost to the environment. When burned directly, as in a log on a fire, chemical energy is transformed into light and heat, or it can be converted into other forms like electrical or mechanical energy.

Some potential sources of energy, such as wood, can be replaced in a relatively short period and are called *renewable* sources, whereas *nonrenewable* sources such as fossil fuels (gas, oil and coal) take thousands and sometimes millions of years to replace and so are finite.

Questions

1. Whenever the Creator gives the people what they need, they live in peace for a time. But what happens every time the people become dissatisfied?
2. What does their fighting and greed lead to? What is greed? If you were the Creator, how would you handle greedy people?
3. Several times in the story the people are living in peace. What does it mean to share the land? To live in community? What is peace? How is Loo-Wit rewarded for her peace-loving and generous ways? Why do you think people become dissatisfied with peace and sharing?
4. Fire and sunlight are very important to the Indians. How did they use fire? What kinds of "fire" or energy do we use today?
5. Loo-Wit becomes what we know as Mount St. Helens and she wants the people to treat the land, the river and each other with respect, to act as good *stewards*. What happened to Mount St. Helens in the summer of 1980? What does this mean to the Indians?

Activities
The Energy Experience

ACTIVITY: (A) Make a simple machine to demonstrate three forms of energy: heat, light (radiant energy) and motion (mechanical energy). (B) Concentrate sunlight with a magnifying lens to create intense heat.

GOALS: Learn three forms of energy: heat, light (radiant

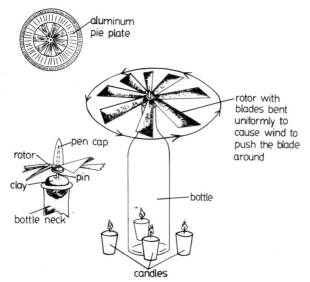

Figure 6-1. Heat, Light and Motion Machine.

aluminum pie plate

rotor with blades bent uniformly to cause wind to push the blade around

pen cap

rotor

pin

clay

bottle

bottle neck

candles

energy) and motion (mechanical energy).

AGE: Younger Children and Older Children

Use information from the "Discussion" section to define energy for the children and describe its various forms and properties. Then perform the following demonstrations.

PROCEDURE A: *Heat, Light and Motion Machine.* Fashion the rotor blades from an aluminum pie plate or other thin metal (Figure 6-1). You can also use cardboard pieces covered with aluminum foil. Mark the center of the blades, use the awl to make a hole there and push the pen cap through from the bottom. The blades must be well balanced so you may need to trim a little off along the edges to create an even weight distribution. Push some modeling clay into the neck of the bottle and set the pin or nail firmly into the clay with the point up. If you use a nail, you will need to file any rough edges off the point so the rotor will spin freely. When a pin or short nail is used, the pen cap will need to be cut down in length so that it will not slip completely over the pin and drag in the clay. Slip the pen cap over the pin or nail to balance the rotor blades on the tip of the point. Place some candles, evenly spaced, around the base of the bottle and beneath the rotor blades. Light the candles and the rotor will begin to spin. The rotor spins faster when more candles are used. The candles should be far enough below the rotor to prevent it from catching on fire.

Encourage the children to figure out why the rotor turns. Warm air from the candles (warm air rises) creates an updraft that blows on the angled rotor blades and causes them to spin.

PROCEDURE B: *Sun Burning. For older children only.* By holding a magnifying lens perpendicular to the direction of the sun's rays and focusing the light onto a single, tiny point, the children can burn paper, wood or other substances. Have them write their names on small pieces of wood and then use a hand lens and sunlight to burn the letters into the wood. *Caution: This activity needs to be closely supervised. Tell the children never to look directly at the sun and especially not through their hand lenses because the beam will burn their eyes. It is best to have them wear sunglasses during the activity because the focused beam of the sun that they will use for burning is very bright.*

MATERIALS: (A) large candles; tall soda pop or juice bottle; aluminum pie plate or cardboard and aluminum foil; awl; ruler; modeling clay; pin or finish nail; metal file; pen cap; scissors; matches; a pair of cutting pliers to cut the pen cap (needed if a pin or short nail is used). (B) magnifying lens, pencil, wood or paper, sunshine.

Energy: Lose It as You Use It

ACTIVITY: Watch a demonstration that distinguishes renewable and nonrenewable energy sources. Practice conserving energy at home and write a report about the experience. Calculate the total amount of gasoline used by families of the group each week and encourage families to conserve gasoline.

GOAL: Understand that chemical energy can be converted into other forms of energy: heat, light and motion. Understand that energy flows through a system and must be replaced once it passes through. Experience ways that energy is harnessed to do work. Learn the difference between renewable and nonrenewable energy sources and learn how to conserve energy.

AGE: Older Children

PROCEDURE: Explain that chemical energy can be converted into other forms of energy (light, heat and motion) and that it becomes dispersed in the process. As an example, explain that chemical energy is stored in a piece of paper, which is made from wood. Burn the paper and show how the energy is given off as heat and light, reducing the paper to a small pile of ashes. Explain that more trees can be grown to replace the paper and its energy.

Light the oil lamp or kerosene lamp. Discuss that the fuel formed from the remains of plants and animals over millions of years, and that it cannot be replaced in time considered in terms of our lives, or even human history. Relate this to gasoline and natural gas and our limited supplies of these fuels. Explain how some societies use mostly renewable fuels such as wood and animal dung, while many North Americans and people in other industrialized societies use mostly nonrenewable energy such as gas, coal, oil and their refined products like gasoline and kerosene.

Have the children write down one way that they could use less of each of these three forms of energy: light, heat (hot water, room heat, cooking heat, etc.) and motion (especially automobiles). Ask the children to conserve energy as much as possible for one day, then write a report about what it is like to live using less energy. Encourage this practice at home by setting a good example for energy conservation. Facilitate a brainstorming session to help the children collect ideas on how to conserve energy—such as shutting off unused lights, putting on warm clothes and turning the heat down and taking shorter hot showers.

As part of this exercise, have each child find out how

much gasoline the tank holds in the family car(s). Calculate the average gas tank volume for the group, and fill up an equivalent number of gallon or liter jugs with water to show how much the gas tanks really hold. Now have each child keep track of one week's worth of gasoline used by his or her family as well as the total mileage driven that week. At the week's end, have each child throw one bean in a large pot to represent each gallon or liter of gasoline used by his or her family. How many gallons or liters were used in one week by all of the families in your group? How many miles or kilometers of driving does this represent? Have the children create a list of ways that their families could manage with less driving. The children can talk to their parents about their findings and try to get them to make a commitment to use less gasoline.

MATERIALS: Graphic, to help explain renewable and nonrenewable energy sources (pictures of trees, oil fields, etc.) or samples of the energy sources themselves, paper to burn, oil lamp or kerosene lamp, matches, metal pan to burn the paper in, pencils, writing paper, dried beans, large pot, gallon or liter containers.

Care Pairs

ACTIVITY: Develop and maintain an empathic relationship with (A) another person, and (B) a part of nature.
GOALS: Understand that empathy is an important part of caring that helps us to understand how another person thinks and feels, and how our actions affect other people and the natural world. Understand that these relationships form a small caring community in which peace and sharing are important.
AGE: Younger Children and Older Children
PROCEDURE A: *Person to Person.* Help children to pair up with a friend.

Have each child draw a picture or write or tell a story about something he or she likes very much. Or each child may bring in an object that represents a positive experience. Then the pairs can talk about the picture, object or story and the experience behind it. Allow time for discussion after the sharing.

Repeat the same exercise, only have the children describe an experience that they did not, or do not like.

Encourage the children to share with each other how they think and feel about other things that happen in their lives. Be sure to explain that a feeling is different from an attitude. For instance, a feeling can be stated directly: "I feel unhappy, happy, angry, etc." Whereas attitudes are usually stated: "I feel (think) *that* this has

been a good day."

Once a week for several weeks have the partners do something nice that they believe their partner would enjoy. Have them work on projects to give one another or write a nice letter to their Care Partner.

It is important to be clear about behavior that promotes positive interactions. If a child is mistreating another by saying or doing nasty things, point out that this is not the way to care for someone and give reasons why this is so. Then, help the child to discover ways of acting in a caring manner.

PROCEDURE B: *We've Got the Whole Earth in Our Hands.* While the children are in their Care Pairs have them visit the outdoors. Together they will try to imagine how a tree, bird, rock, squirrel, caterpillar or other part of the Earth would "feel" if it were not treated well. Children will imagine that they *are* that part of nature. Have them demonstrate (with a picture, story, poem or verbal response) something that would please that living thing or object. Review their projects and, if it is possible for them to do that or those things for their natural partners and in your estimate they will be positive things to do, have the children carry them out. These projects may range from building nesting boxes for wood ducks or bluebirds, to brush piles that shelter woodland mice, to putting up bird feeders and caring for the birds through the winter and spring. (See the activities in Chapters 5 and 21 for more ideas.) Repeat this experience by having the children imagine what their natural partner would *not* like to have happen to it. Projects will consist of working to keep these negative things from happening or stopping them if they are now occurring.

MATERIALS: (A) pencils, paper, crayons, materials as needed for their projects. (B) similar materials as in part A plus a natural area to visit.

Extending the Experience

• Place some ice cubes in small containers and insulate them using different kinds of materials. Return periodically to unwrap the ice cubes to discover which materials make better insulators.
• Show your children your home heating system so they can see where their heat comes from and what kind of heating fuel is being used.
• Visit a busy gasoline station and calculate how much gasoline is sold in fifteen minutes. Multiply this by the number of hours that the station is open to estimate daily sales. Multiply this by the number of days the station is open each week to get weekly sales. Ask the management to provide their averages for volume sold each week in order to verify your findings.

• Have the children create illustrations to go with the rich imagery of the story of *Loo-Wit, The Fire-Keeper*.

• Discuss the fighting that occurs in this story between the Multnomahs and Klickitats. Develop alternative ways that these people could have resolved their conflicts and rewrite the story giving it a peaceable solution.

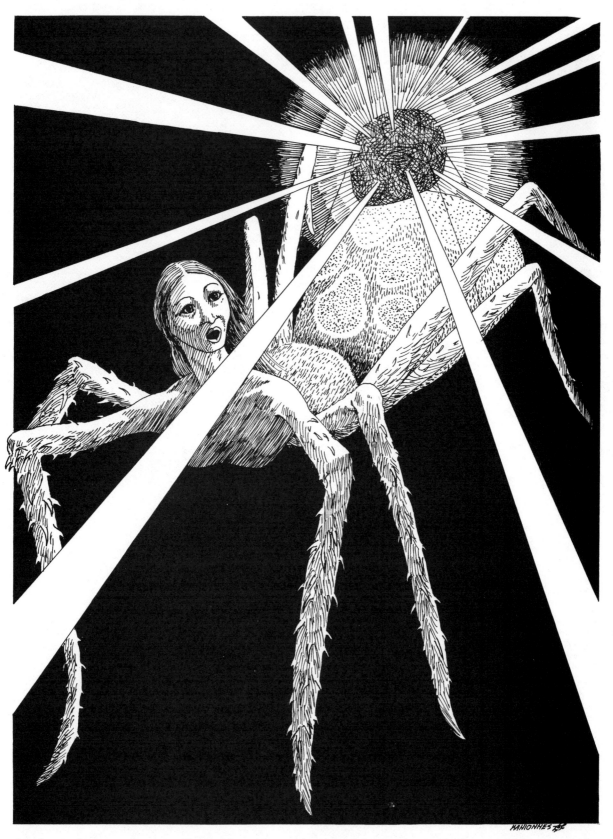

Grandmother Spider wove a bag out of her webbing. She put the piece of the sun into her bag and carried it back with her.

CHAPTER 7

How Grandmother Spider Stole The Sun

(Muskogee [Creek]—Oklahoma)

When the Earth was first made, there was no light. It was very hard for the animals and the people in the darkness. Finally the animals decided to do something about it.

"I have heard there is something called the Sun," said the Bear. "It is kept on the other side of the world, but the people there will not share it. Perhaps we can steal a piece of it."

All the animals agreed that it was a good idea. But who would be the one to steal the Sun?

The Fox was the first to try. He sneaked to the place where the Sun was kept. He waited until no one was looking. Then he grabbed a piece of it in his mouth and ran. But the Sun was so hot it burned his mouth and he dropped it. To this day all foxes have black mouths because that first fox burned his carrying the Sun.

The Possum tried next. In those days Possum had a very bushy tail. She crept up to the place where the Sun was kept, broke off a piece and hid it in her tail. Then she began to run, bringing the Sun back to the animals and the people. But the Sun was so hot it burned off all the hair on her tail and she lost hold of it. To this day all possums have bare tails because the Sun burned away the hair on that first possum.

Then Grandmother Spider tried. Instead of trying to hold the Sun herself, she wove a bag out of her webbing. She put the piece of the Sun into her bag and carried it back with her. Now the question was where to put the Sun.

Grandmother Spider told them, "The Sun should be up high in the sky. Then everyone will be able to see it and benefit from its light."

All the animals agreed, but none of them could reach up high enough. Even if they carried it to the top of the tallest tree, that would not be high enough for everyone on the Earth to see the Sun. Then they decided to have one of the birds carry the Sun up to the top of the sky. Everyone knew the Buzzard could fly the highest, so he was chosen.

Buzzard placed the Sun on top of his head, where his feathers were the thickest, for the Sun was still very hot, even inside Grandmother Spider's bag. He began to fly, up and up toward the top of the sky. As he flew the Sun grew hotter. Up and up he went, higher and higher, and the Sun grew hotter and hotter still. Now the Sun was burning through Grandmother Spider's bag, but the Buzzard still kept flying up toward the top of the sky. Up and up he went and the Sun grew hotter. Now it was burning away the feathers on top of his head, but he continued on. Now all of his feathers were gone, but he flew higher. Now it was turning the bare skin of his head all red, but he continued to fly. He flew until he reached the top of the sky, and there he placed the Sun where it would give light to everyone.

Because he carried the Sun up to the top of the sky, Buzzard was honored by all the birds and animals. Though his head is naked and ugly because he was burned carrying the Sun, he is still the highest flyer of all, and he can be seen circling the Sun to this day. And because Grandmother Spider brought the Sun in her bag of webbing, at times the Sun makes rays across the sky which are shaped like the rays in Grandmother Spider's web. It reminds everyone that we are all connected, like the strands of Grandmother Spider's web, and it reminds everyone of what Grandmother Spider did for all the animals and the people.

Fox and Possum both try and fail to bring the Sun to the dark side of the Earth. Then Grandmother Spider succeeds by weaving a web to hold the Sun.[1] Buzzard makes a great sacrifice when he brings the Sun to the highest point in the sky for all to see. The feathers on his head burn off and his skin becomes red. He is honored for the gift of his sacrifice, which helped to bring the Sun to others.

(Grandmother Spider also appears in Chapter 10, "The Hero Twins and the Swallower of Clouds.")

Discussion

In this chapter the questions and activities focus on the importance of the sun's energy for supporting life on Earth, the concept of energy flow among plants and animals, and the causes of the day-and-night cycle.

Figure 7-1. During photosynthesis green leaves convert sunlight into the food energy that feeds virtually all living things.

The sun is the source of energy for all life on Earth except for some bacteria and a few highly specialized marine animals that live near hot springs deep in the sea: some 10-foot-long (3-meter) tube worms along with giant clams and crabs. When sunlight strikes green plant leaves, a vital reaction occurs called *photosynthesis*. During this reaction, which takes place in the green chlorophyll of the leaf, water and carbon dioxide are changed into glucose, protein, starches and other nutrients that trap the sun's energy. Water is also produced, and oxygen, a gas, is released.[2] Here is the formula for photosynthesis:

water + carbon dioxide + chlorophyll (green pigment in leaves) in the presence of sunlight yields→oxygen + nutrients (simple sugars, starches, fats, proteins, vitamins, etc.) + water

Plants are the producers of energy for other living things. Animals get energy from the sun either by eating the plants directly (*herbivores*) or by eating other animals (*carnivores*). *Omnivores* eat both plants and animals. Some animals (*scavengers*) and plants (*saprophytes*) eat the dead remains and wastes of plants and/or animals.[3] All of these organisms are called *consumers*—their sources of energy can ultimately be traced back to plants. *Respiration* is the process during which plants and animals metabolize food to get energy for growth and maintenance.

Energy flows from the sun to the plants and animals. A simple *food chain* would be seeds → mouse→red-tailed hawk (Figure 7-2). Of course, mice also eat grass and other plant parts, and red-tailed hawks consume other small animals. For this reason, food chains weave together to form a *food web*. The term *niche* refers to the role or roles an organism plays in an environment, such

Figure 7-2. Simple food chain.

as producer, consumer, decomposer, pollinator or planter of seeds. For instance, a squirrel is an herbivore, a kind of consumer, that lives in the forest, and it also spreads seeds which get caught in its fur, deposited in its droppings and planted when it stores nuts in the ground.

Much energy is dissipated as food passes from each source to the next energy level. Roughly 90 percent of the energy is expended by the consumer's growth, physical motion, metabolic processes such as breathing and digestion and by the production of heat. One hundred pounds (45.4 kilograms) of seeds can produce around 10 pounds (4.5 kilograms) of mice and one pound (.45 kilogram) of red-tailed hawk. The 90 percent figure varies greatly from 2–40 percent according to the food energy found in the plant or animal eaten, the season, and the efficiency of the consumer. In this way a *food pyramid* forms, with any given area being capable of feeding fewer animals on the top levels of the food web. (Figure 7-3)

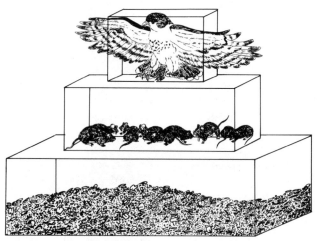

Figure 7-3. Food pyramid

But the sun does not shine constantly on the green plants that produce our food energy. The cycle of night and day, which affects all life, results from the Earth's rotation on its axis. A complete day/night cycle occurs every 24 hours. As the Earth turns on its axis, someone standing at the equator is moving at the speed of more than 1,000 miles (1,609 kilometers) every hour!

Questions

1. What happens to Fox and Possum when they try to carry the Sun? How does Grandmother Spider succeed in bringing the Sun to the dark side of Earth?
2. What does the story explain about the Fox's mouth, the Possum's tail and the Buzzard's head?
3. Buzzard makes a great sacrifice to place the Sun high in the sky. What is this sacrifice? What would you do in Buzzard's situation?
4. Why do the Indians have a story about the sun?
5. Could we live without the sun? Why not? What are the most important things that the sun gives to us?
6. What do plants use, and produce, during photosynthesis?
7. What would happen to the animals if green plants were gone?
8. What causes night and day? How long is each day?

Activities

Sun Circle

ACTIVITY: Form a circle and use oranges to symbolize the sun. Recall the many gifts that we receive from the sun.

GOALS: Understand the important things that the sun provides for us, such as food, energy, heat and light. Understand that we can show our appreciation for these gifts.

AGE: Younger Children and Older Children

PROCEDURE: Have the children stand in a circle with their eyes closed. Have each child hold one hand open, palm up, in front of him or her. Take chilled orange sections, or pieces of other bright, sunshinelike fruit, and place one in each waiting hand. Ask the children to guess what you have passed out. Once someone has guessed correctly instruct the children to open their eyes but to not eat the oranges yet. Hold up a whole orange and tell the children that it represents the sun. Have each child name one thing that we receive from the sun; then he or she can eat the orange slice. Remind the children that it is the food energy created from sunlight by plants that enables people to do this, or any other activity.

MATERIALS: Sunny area, enough chilled and peeled oranges to provide one section for each child, a whole orange.

Vored to Death

ACTIVITY: Go on a scavenger hunt to find plants and animals. Discuss green plants as producers of energy and animals as consumers, and classify each animal as an herbivore, carnivore or omnivore. Make a human pyramid to represent energy flow. Discuss photosynthesis.

GOALS: Understand that, through photosynthesis, sunlight grows the green plants that are the primary food for animals. Understand the concepts of producer, consumer, food chain and food pyramid. Be familiar with the meaning of the terms herbivore, carnivore and omnivore.

AGE: Younger Children and Older Children

PROCEDURE: Beforehand: Make up scavenger hunt cards listing plants, animals and signs of animals living in a habitat nearby, such as a field, forest or pond. For instance, these cards may list grass, milkweed, a maple tree, grasshopper, cricket, mouse, deer, swallow, pigeon, fox and hawk. Leave room on the cards for children to write in their own discoveries.

Have the children work in small groups of about three as they go outside on a scavenger hunt using the cards you have prepared. Ask the children to look for, but not collect, the plants and animals. The children will place marks next to those things on the list that they find, and write in any new sightings. After about ten minutes, collect the children and have each small group report on what they have found. If they report any interesting or exciting findings they can lead the group to that spot and share their discovery. Groups will then write the names of all plants and animals found on separate file cards.

Define and discuss the concepts of photosynthesis, energy producers and some major kinds of consumers: herbivores, carnivores and omnivores. Use the field guides and other books to research each animal's food habits. Classify each animal as either an herbivore, carnivore or omnivore. Have the children write this classification on the back of each card that contains the corresponding animal's name.

Now combine the children into groups of six. Each group needs six cards labeled with plant and animal names: three plants and three animals (two herbivores and one carnivore *or* one herbivore, one omnivore and one carnivore). Tell the children that each animal is one kind of *Vore* that eats other living things, and that in any field, forest or pond the plants and animals are being "Vored to Death." Describe how energy is used for heat, growth and work as the animals feed and are active in other ways, and how energy is dissipated each time the animals eat plants or other animals. Because the available energy is diminished as it moves along the food chain, plants can only support so many herbivores and even fewer carnivores. That is why each group in this activity has only one carnivore. Use a drawing of a food pyramid constructed from the animals found near the home to make your point.

Explain the concept of food pyramid to the children. To reinforce the lesson, have each group of six make a pyramid with the three plants on the bottom, the herbivores (and in some cases an herbivore and an omnivore) on the second level and the carnivore on top.

You can combine groups to make still larger pyramids. While they are in the pyramid shape, and beginning with the children on the bottom, have them introduce themselves, explaining the kind of "vores" that they are and the roles they play in the food pyramid.

Ask the children what would happen if someone came along and took all of the plants away and there was no food left to eat. Pull a "plant" out from under one of the small pyramids and see what happens, but be careful because the children will come tumbling down.

No matter how much fun the children have, they are still going to be "Vored to Death."

MATERIALS: Scavenger hunt cards, pencils, 5x7-inch (12.7x17.8-centimeter) file cards, string to hang the cards around the childrens' necks, field guides and books for background information on common plants and animals, drawing of a food pyramid composed of animals found near your home.

Daylight—Night

ACTIVITY: Demonstrate the causes of day and night by (A) using a flashlight and globe, and (B) dividing the room in half, creating a dark and light side, and forming a circle of children that rotates through the "daytime" and "nighttime."

GOAL: Visualize how the Earth's rotation on its axis brings night and day as the different regions of the Earth become exposed alternately to sunlight and shadow.

AGE: Younger Children and Older Children

PROCEDURE A: *As the World Turns.* Equip the flashlight with a tube to focus the beam (Figure 7-4). A narrow tube like a juice can will do in most cases, or you may need to use a coffee can or to make your own tube out of cardboard if the flashlight beam is wide.

Mark the spot on the globe where your town or city is located. If you are using the beach ball to represent the Earth, mark any place about one third of the way down from the uppermost point. Then sit the ball in a large salad bowl and place it on a Lazy Susan or other suitable rotating stand. Darken the room and focus the beam onto one side of the "Earth" while someone slowly turns the globe and creates "night" and "day." Point to your location on the map and watch that spot move from light to dark and back again as the world turns.

PROCEDURE B: *The Edge of Night.* Divide the room in half by hanging blankets from ceiling to floor and leave a door-sized space at each end of the row of blankets on each side of the room. Arrange the children in a circle passing through the two openings with the curtain in the

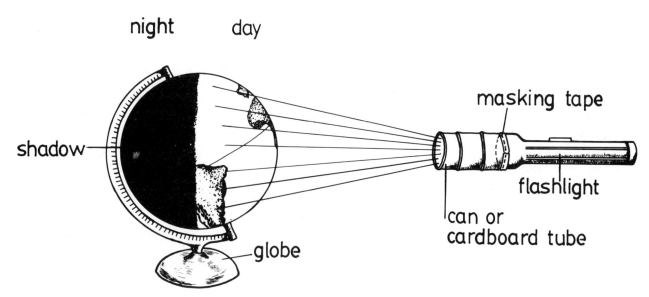

night   day

masking tape

shadow

flashlight

can or
cardboard tube

globe

globe

Figure 7-4. Demonstrating day and night with As the World Turns.

center. Light up one side of the room and keep the other side dark. Use a lamp with a yellow lightbulb or colored globe or lampshade for a sunlight effect. Tell the children that the circle represents the surface of the Earth as it rotates into and out of the sunlight (day) and shadow (night). Stop the group occasionally and ask the children what time of day they are in.

MATERIALS: (A) flashlight; a tube that is open at both ends, such as an empty frozen juice can, coffee can or a piece of cardboard rolled and taped; masking tape; globe or large beach ball; large salad bowl; Lazy Susan or other rotating stand. (B) enough blankets to divide the room in half from ceiling to floor, nails and hammer to tack up blankets or rope to hang the blankets from, desk or floor lamp with a yellow light (bulb, globe or lampshade).

Extending the Experience

•　Grow some vegetable seeds. Place some in the sunlight and some in a dark place. Watch and record their progress, noting the effects of sunlight deprivation on growing plants over a period of several weeks.

•　Take a night hike and experience that world and how the eyes can adapt to the dark, a process which takes about 30 minutes when the eyes are adjusted to a lighted area at the outset. At dusk, when it is almost dark, have the children look into the forest at some trees about 10 feet (3 meters) away. Tell the children not to blink their eyes. In a short time, the trees will appear to fade into the background and disappear!

•　Use a prism to show how light can be separated into the spectral colors: red, orange, yellow, green, blue, indigo and violet. Hang a crystal prism in a sunny window and it will cast colors about the room on sunny days.

•　Make a simple sundial by driving a stake into the ground and marking the shadow where it is cast at different times of day. When the sundial is completed, it can be used to tell time with reasonable accuracy. Keep in mind that the position of the shadow will drift relative to time because the sun's angle changes as the season progresses.

Notes

1.　See Chapter 14 for information about the nature of the sun as a solar body.

2.　See Chapter 4, page 27, for more information about the gas exchange between plants and animals and an activity on this theme.

3.　See Chapter 16 for a description of how nutrients cycle, via the decomposers, from soil to plants to animals and back to the soil, in a constant circle of life and death.

✦ EARTH ✦

GA-DA-RUM. GA-DA-RUM. The big rock was rolling down the hill after Coyote.

CHAPTER 8

·Tunka-shila, Grandfather Rock·

(Lakota [Sioux]—Great Plains)

The Lakota (Sioux) people say that in the beginning everything was in the mind of Wakan-Tanka. All things which were to be existed only as spirits. Those spirits moved about in space seeking a place to manifest themselves. They traveled until they reached the sun, but it was not a good place for creation to begin because it was too hot. Finally they came to the Earth, which was without life and covered with the great waters. There was no dry land at all for life to begin upon. But then, out of the waters, a great burning rock rose up. It made the dry land appear, and the clouds formed from the steam it created. Then the life on Earth could begin. So it is that the rock is called Tunka-shila, "Grandfather Rock," for it is the oldest one. Because of that, the rocks must be respected. In the sweat lodge,¹ when the water strikes the heated stones and that mist rises once again, it brings back the moment of creation as the people in the lodge sing to Tunka-shila, the Grandfather, the old one.

In "Tunka-shila, Grandfather Rock," there is a great awareness of basic geological concepts. Grandfather Rock is burning when he rises up from beneath the oceans, just as rock from the depth of the Earth's crust that surfaces gradually or suddenly (as lava) is hot and cools to the surface temperature. Volcanoes are places where the Earth's crust is very thin and molten rock emerges dramatically during an eruption, along with steam, heat, ash and fire. As in this first story, science tells us that over four billion years ago the hot, molten rock of the Earth's crust gave off water vapor that formed clouds and rain.

·Old Man Coyote and the Rock·

(Pawnee—Great Plains)

Old Man Coyote was going along. It was quite a while since he had eaten and he was feeling cut in half by hunger. He came to the top of a hill and there he saw a big rock. Old Man Coyote took out his flint knife.

"Grandfather," Old Man Coyote said to the rock, "I give you this fine knife. Now help me in some way, because I am hungry."

Then Old Man Coyote went along further. He went over the top of the hill and there at the bottom was a buffalo that had just been killed.

"How lucky I am," Old Man Coyote said. "But how can I butcher this buffalo without a knife? Now where did I leave my knife?"

Then Old Man Coyote walked back up the hill until he came to the big rock where his knife still lay on the ground.

"You don't need this knife," he said to the big rock. Then he picked his flint knife up

The big rock rolled right over him and flattened him out.

and ran back to where he had left the buffalo. Now, though, where there had been a freshly killed buffalo, there were only buffalo bones and the bones were very old and grey. Then, from behind him, Old Man Coyote heard a rumbling noise. He turned around and looked up. The big rock was rolling down the hill after him. GA-DA-RUM, GA-DA-RUM.

Old Man Coyote began to run. He ran and ran, but the stone still rumbled after him. GA-DA-RUM, GA-DA-RUM. Old Man Coyote ran until he came to a bear den.

"Help me," he called in to the bears.

The bears looked out and saw what was chasing Old Man Coyote. "We can't help you against Grandfather Rock," they said.

GA-DA-RUM, GA-DA-RUM. The big rock kept coming and Old Man Coyote kept running. Now he came to a cave where the mountain lions lived and he called out again.

"Help me," Old Man Coyote said. "I am about to be killed!"

The mountain lions looked out and saw what was after Old Man Coyote. "No," they said, "we can't help you if you have angered Grandfather Rock."

GA-DA-RUM, GA-DA-RUM. The big rock kept rumbling after Old Man Coyote and he kept running. Now he came to the place where a bull buffalo was grazing.

"Help me," Old Man Coyote yelled. "That big rock said it was going to kill all the buffalo. When I tried to stop it, it began to chase me."

The bull buffalo braced his legs and thrust his head out to stop the big rock. But the rock just brushed the bull buffalo aside and left him standing there dazed, with his horns bent and his head pushed back into his shoulders. To this day all buffalo are still like that.

GA-DA-RUM, GA-DA-RUM. The big rock kept rolling and Old Man Coyote kept running. But Old Man Coyote was getting tired now and the rock was getting closer. Then Old Man Coyote looked up and saw a nighthawk flying overhead.

"My friend," Old Man Coyote yelled up to the nighthawk, "this big rock that is chasing me said you are ugly. It said you have a wide mouth and your eyes are too big and your beak is all pinched up. I told it not to say that and it began to chase me."

The nighthawk heard what Old Man Coyote said and grew very angry. He called the other nighthawks. They began to swoop down and strike at the big rock with their beaks. Each time they struck the big rock a piece broke off and stopped rolling. GA-DA-RUM, GA-DA-RUM. The rock kept rolling and Old Man Coyote kept running, but now the rock was much smaller. The nighthawks continued to swoop down and break off pieces. Finally the big rock was nothing but small pebbles.

Old Man Coyote came up and looked at the little stones. "My, my," he said to the nighthawks, "Why did you wide-mouthed, big-eyed, pinch-beaked birds do that to my old friend?" Then Old Man Coyote laughed and started on his way again.

Now the nighthawks were very angry at Old Man Coyote. They gathered all of the pieces of the big rock and fanned them together with their wings. The next thing Old Man Coyote knew, he heard a familiar sound behind him again. GA-DA-RUM, GA-DA-RUM. He tried to run, but he was so tired now he could not get away. The big rock rolled right over him and flattened him out.

In this story, Old Man Coyote angers Grandfather Rock by taking back the knife that he presents as a gift for help in finding food. Then, as he is chased by Grandfather Rock, Coyote asks the bears, the mountain lions, the buffalo and the nighthawks for help. He tricks the buffalo and the nighthawks by lying to them to get their help. Finally, he insults the nighthawks and, as a result, ends up being caught and squashed by Grandfather Rock.

(Old Man Coyote also appears in Chapter 5, "Four Worlds, The Dine [Navajo] Story of Creation," and in Chapter 13, "How Coyote Was the Moon.")

Discussion

The questions and activities in this chapter investigate the three major kinds of rocks, their properties and the dynamics of geology such as weathering and rock formation. The components of soil, soil formation and the importance of soil for growing the plants that support life on Earth are also explored.

There are three major kinds of rocks. *Igneous* rocks form from molten rock (*magma*) that has cooled; for example granite, quartz and pumice (lava that has cooled and solidified). (Quartz and pumice are both types of igneous rock, but they should never be "taken for granite.") Igneous rocks are hard because they mostly consist of interlocking crystals formed as the molten magma slowly cooled. Volcanic lava cools too quickly for the molecules to arrange themselves into crystals. When sediments are compressed by the layers above them, they solidify and harden to form *sedimentary* rocks like sandstone and limestone. Sedimentary rocks are usually composed of layers that were originally laid down by wind or water. Limestone, which has a high calcium content, is a sedimentary rock that forms from the shell remnants of sea creatures. Sedimentary or igneous rocks that are altered by heat, pressure or chemical action change into *metamorphic* rocks. For instance, sandstone forms quartzite and limestone will change into marble. Metamorphic rocks are crystalline and often appear as wavy bands and stripes.

Earth's continents are part of large crustal plates that are gradually moving as they drift upon the partially molten rock below. Points of contact along the edges of these plates, where they are grinding together or pulling apart, are places where earthquakes occur and mountains and volcanoes are formed. Wherever two plates push against one another, one rides over the other and mountains and volcanoes are thrust up. The other plate is depressed and those rocks are heated and melted to form magma. In this way a *rock cycle* occurs over millions of years as rock is heaved up, eroded into sediments, pressed down into the Earth's crust and finally uplifted once again (Figure 8-1).

Surface rocks experience heat, cold, water, wind and ice. These forces cause *weathering* of the rocks, breaking them down into smaller pieces over time

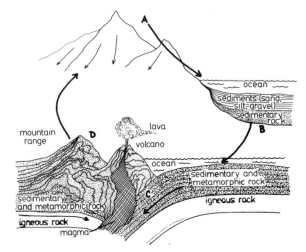

Figure 8-1. The rock cycle. A. Erosion and weathering produce sediments of sand, silt and gravel from volcanic slopes and mountain sides, which are carried to the ocean by streams and rivers. B. As sediments build up they become compressed, hardened and cemented to form sedimentary rocks. Further pressure, heat and chemical action creates metamorphic rocks. C. Sedimentary and metamorphic rocks are compacted, heated and melted where two plates of the Earth's crust meet and one plate becomes buried beneath the other. Wherever this molten material or magma cools and solidifies it forms igneous rocks. D. Volcanoes and mountains form as rocks on the overriding plate are pushed up and folded. The rock cycle begins again with erosion and weathering on these slopes.

which form the mineral basis for *soil.* Lichens (plants that are really an association of an alga and a fungus) can grow on bare rock by producing food from sunlight and obtaining minerals from the rock with their strong dissolving acids. Whenever small pockets of soil accumulate in the cracks and crevices of rocks, they afford places for the windblown spores of mosses and plant seeds to germinate. Weathered rocks and dead plant and animal remains, called *organic matter,* continue to build the soil over time. This process is called *primary succession.* Soil supports the plant growth which makes life on Earth possible.

Questions

1. Why does Grandfather Rock get angry at Old Man Coyote?

2. How many times does Old Man Coyote lie during the story? Why does he lie? Do you know any people who lie and trick people to get their way? How do you feel when someone does this to you?

3. Does Old Man Coyote end up getting his way? What finally happens to him?

4. What are some things that Old Man Coyote could have done to get food and not anger Grandfather Rock?

5. What are rocks? Do you know the names of any kinds of rocks? How do the three major rock types—sedimentary, metamorphic and igneous—form?

6. How does soil form? Why is soil important to plants, animals and people?

Activities
Rock to Rock: A Fantasy Journey

ACTIVITY: Listen to a story and imagine that you are becoming different kinds of rocks over a long period of time. Look at the three major kinds of rocks and discuss the rock cycle.

GOALS: Understand the three main kinds of rocks—sedimentary, metamorphic and igneous—and the differences between them. Realize that rocks change over time and that the process of weathering breaks rocks down into finer pieces, which, over thousands and sometimes millions of years, can change into different kinds of rocks. Understand the rock cycle.

AGE: Older Children

PROCEDURE: Read the following story while the children sit with their eyes closed. Emphasize that these events would happen over thousands or even millions of years. Later, have them draw pictures of their experiences as a rock as imagined during the fantasy journey. Then look at samples of the three rock types and use the diagram in Figure 8-1 to explain the rock cycle.

Rock to Rock

Imagine that you are a rock as big as a baseball. Your home is on a sunny hillside and you can see down into a deep valley with a river roaring far below. You like your home. Sometimes it is very hot there. Can you feel the sunlight warming you?

During the winter you get worried about the ice that freezes in the crack on top of you. This crack grows bigger each year because the ice pushes hard on the sides of the crack.

One spring it is very wet, wetter than you can ever remember. The rain pours in little streams rushing down the hillside. Feel the water flowing over you and into the soft mud below.

Suddenly you feel a rumbling and the Earth begins to shake. You look uphill and a large wall of mud rushes down and sweeps you up. You begin to roll down, down, down into the valley. Ow! You hit another rock and you split along the crack. Now you are two halves rolling down the hill.

Splash! You land in the river. For days and days you are pushed by the swift, strong waters. Rolling and bumping along you are getting all broken up into gravel and sand. Finally the river enters the ocean and your many pieces settle onto a large, flat area along with millions of pieces of sand, gravel and silt.

Some pieces settle on top of you and you are getting squished. You yell out, "Stop pushing!" but more and more weight presses down. Your pieces get pushed and stuck together with other pieces. You are now hardening and becoming a *sedimentary rock.*

The pressure grows and you begin to get warmer and warmer. You change color and form into many hard crystals. Now you're a *metamorphic rock.*

You keep getting pushed farther down. It is hot. It is boiling hot! Everything begins to melt and you are part of a hot mass of melted rock called *magma* deep underground. It seems like forever that you are part of this big melted sea of rock. Will you ever see the sun again? You want to be back on your hillside feeling the hot sun and cool wind and rain.

Wait, you're being pushed up and the Earth is shaking and rumbling again. You can feel yourself rising higher and higher. Fire, ash, dust and steam surround you and, with a loud explosion, you burst up out of the top of a volcano. Red-hot lava is all around. You are a scalding, steamy piece of lava shooting through the air when, suddenly, you land on a high point of the volcano away from the hot flow of lava below.

Slowly the volcano begins to quiet down and the lava cools and hardens. You are now a cold, grey *igneous rock* on top of a high volcano looking down at a river flowing far below. When the dark ashes blow away and the sky clears, the sun comes out and warms you high up on the volcano—your new home.

MATERIALS: Story "Rock to Rock," pencils, crayons, paper, samples of the three basic rock types, Figure 8-1.

Rock Charades

ACTIVITY: Examine the three major types of rocks for differences in their physical properties. Discuss how each kind of rock forms. Pantomime the three kinds of rocks.
GOALS: Understand that there are three main kinds of rocks and that each kind has its own characteristic properties and process of formation.
AGE: Younger Children
PROCEDURE: Beforehand: Create diagrams of the basic structure of the three types of rocks: sedimentary, metamorphic and igneous.

Pass the rock samples around and talk about how each kind forms. Discuss the properties of each kind of rock. Have the children pick at the rocks with nails to see how hard or soft the rocks are.

Now display the diagrams showing the basic structure of the three types of rocks. Form the whole group into a circle and have them squeeze together to imitate the particles of a sedimentary rock that are stuck together. Divide the children into smaller groups of four each. Have each group "make" a metamorphic rock out of their bodies by imitating the way that kind of rock forms. Now have each small group "melt" and then harden to form an igneous rock.
MATERIALS: Samples of sedimentary rock with many pieces stuck together, usually in layers, metamorphic rock with minute, aligned crystals and igneous rock, a solid mass which may have large crystals; nails for picking at the rocks; diagrams showing how each rock type is structured.

Making Soil[2]

ACTIVITY: Discuss the ingredients of soil, how soil forms and its importance to life on Earth. Examine soil outdoors.
GOALS: Understand the five major components of soil and the process of soil formation. Be aware that the thin crust of topsoil on the Earth supports the plant life that in turn feeds the animals and makes continuing life possible.
AGE: Younger Children and Older Children
PROCEDURE: Prepare the soil by combining each of the ingredients in the large pan. Start with the rocks first and talk about weathering by ice, rain, wind and the sun's heat. As you add the other soil ingredients, discuss the role each plays in the life of the soil community. Emphasize the importance of soil for growing plants, which in turn feed animals. When your "soil" is prepared, show it to the group and ask whether they think it is real soil. Emphasize that soil development is a natural process that takes many years. Then use the activities listed at the end of this chapter to study soil outdoors.
MATERIALS: Spoon, large metal pan, soil ingredients: rocks (mineral), leaves and twigs (organic matter), water, air, clay models of living things such as worms, soil insects, etc.

Extending the Experience

• Study the soil life outside using hand lenses, small garden spades and collecting jars.
• Take the temperature at the soil surface and about six inches (15.2 centimeters) below. Record and discuss the reasons for the differences in these temperatures.
• Find a road cut or eroded river bank and create a vertical slice of soil with a shovel to study the three layers, which are called *horizons* (See Figure 8-2). The

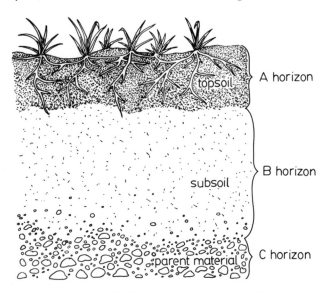

Figure 8-2. Soil profile. Topsoil is dark brown, rich in humus and other organic matter, and often well-aerated. It usually has a thin layer of partly decomposed plant and animal remains on the surface (A horizon). Subsoil is lighter in color than topsoil, has a high mineral content, is often colored by compounds leached from above and is a less favorable environment than topsoil for the growth of plant roots (B horizon). Parent material consists of rocks in various stages of weathering, which are usually derived from bedrock, and from which soil particles form (C horizon).

A horizon is the rich, brown, organic *topsoil* which is high in humus and decomposing plants and animals. Below this is the *B horizon* or *subsoil*, which is lighter in color and often takes on hues from compounds leached down from above. Finally, the *C horizon* consists of rocks and other *parent material* from which the soil was derived, usually coming from the bedrock.

• Start a rock collection.

• Play rock friends. Have each child find a small rock of about 1 inch (2.5 centimeters) in diameter and have her or him get to know the rock very well by the feel of it, especially its shape, weight and texture. Each child should initial the rock to identify it. Collect the rocks in a hat or bag. The children must pick their own rocks out by the sense of feeling alone. Discourage peeking.

• Visit an area where rocks are abundant. Hand out cards with descriptive words such as rough, sharp, red, bumpy, smooth and heavy. Have the children collect rocks that fit these descriptions.

• Look at rocks under an ultraviolet light. Many rocks that look very dull in normal daylight, such as calcite, will glow under ultraviolet light.

Notes

1. The sweat lodge is a small structure where people gather in a cleansing ritual. The intense heat of the steam rising from heated stones purifies the body. This experience, along with the rituals of the "sweat," purifies the spirit.

2. See Chapter 16 for more information and activities about soil.

✤ WIND AND WEATHER ✤

Now the wind was so strong that it blew off his hair, but Gluscabi still kept walking, facing into the wind.

Chapter 9

⋄ Gluscabi and the Wind Eagle ⋄

(Abenaki—Northeast Woodlands)

Long ago, Gluscabi lived with his grandmother, Woodchuck, in a small lodge beside the big water. One day Gluscabi was walking around when he looked out and saw some ducks in the bay.

"I think it is time to go hunt some ducks," he said. So he took his bow and arrows and got into his canoe. He began to paddle out into the bay and as he paddled he sang:

Ki yo wah ji neh
yo hey ho hey
Ki yo wah ji neh
Ki yo wah ji neh.

But a wind came up and it turned his canoe and blew him back to shore.

Once again Gluscabi began to paddle out and this time he sang his song a little harder:

KI YO WAH JI NEH
YO HEY HO HEY
KI YO WAH JI NEH
KI YO WAH JI NEH.

But again the wind came and blew him back to shore. Four times he tried to paddle out into the bay and four times he failed. He was not happy. He went back to the lodge of his grandmother and walked right in, even though there was a stick leaning across the door, which meant that the person inside was doing some work and did not want to be disturbed.

"Grandmother," Gluscabi said, "What makes the wind blow?"

Grandmother Woodchuck looked up from her work.

"Gluscabi," she said, "Why do you want to know?"

Then Gluscabi answered her just as every child in the world does when they are asked such a question.

"Because," he said.

Grandmother Woodchuck looked at him. "Ah, Gluscabi," she said. "Whenever you ask such questions I feel there is going to be trouble. And perhaps I should not tell you. But I know that you are so stubborn you will never stop asking until I answer you. So I shall tell you. Far from here, on top of the tallest mountain, a great bird stands. This bird is named Wuchowsen, and when he flaps his wings he makes the wind blow."

"Eh-hey, Grandmother," said Gluscabi, "I see. Now how would one find that place where the Wind Eagle stands?"

Again Grandmother Woodchuck looked at Gluscabi. "Ah, Gluscabi," she said, "Once again I feel that perhaps I should not tell you. But I know that you are very stubborn and would never stop asking. So, I shall tell you. If you walk always facing the wind you will come to the place where Wuchowsen stands."

"Here, Grandfather," he said, "let me wrap this around you so I can lift you more easily."

"Thank you, Grandmother," said Gluscabi. He stepped out of the lodge and faced into the wind and began to walk.

He walked across the fields and through the woods and the wind blew hard. He walked through the valleys and into the hills and the wind blew harder still. He came to the foothills and began to climb and the wind still blew harder. Now the foothills were becoming mountains and the wind was very strong. Soon there were no longer any trees and the wind was very, very strong. The wind was so strong that it blew off Gluscabi's moccasins. But he was very stubborn and he kept on walking, leaning into the wind. Now the wind was so strong that it blew off his shirt, but he kept on walking. Now the wind was so strong that it blew off all his clothes and he was naked, but he still kept walking. Now the wind was so strong that it blew off his hair, but Gluscabi still kept walking, facing into the wind. The wind was so strong that it blew off his eyebrows, but still he continued to walk. Now the wind was so strong that he could hardly stand. He had to pull himself along by grabbing hold of the boulders. But there, on the peak ahead of him, he could see a great bird slowly flapping its wings. It was Wuchowsen, the Wind Eagle.

Gluscabi took a deep breath. "GRANDFATHER!" he shouted.

The Wind Eagle stopped flapping his wings and looked around. "Who calls me Grandfather?" he said.

Gluscabi stood up. "It's me, Grandfather. I just came up here to tell you that you do a very good job making the wind blow."

The Wind Eagle puffed out his chest with pride. "You mean like this?" he said and flapped his wings even harder. The wind which he made was so strong that it lifted Gluscabi right off his feet, and he would have been blown right off the mountain had he not reached out and grabbed a boulder again.

"GRANDFATHER!!!" Gluscabi shouted again.

The Wind Eagle stopped flapping his wings. "Yesss?" he said.

Gluscabi stood up and came closer to Wuchowsen. "You do a very good job of making the wind blow, Grandfather. This is so. But it seems to me that you could do an even better job if you were on that peak over there."

The Wind Eagle looked toward the other peak. "That may be so," he said, "but how would I get from here to there?"

Gluscabi smiled. "Grandfather," he said, "I will carry you. Wait here." Then Gluscabi ran back down the mountain until he came to a big basswood tree. He stripped off the outer bark and from the inner bark he braided a strong carrying strap which he took back up the mountain to the Wind Eagle. "Here, Grandfather," he said. "let me wrap this around you so I can lift you more easily." Then he wrapped the carrying strap so tightly around Wuchowsen that his wings were pulled in to his sides and he could hardly breathe. "Now, Grandfather," Gluscabi said, picking the Wind Eagle up, "I will take you to a better place." He began to walk toward the other peak, but as he walked he came to a place where there was a large crevice, and as he stepped over it he let go of the carrying strap and the Wind Eagle slid down into the crevice, upside down, and was stuck.

"Now," Gluscabi said, "It is time to hunt some ducks."

He walked back down the mountain and there was no wind at all. He waited till he came to the treeline and still no wind blew. He walked down to the foothills and down to the hills and the valleys and still there was no wind. He walked through the forests and through the fields, and the wind did not blow at all. He walked and walked until he came back to the lodge by the water, and by now all his hair had grown back. He put on some fine new clothing and a new pair of moccasins and took his bow and arrows and went down to the bay and climbed into his boat to hunt ducks. He paddled out into the water and sang his canoeing song:

Ki yo wah ji neh

yo hey ho hey

Ki yo wah ji neh

Ki yo wah ji neh.

But the air was very hot and still and he began to sweat. The air was so still and hot that it was hard to breathe. Soon the water began to grow dirty and smell bad and there was so much foam on the water he could hardly paddle. He was not pleased at all and he returned to the shore and went straight to his grandmother's lodge and walked in.

"Grandmother," he said, "What is wrong? The air is hot and still and it is making me sweat and it is hard to breathe. The water is dirty and covered with foam. I cannot hunt ducks at all like this."

Grandmother Woodchuck looked up at Gluscabi. "Gluscabi," she said, "what have you done now?"

And Gluscabi answered just as every child in the world answers when asked that question, "Oh, nothing," he said.

"*Gluscabi,*" said Grandmother Woodchuck again, "Tell me what you have done."

Then Gluscabi told her about going to visit the Wind Eagle and what he had done to stop the wind.

"Oh, Gluscabi," said Grandmother Woodchuck, "will you never learn? Tabaldak, The Owner, set the Wind Eagle on that mountain to make the wind because we need the wind. The wind keeps the air cool and clean. The wind brings the clouds which gives us rain to wash the Earth. The wind moves the waters and keeps them fresh and sweet. Without the wind, life will not be good for us, for our children or our children's children."

Gluscabi nodded his head. "Kaamoji, Grandmother," he said. "I understand."

Then he went outside. He faced in the direction from which the wind had once come and began to walk. He walked through the fields and through the forests and the wind did not blow and he felt very hot. He walked through the valleys and up the hills and there was no wind and it was hard for him to breathe. He came to the foothills and began to climb and he was very hot and sweaty indeed. At last he came to the mountain where the Wind Eagle once stood and he went and looked down into the crevice. There was Wuchowsen, the Wind Eagle, wedged upside down.

"Uncle?" Gluscabi called.

The Wind Eagle looked up as best he could. "Who calls me Uncle?" he said.

"It is Gluscabi, Uncle. I'm up here. But what are you doing down there?"

"Oh, Gluscabi," said the Wind Eagle, "a very ugly naked man with no hair told me that he would take me to the other peak so that I could do a better job of making the wind blow. He tied my wings and picked me up, but as he stepped over this crevice he dropped me in and I am stuck. And I am not comfortable here at all."

"Ah, Grandfath . . . er, Uncle, I will get you out."

Then Gluscabi climbed down into the crevice. He pulled the Wind Eagle free and placed him back on his mountain and untied his wings.

"Uncle," Gluscabi said, "It is good that the wind should blow sometimes and other times it is good that it should be still."

The Wind Eagle looked at Gluscabi and then nodded his head. "Grandson," he said, "I hear what you say."

So it is that sometimes there is wind and sometimes it is still to this very day. And so the story goes.

Gluscabi cannot paddle as strong as the wind can blow so he decides to do something about it. When he learns from Grandmother Woodchuck where the Wind Eagle, Wuchowsen, lives, Gluscabi schemes to stop the wind. He tricks the Wind Eagle, but once the wind stops Gluscabi learns that the wind also brings some good things with it that he had not thought about before. Grandmother Woodchuck tells him of the many ways that life would not be good without wind. Gluscabi listens and goes to free the Wind Eagle. He pretends to be someone else. The Wind Eagle recognizes him but still he listens to Gluscabi's advice. Today the wind blows sometimes and doesn't blow at other times.

(Gluscabi also appears in Chapter 3, "The Coming of Gluscabi," Chapter 20, "Gluscabi and the Game Animals," and as Koluscap in Chapter 10, "Koluscap and the Water Monster." Grandmother Woodchuck also appears in Chapter 20, "Gluscabi and the Game Animals.")

Discussion

The importance of wind and weather is emphasized throughout this chapter: the causes and benefits of the wind, large-scale wind patterns, local and regional influences upon wind patterns, wind and weather and the relationship between the wind and air pollution.

Wind is created when air moves from places of higher air pressure to places of lower air pressure. These differences in pressure are caused by the uneven heating and cooling of air. Warm air is lighter than cold air so it rises. For instance, during the day along the coastline, the land heats up faster than the water and this warmer air rises. The heavier cool air from the sea rushes in beneath the rising warm air on land and a *sea breeze* or *lake breeze* forms. At night the land cools faster than the water, and the warmer air over the water rises and is replaced by cooler air blowing in from the land, forming a *land breeze* (Figure 9-1). In mountainous and hilly areas, air in the valley warms during the day and rises, causing an upslope *valley breeze*. As the air cools and sinks at night, a *mountain wind* blows downslope.

Clouds form when a rising warm air mass meets a cold air mass at a temperature below the *dew point* of the warm air—the temperature at which water vapor con-denses into liquid and forms visible droplets. The warm air cools and can no longer hold as much moisture. Clouds are constantly both forming and being evaporated by the sun's heat.

There are other forces that affect the wind. The Earth's spinning motion creates the *Coriolis effect*, which causes winds to be deflected to the right in the Northern Hemisphere and to the left in the Southern Hemisphere. This creates the *westerlies*, the general wind pattern blowing from west to east in the middle latitudes of the northern and southern hemispheres. This pattern is familiar to most people because we generally look to the west to see what kind of weather lies ahead. Wind direction is indicated by saying where the wind is coming *from*. An easterly wind blows from east to west.

Besides playing an important role in determining weather patterns, wind also dilutes air pollution that is produced by automobile exhausts, electrical generating plants, industrial emissions and more. Wind blows across lakes and ponds to free them of floating debris and it mixes vital oxygen into the water.

Questions

1. Why does Gluscabi travel to visit the Wind Eagle?

a. sea or lake breeze (daytime)

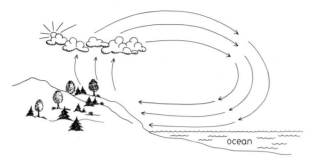

b. land breeze (nighttime)

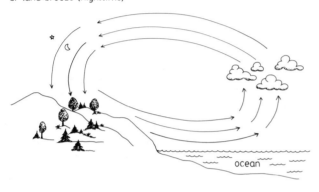

Figure 9-1. Wind patterns found along the shore. A. Sea breeze or lake breeze (daytime). Warm air over the land rises. Cooler offshore air rushes inland beneath this rising warm air. Clouds often form inland. B. Land breeze (nighttime). Warm air over the water rises. Cooler air from land rushes out to replace this rising warm air. Clouds often form over water.

What happens to him along the way?

2.   Is it a good idea for Gluscabi to tie up the Wind Eagle? Why or why not?

3.   Gluscabi plays a trick to get his way and he stops the wind so he can paddle his canoe. What else could Gluscabi have done instead of tying up the Wind Eagle?

4.   Once Grandmother Woodchuck tells Gluscabi what has happened because the wind is no longer blowing, Gluscabi feels foolish and he listens to Grandmother Woodchuck. What lessons does Gluscabi learn?

5.   What is the scientific explanation for what causes the wind to blow?

6.   How does the wind benefit people and other living things?

Activities
Catch the Wind

ACTIVITY: (A) Watch a demonstration of how wind cleans the air by dissipating pollution and how warm air rises and how clouds form. (B) Watch clouds "disappear" from the sky. (C) Sail a boat by wind power to see how wind cleans the surface of the waters. (D) Race windblown seeds.

GOALS: Understand that wind energy helps to keep the air clean, to bring the clouds, to keep the surfaces of the waters clean and to spread plant seeds.

AGE: Younger Children

PROCEDURE: Beforehand: Assemble the boats for Activity C on the day before the field trip making sure that the mast is attached closest to the front of the boat (Figure 9-2).

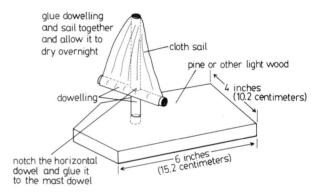

Figure 9-2. Boat assembly for Sail Away.

Take the children outdoors on a mildly windy day that is partly cloudy with cottony cumulus clouds overhead. Ask them to name several things that the wind does for us and for plants and animals. Be sure that the four main goals of the activity are covered. Discuss and show some kinds of seeds that blow on the wind (such as aster, milkweed, dandelion). Tell how the wind blows away air pollution and makes it less severe. Emphasize that the pollution is diluted and blown away but still exists downwind. Point out how the clouds are blowing across the sky and the surface of the water is free of debris because of the wind.

Lead the following activities:

PROCEDURE A: *Clouds and Clean Air.* Start a fire with dry wood and then place some green wood on top to generate a lot of smoke. Watch the rising smoke dissipate more and more as it is blown by the wind. Now douse the fire with water and watch the thick steam billow upward. Point out that the hot air is lighter and rises and that clouds form much the same way, except that the air is heated by the sun instead of the fire. Explain that warm air masses will rise until they get to where they are so cold that the water condenses out as visible vapor. This is similar to the way we can see our hot breath steaming on a cold day.

PROCEDURE B: *Now You See It—Now You Don't.* Have everyone lie down on their backs and look up at the clouds. Tell each person to pick a small, wispy cumulus cloud and watch it for a few minutes. The cloud will disappear. The "disappearing" clouds are really evaporating.

PROCEDURE C: *Sail Away.* This is a fun demonstration of how the wind clears the surface of the water. Place toy sailboats (See Figure 9-2) or folded paper boats into the water on the windward side and watch them sail across the pond.

PROCEDURE D: *Wind-Sown.* Pass out to each child a seed from a dandelion, milkweed or any other seed with a parasol or other adaptation for being carried on the wind. Line the children up shoulder to shoulder with their backs to the wind. Tell them they will be helping the wind to spread seeds. Lay a rope on the ground parallel to the line of children and about 20 feet (6.1 meters) downwind. This is the finish line. The rules are that when you say the words, "sow your seed," they are to release their seeds, but they are not to throw the seeds or blow them. The first seed to cross the finish line wins. If someone's seed lands before it crosses the finish line, have that person pick up the seed and release it again from where it landed.

MATERIALS: (A) dry wood and tinder, matches, green wood, pail of water, fireplace or fire ring and open area safe for starting a fire. (B) flat open area, cumulus clouds on a partly cloudy day. (C) lightweight wood (such as white pine) cut 4 inches (10.2 centimeters) wide by 6 inches (15.2 centimeters) long and pointed at one end, pencil, saw, drill and bit, carving knife, ruler, dowelling same size as the drill bit, cloth for the sail, glue, sandpaper. (D) seeds that have parasols and/or other adaptations for being carried on the wind, rope, flat open area.

From Whence the Wind?

ACTIVITY: (A) Watch a demonstration of how wind forms when hot and cold air fronts meet. (B) Make a rocket ship and harness air pressure to make the rocket blast off.

GOALS: Understand how wind is generated when adjacent air masses are unevenly heated, thus resulting in differences in air pressure. Learn how wind can be harnessed for fun and work.

AGE: Older Children

PROCEDURE A: *Blow In, Blow Out.* Find two rooms that are cooled and heated separately and are connected by a doorway. Shut the door and heat one room up while cooling the other down until the temperature difference is at least 25°F to 30°F (14°C to 16.7°C). Larger temperature differences will make this activity more effective. Now hang the blanket in the doorway on the side that the door *does not* open into. Leave a 6-inch (15.2-centimeter) space on the top and bottom of the blanket for air exchange. When you open the door, the warm air will blow over the blanket into the cold room, and the cold air will blow under the blanket into the warm room. Hold the tissue paper in the wind to show how the wind blows. Explain that these winds are caused because warm air is lighter than cool air, so it rises up over the cool air and blows over the blanket, while the heavier cool air pushes under the blanket below the warm air in the next room.

Discuss and look at the diagrams of land and sea breezes (see "Discussion" section in this chapter for details) and how these breezes relate to the wind you have just created. Keeping in mind the air flow over and under the blanket, ask the children which room would represent the sea and which the land if it were daytime. Ask the same question for nighttime.

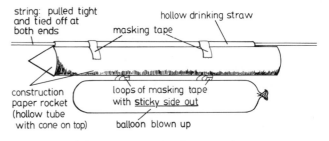

1) Blow balloon up and push onto masking tape loops while holding end of **balloon** closed.
2) Let go of end of balloon and blast off!

Figure 9-3. Assembly and operation for Blast Off: Air Pressure Rocket Ships.

PROCEDURE B: *Blast Off: Air-Pressure Rocket Ships.* This demonstration shows how air moves from a high-pressure system (inside the inflated balloons) to an area of lower pressure. Draw a large diagram of the illustration showing how to make rocket ships and help the children to assemble them while working in pairs (Figure 9-3). Set up several strings across the room and have the children take turns sending their rocket ships into flight. *Note:* Once a rocket is strung onto the track, fasten the masking tape loops onto the bottom of the *rocket.* Blow the balloon up and, while it is still inflated, hold the end closed but do not tie it. Then stick the inflated balloon firmly onto the loops of tape. Let go of

the open end of the balloon and Blast Off!
MATERIALS: (A) two adjacent rooms that have significant temperature differences of at least 25°F to 30°F (14°C to 16.7°C) and that are connected by a door, nails or tacks, blanket big enough to cover the doorway, tissue paper, Figure 9-1. (B) construction paper, masking tape, pencils, glue or paste, string, scissors, drinking straws, long thin balloons.

Things that Blow in on the Wind

ACTIVITY: (A) Discuss warm fronts, cold fronts and general and local weather patterns. Monitor the weather in your area and forecast the weather. (B) Sample the pollution from a car exhaust and discuss the forms of air pollution caused by burning fossil fuels. Measure wind direction and identify the sources of pollution blowing into your area from communities upwind, and the destination of your pollution blowing downwind.
GOALS: Understand the general wind and weather patterns moving from west to east in the middle latitudes of the northern and southern hemispheres. Be familiar with local variations in wind and weather patterns due to the affects of mountain ranges, oceans and other regional influences. Understand that the forthcoming weather conditions and air quality can often be estimated accurately by looking to the west.
AGE: Older Children
PROCEDURE A: *Weather Wise.* Discuss how air masses meet along *fronts*—places marking the leading edges of air masses where storms often occur. A warm air mass pushing against a heavier cold air mass rides over the cold air (*warm front*), while a cold air mass pushing against a warm air mass forces the lighter warm air upward (*cold front*). The weather map symbols for both a warm front and cold front are shown in Figure 9-4. Use the "Discussion" to explore the effects on wind and weather patterns caused by local and regional influences such as mountains, lakes and oceans.

Monitor the weather patterns to the west of your home, or in the direction of the prevailing winds in your region. Use newspapers, radio and television weather

reports, and information available from the local weather bureaus. Many newspapers print weather maps showing storm fronts. Predict what your weather will be like for the next day or two by studying approaching weather patterns upwind from your area. How do your predictions compare with those of the professional weather forecasters? Monitor the weather to see how accurate your predictions were: wind direction (measure this with the wind sock), wind speed, temperature, cloud cover, barometric pressure, etc.
PROCEDURE B: *Smut Goes Up, Must Come Down.* Take the group outdoors and over to an automobile on which the engine and exhaust pipe have cooled down. Rub the white cloth around the inside of the end of the exhaust pipe to collect a sample of the pollution that cars put into the air. Discuss how car exhausts contain carbon monoxide. This gas bonds to the hemoglobin in our blood 200 times more readily than oxygen, a situation which decreases the oxygen supply to body tissues. Exhaust emissions also produce nitrogen oxides and sulfur dioxide, which can change into nitric and sulfuric acids in the atmosphere, contributing to *acid rain*. There are many other forms of *air pollution* from industry, power plants and other sources, some of which can be very toxic and, in some cases, radioactive.

Now take a map of your region and look both upwind (windward) and downwind (leeward) to see where air pollution in your area is coming from and

warm front

cold front

Figure 9-4. Weather map symbols.

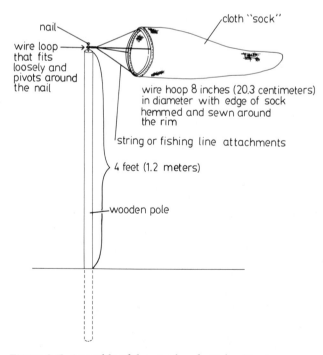

Figure 9-5. Assembly of the wind sock and support.

going to. Calculate wind direction using the simple wind sock described in the activities listed at the end of this chapter.

As a follow-up to this activity, have the children produce research reports on air pollution: as a general topic, as a local issue and as an issue in their lives that they can do something about. Have them include a list of specific ideas for how they can each work for cleaner air.

MATERIALS: (A) Figure 9-4; weather reports from newspapers, radio, television and weather bureau reports; thermometers; barometer; anemometer (wind speed gauge); wind sock (see Figure 9-5 for directions on how to make a wind sock); pencils; paper. (B) automobile, white cloth, regional map, wind sock, references, pencils, paper.

Extending the Experience

• Make a wind sock to hang outside (Figure 9-5). The closed tip of the sock will point in the direction the wind is *blowing toward*.
• Visit a local weather station where measurements and forecasts are made.
• Have fun with the wind:
—Hang wind chimes outside your home.
—Make pinwheels.
—Fly a kite.
—Blow soap bubbles into the wind.

✦ WATER ✦

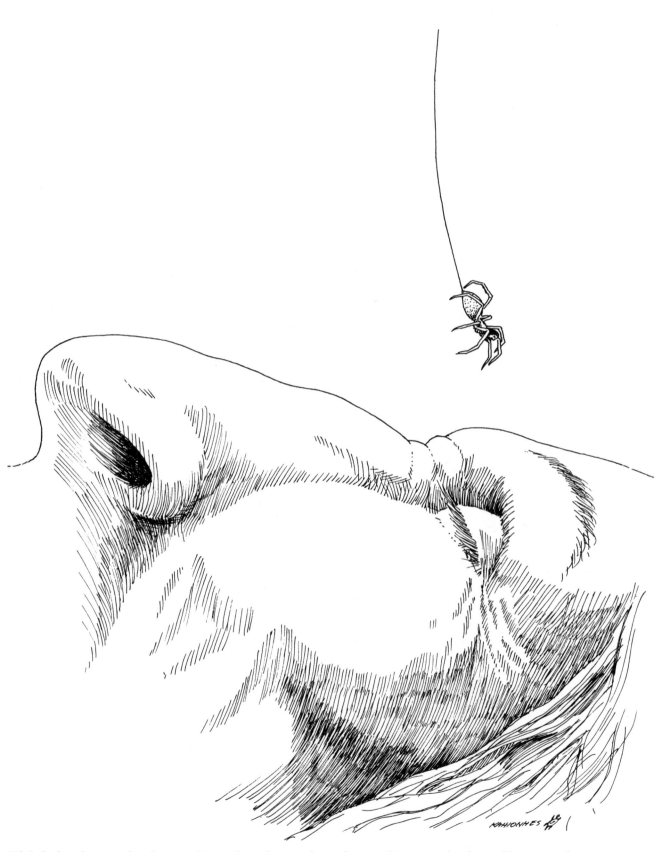

While he kept his eyes closed, pretending to sleep, she wove her web across his eyes so that he could not open them.

CHAPTER 10

The Hero Twins and the Swallower of Clouds

(Zuni—Southwest)

To the American Indian people of the dry Southwest, few things are more important than rain. The people speak of different kinds of rain: the *male rain*, which strikes hard on the Earth and washes away; the *female rain*, which falls gently and steadily, soaking the soil. Many stories are told of the rain, and songs relate to the coming of the rain. One of the corn-grinding songs of the Zuni people praises the mountains, from which the clouds come:

> Clouds come rising out of my beautiful mountain.
> Up in the sky, the rain makers are sitting.
> One after another rain clouds are coming.
> Over there the flowers are coming.
> Here the young corn is growing.

The clouds are powerful and benevolent, connected to the kachinas, those helping spirits of the ancestors. So when the Zuni tell the story of the giant, Swallower of Clouds, they tell of a very terrible monster indeed.

When the world was young, they say, a giant lived in the cliffs above Cañon de Chelly. The food he lived on was human beings, and he caught the clouds and squeezed them into his mouth for drink. The people called him Swallower of Clouds, and the bravest of the men tried to destroy him. However, anyone who went out to kill the giant was never seen again. Before long, because he was swallowing all the clouds, the snow stopped falling to the north. Because he was swallowing all the clouds, the rain no longer came from the west. Because he was swallowing all the clouds, the mist above the mountains to the east disappeared. Because he was swallowing all the clouds, the springs to the south dried up. The crops dried up and died. The people were suffering and some began to die.

The Hero Twins saw what was happening.

"We will go and kill Swallower of Clouds," they said. Then they started on their way to the cliffs where he lived. But as they were following the path to the cliffs, they saw a spider web next to the trail.

"Grandmother Spider," they said, greeting the maker of webs, "Are you well?"

"I am well, Grandchildren," said the spider. "Where are you going?"

"We are going to kill the giant, Swallower of Clouds," they said.

"That is good," Grandmother Spider said, "but first let me warn you. The giant has a trick. He stretches himself out on top of the cliffs. He pretends to be sleeping and then

Then the Twins leaped up and struck him with their clubs.

tells whoever comes to pass under his legs, which are arched over the trail. As soon as someone passes under, though, he grabs them and throws them over the cliff."

"Grandmother," said the Hero Twins, "what should we do?"

"Let me go ahead of you," said Grandmother Spider. "Wait for a while and then follow."

Then Grandmother Spider set out. She did not go far before she came to the giant. He was stretched out on top of the cliff with his legs over the trail. He was as huge as a hill and his legs were bigger than tree trunks. He pretended to sleep, for he had heard the Hero Twins were coming to fight him. Grandmother Spider, though, was so small the giant did not see her. She climbed up a rock behind him and then let herself down on his forehead with a strand of silk. While he kept his eyes closed, pretending to sleep, she wove her web across his eyes so that he could not open them up.

Now the Hero Twins, having waited for a while, started on their way. When they came close to the place where Swallower of Clouds lay, they began to sing a war song.

"Who is that?" said Swallower of Clouds as the Hero Twins came closer, "I am old and tired, too old and tired to move out of the way. Just pass under my legs."

But when the Hero Twins came close to the giant, they split up. One ran to the right and one ran to the left. The giant tried to open his eyes to see what they were doing, but he was blinded by the spider web.

"Where are you, Little Ones?" he said, striking at them and missing. "Just pass under my legs."

Swallower of Clouds struck again at the Hero Twins, but he could not see them and he missed. Then the Twins leaped up and struck him with their clubs. One struck him in the head. The other struck him in the stomach. They killed Swallower of Clouds with their clubs. Then they threw him over the same cliffs where he had thrown all the people he had killed. Now the clouds were able to pass again through the mountains. The snow returned to the north. The rain came again from the west. The mists formed once more above the mountains to the east. The springs to the south flowed once more. Again the crops of the people grew and the people were well and happy.

It is said that when the giant fell, he struck so hard that his feet drove into the Earth. He still stands there to this day with his blood dried red all along his great stiff body. Though some call that great stone by other names, the Zunis know it is the Swallower of Clouds. When they see it they are thankful for the deed of the Hero Twins and the life-giving rain.

⋅Koluscap and the Water Monster⋅

(MicMac and Maliseet—Nova Scotia)

Once there was a great drought. The rain stopped falling and the Earth became dry. Finally the streams themselves stopped flowing. There was a village of people who lived by the side of a stream, and life now became very hard for them. They sent someone

Now Koluscap was taller than the dam, taller even than the monster who sat in the deep water.

upstream to see why the stream had stopped. Before long, the man came back.

"There is a dam across the stream," he said. "It is holding back all the water. There are guards on the dam. They say their chief is keeping all the water for himself."

"Go and beg him for water," said the elders of the village. "Tell him we are dying without water to drink." So the messenger went back again. When he returned, he held a bark cup filled with mud.

"This is all the water their chief will allow us to have," he said.

Now the people were angry. They decided to fight. They sent a party of warriors to destroy the dam. But as soon as the warriors came to the dam, a great monster rose out of the water. His mouth was big enough to swallow a moose. His belly was huge and yellow. He grabbed the warriors and crushed them in his long fingers which were like the roots of cedar trees. Only one warrior escaped to come back to the people and tell them what happened.

"We cannot fight a monster," the people said. They were not sure what to do. Then one of the old chiefs spoke. "We must pray to Gitchee Manitou," he said. "Perhaps he will pity us and send help." Then they burned tobacco and sent their prayers up to the Creator.

Their prayers were heard. Gitchee Manitou looked down and saw the people were in great trouble. He decided to take pity and help them and he called Koluscap. "Go and help the people," Gitchee Manitou said.

Koluscap then went down to the Earth. He took the shape of a tall warrior, head and shoulders taller than any of the people. Half of his face was painted black and half was painted white. A great eagle perched on his right shoulder and by his side two wolves walked as his dogs, a black wolf and a white wolf. As soon as the people saw him they welcomed him. They thought surely he was someone sent by the Creator to help them.

"We cannot afford you anything to drink," they said. "All the water in the world is kept by the monster and his dam."

"Where is this monster?" Koluscap said, swinging his war club, which was made of the root of a birch tree.

"Up the dry stream bed," they said.

So Koluscap walked up the dry stream bed. As he walked he saw dried up and dead fish and turtles and other water animals. Soon he came to the dam, which stretched between two hills.

"I have come for water," he said to the guards on top of the dam.

"GIVE HIM NONE, GIVE HIM NONE!" said a big voice from the other side of the dam. So the guards did not give him water.

Again Koluscap asked and again the big voice answered. Four times he made his request, and on the fourth request Koluscap was thrown a bark cup half-full of filthy water.

Then Koluscap grew angry. He stomped his foot and the dam began to crack. He stomped his foot again and he began to grow taller and taller. Now Koluscap was taller than the dam, taller even than the monster who sat in the deep water. Koluscap's club was now bigger than a great pine tree. He struck the dam with his club and the dam burst open and the water flowed out. Then he reached down and grabbed the water monster. It tried to fight back, but Koluscap was too powerful. With one giant hand Koluscap squeezed the water monster and its eyes bulged out and its back grew bent. He rubbed it with his other hand and it grew smaller and smaller.

"Now," Koluscap said, "no longer will you keep others from having water. Now you'll just be a bullfrog. But I will take pity on you and you can live in this water from now on." Then Koluscap threw the water monster back into the stream. To this day, even though he hides from everyone because Koluscap frightened him so much, you may still hear the bullfrog saying, "Give Him None, Give Him None."

The water flowed past the village. Some of the people were so happy to see the water that they jumped into the stream. They dove so deep and stayed in so long that they became fish and water creatures themselves. They still live in that river today, sharing the water which no one person can ever own.

These stories come from cultures living in very different and distant environments in North America, yet both stories emphasize the importance of water. They begin with a drought and end with the water's return.

In "The Hero Twins and the Swallower of Clouds," the opening poem shows an understanding of the connection between clouds, rain and mountains. When the Cloud Swallower consumes all of the clouds, the rain and snow stop and a drought comes over the Earth. The Cloud Swallower has to be slain before the clouds come again. Because he is so big and wily, the Hero Twins and Grandmother Spider must cooperate to slay him.

In "Koluscap and the Water Monster," the stream stops flowing when the Water Monster builds a dam. He will give out only filthy water. When Koluscap turns the Water Monster into a bullfrog and breaks the dam, the water flows past the village once more. Some villagers dive in and become aquatic animals that live in the water from that day on.

(The Hero Twins also appear in Chapter 5, "Four Worlds, The Dine [Navajo] Story of Creation." Grandmother Spider also appears in Chapter 7, "How Grandmother Spider Stole The Sun.")

(Gitchee Manitou also appears in Chapter 14, "How Fisher Went to the Skyland: The Origin of the Big Dipper," and in Chapter 17, "Manabozho and the Maple Trees." Koluscap appears as Gluscabi in Chapter 3, "The Coming of Gluscabi," in Chapter 9, "Gluscabi and the Wind Eagle" and in Chapter 20, "Gluscabi and the Game Animals.")

Discussion

Drought is a serious, life-threatening problem in many regions of the world, including the southwestern United States, the lands lying east of the Rocky Mountains in the United States and Canada and the numerous deserts and arid lands around the world.

The issue of *water rights* arises in both stories. Who owns the water? This is a serious problem when people living downstream must accept the consequences of the water-use practices of upstream communities. For years Mexico has received the Colorado River from the United States as a greatly reduced flow of *polluted water* high in salts and other contaminants. Some of the activities in this chapter explore the issues of water supply, waste-water treatment and the conservation of fresh water.

Rain is part of the *water cycle*. In this continuous cycle, water falls from the clouds as rain and is then evaporated from the land, plants, animals, rivers and lakes by the sun's energy. This water then condenses as clouds that rain down on the land once again. Some water enters the *ground water* stores and may remain there for anywhere from a short time to many years. Water in the great Ogallala aquifer, underlying the Great Plains in the western United States, is only renewable when considered in terms of geologic time, yet we are using it up in decades.

In mountainous areas, air masses travel up the slopes, the air cools and moisture condenses to form clouds. As a result, there is usually a lot of rain that falls on the windward sides of mountains (Figure 10-1). A dry region called a *rain shadow* forms on the leeward slopes and beyond because the air has little moisture left to fall as rain.

The surface water that collects in lakes, ponds,

Figure 10-1. As an air mass moves up a mountain slope the air cools, moisture condenses out and clouds form.

rivers and wetlands is full of life: an abundance and variety of plants and animals depend on these habitats to live. These organisms must be adapted to life conditions in fresh water: oxygen levels (dissolved oxygen), temperature, pH (acid, neutral or alkaline conditions), availability of food, water quality and water movement (waves and currents) are all important. Plant and animal adaptations must enable them to perform all or some of these vital functions to live: exchanging gases, moving, finding optimal temperatures, maintaining correct body fluid concentrations, getting nourishment, excreting waste, reproducing, surviving in the current and adapting to seasonal changes.

Questions

1. How would you describe the characters of the Cloud Swallower and Water Monster? Why do the Indians believe that horrible monsters are taking the water when it disappears during a drought?
2. Koluscap is strong enough to defeat the Water Monster alone, but the Hero Twins are only able to defeat the Cloud Swallower because they cooperate with Grandmother Spider. What does it mean to cooperate? Why is this a good way to do things?
3. What are some of the terrible things that start to happen when no rain comes in the first story, when the giant is swallowing all the clouds? In what ways is water so important to living things?
4. Is there enough water in your neighborhood? Where does your water come from?
5. Can anyone own the water? Would you take water that someone else needs? How would you feel and what would you do if someone began to take the water you need to live?
6. Where does the water go to once you have used it? Is there an unlimited supply of water in the world? What could you do to conserve your water supply?

Activities
Rain Making

ACTIVITY: (A) Create the sounds of an imaginary

Figure 10-2. This frog is well adapted to aquatic life. Young frogs like this one, that have not yet completely absorbed their tadpole tails, are sometimes called "frogpoles" or "frogiwogs."

rainstorm. (B) Take a fantasy journey as a speck of dust that becomes a raindrop.

GOALS: Understand how a raindrop forms in the atmosphere and falls to the earth. Appreciate the sequence of events that we call a rainstorm.

AGE: Younger Children and Older Children

PROCEDURE A: *Making Rain.* Arrange the children so they are all facing you. Ask if anyone has ever made a rainstorm before. Then say that they are going to work together to make a storm. Tell them to imitate what you are doing whenever you walk in front of them, and have them *keep doing it* until you come by again doing something else. Each time you begin making a different sound you will start on one side of the group, walk across the front to the other side and then return to the starting point to start the next sound. Tell the children that they will first hear the wind, then drizzle, hard rain, thunder and then the storm as it gradually blows away. Your sequence of sound-making activities should go like this: (1) rub your hands gently, (2) snap your fingers (those who cannot snap their fingers can tap their

fingernails together), (3) slap your hands on your thighs, (4) keep slapping your hands on thighs plus stamp your feet, (5) return to just slapping hands on thighs, (6) snap fingers, (7) rub hands, (8) stop all movement.

PROCEDURE B: *From Dust to Raindrop.* Have the children lie face-up on their backs, close their eyes, take a few deep breaths and slowly exhale and clear their minds of all thoughts. Read the following story about the birth of a raindrop and have them imagine that they are becoming the raindrop. After the story has been read, discuss how a raindrop forms. Then have the children write their own conclusions to the story.

Birth of a Raindrop

You are a tiny speck of dust sitting on top of a dried-up weed in the middle of a big field. It is early October and a cold, strong wind blows. This fall, when the children were going back to school, you landed on the weed while it was still alive and green. Now you are wondering, "Will I ever become unstuck from this dried-up old weed?"

The cold wind blows longer and harder, causing your weed stalk to wave back and forth. Suddenly you are thrown off the weed and blown right toward a grove of trees. The bare branches of the trees look closer as the wind carries you toward them. At the last instant before you crash, you are lifted up over the treetops and into the open sky.

As you rise higher and higher you feel light as a feather. Down below, the field that you came from looks like a dot on the Earth. The wind carries you into a dark gray cloud. You hear a loud cry and almost bump into a large, black bird with a white head. Here in the cloud there are millions and billions of dust particles rushing around and bumping into one another. "Hey, watch it!" you yell as a careless piece of dust bumps into you. "Ouch! It's too crowded here!"

It's also very wet in the cloud, and some water vapor begins to cover you, turning you into a tiny droplet of water. Soon you become too heavy and start to fall back to Earth. All around you other raindrops are falling. Lower and lower you sink. In every direction you look there are raindrops. The whole world seems to be wet.

You can't tell where you are going. You begin asking yourself, "Where and when will I ever land?"

MATERIALS: copy of fantasy "Birth of a Raindrop," paper, pencils.

Life in a Pond or Stream

ACTIVITY: (A) Turn a person into an aquatic insect to demonstrate some adaptations needed to survive in fresh water. (B) Visit a pond or stream to study that environment and the plants and animals that live there.
GOALS: Appreciate the abundance and variety of life in fresh water. Understand the conditions for life in freshwater environments. Learn some specific adaptations to aquatic life among freshwater plants and animals.
AGE: Younger Children and Older Children
PROCEDURE A: *Now a Person: Now an Insect.* Beforehand: Prepare the parts of the aquatic insect to have them ready when you are making a child into an "insect."

Ask for a volunteer to come up front. Do the

children think that the volunteer could live underwater for a long period of time? Now say that you are going to turn the volunteer into an aquatic insect. Review, with leading questions, that insects have three body parts (head, thorax and abdomen) and six legs attached to the thorax. (See the "Discussion" in Chapter 18 for information about insects.) Make a list of all the things that the insect will need to do while underwater (such as to get oxygen, eat, move around, hold still in the current and sense the environment [smells, temperature, light levels, sounds, tastes]). Now, for each of these functions, ask the children what the volunteer will need on his/her body in order to be able to do that thing underwater. Each time you listen to the responses, add one or more *adaptations* to the child: gills; breathing tubes and other devices for gas exchange; mouth parts for handling food or attacking prey; legs with hairs or flattened (paddle-like) surfaces for swimming; claws for gripping; antennae or other sensory appendages for sensing temperature changes, scents, vibrations; eyes; etc.
Note: A variation on this activity is to have the children make their friends into aquatic insects. Or, each child could combine the *Materials* to fashion a model of an aquatic insect.
PROCEDURE B: *Detectives at a Pond or Stream.* When you arrive at the water's edge, take a few minutes to review with the children what the water gives to people and other living things. Have the children sit quietly and allow time for each child, in his or her own way, to give thanks for what the water will give on that day.

Pass out the strainers, hand lenses, paper, pencils and *Aquatic Creature Cards* (Figure 10-3) on which the children will record their findings. Have the children fill out one card for each different kind of plant or animal they find. Have the older children fill out the *Freshwater Findings* sheets (Figure 10-4). Notice that there are different questions to answer on a stream visit.

Show the children how to sieve the bottom, how to look under rocks in the stream, and how to wash the debris into a container to search for tiny insects, snails and other creatures. Point out that on shore there are keys to help identify things and buckets of pond or stream water to put their plants and animals into. Walk around and help the children to sample the aquatic life as you try to answer the questions that arise.

Call the children together after about twenty minutes. Ask them to share highlights from their freshwater visit. Discuss the plants and animals found. Now take these collections and, all together, release the plants and animals gently into their correct homes and thank them for what they have given.

Once the release ceremony is over, pass out blank

AQUATIC CREATURE CARD

Draw your creature in
the space below.

Answer the following questions:

1. How big is it? _____

2. How does it eat? _____

_____

What does it eat? _____

What eats it? _____

3. How does it move around? _____

_____

4. How does it get air underwater? _____

_____

5. What was it doing when you found it? _____

_____

6. Does it live in, on or near the water (or in several places)? _____

_____

7. How does it live through the winter? _____

_____

8. Does it prefer the light or dark? _____

9. Is it a young stage of an animal or an adult? _____

If young, what stage is it? _____

10. Give it a name and write it here. _____

Now look up its common name and write it here. _____

Write down anything else you notice about it. _____

_____

_____

Figure 10-3. Detectives at a pond or stream

FRESHWATER FINDINGS

1. Where does the water come from that enters the pond (stream)? _____
_____

2. Where does it go to when it leaves? _____
What are the different ways that water leaves the pond (stream)? _____
_____

3. Where does the energy come from that feeds the plants and animals of the pond (stream)? _____
_____

4. What is the bottom mostly like? (check one or two):
silt and mud ____ ; sand ____ ; rocks and gravel ____ ; bedrock ____

5. What purposes does the bottom serve for those things living in the pond (stream)? _____
_____

6. How deep is the pond (stream)? Measure the depth in three places and average them. _____
_____

7. How much of the pond (stream) is covered by shade, as a percent of the total surface area? _____
_____

8. What is the water temperature? _____
The air temperature? _____

9. Stream Questions:
Calculate the velocity of the water (distance traveled over time). Float an orange down a measured 25-foot (7.6-meter) stretch of the stream and measure the time it takes to complete the journey. Do this three times and take the average.

velocity = feet (meters)/second = _____ feet (meters)/second x 60 = _____ feet (meters)/minute

Plants and Animals

1. Identify at least four kinds of plants growing in the pond (stream) and along the shoreline. Look for algae, moss, floating plants and rooted plants. How are each of these adapted to life in and around the water?
a. _____
b. _____
c. _____
d. _____

2. Search for animals and signs of their presence (tracks, droppings, empty skins and egg cases, etc.).
What kinds of signs do you find? _____
_____
_____

3. Collect some animals and fill out an AQUATIC CREATURE CARD describing each animal.

Figure 10-4. Detectives at a pond or stream

pictures of a pond or stream to younger children, along with pencils and crayons. Have the younger children complete the pictures by drawing in what they saw during the visit. Ask the older children to write one or two haikus about the visit. A haiku has three lines, with five, seven and five syllables respectively. For example:

> mirror reflecting
> reed along the water's edge
> sunlight is dancing

MATERIALS: (A) construction paper, balloons, cardboard, tape, glue, string, pencils, crayons, scissors, pipe cleaners and other material as needed to make the appendages for creating an aquatic creature out of a person, felt-tipped marking pens and newsprint. (B) large tea strainers, hand lenses, keys and reference books for identifying aquatic organisms and for learning about their natural histories, paper with cardboard backing for a firm writing surface, pencils, rulers, collecting jars, large collecting buckets or tubs, *Aquatic Creature Cards* (Figure 10-3), blank line drawings of pond or stream and crayons for younger children, and for older children: thermometers, *Freshwater Findings* sheets (Figure 10-4), yard or meter sticks, plus for a stream visit, string, stopwatch or watch with seconds indicator, measuring tapes and oranges.

Water: Here Today, Where Tomorrow?

ACTIVITY: Trace a water supply from its source to where it goes after it is used and study the kind of wastewater treatment that it undergoes. Practice conserving water at home.
GOALS: Be aware of where your water supply comes from, where that water goes once you have used it, and how the water is disposed of and purified. Understand that all of the water we use ends up back in the environment and needs to be purified. Understand the importance of conserving water and that we can conserve water in our daily lives.
AGE: Older Children
PROCEDURE: Begin with the activity called "A-Maze-Ing Water." Then discuss the schematic drawing of where the wastewater goes when it leaves your home. Visit the site, whether it is a septic system or a sewage treatment plant. Describe how the system works (if it is a septic system) or arrange for a tour of the sewage treatment plant.

Brainstorm ways of conserving water at home, such

as not leaving the water running while brushing your teeth, flushing the toilet only when necessary, putting bricks in the toilet tank to reduce the water volume used per flush and reducing lawn watering. Have the children practice these measures for two or three days and then report on what it means to make a sacrifice and accept inconveniences to conserve a resource. Encourage them to continue these practices.
MATERIALS: Mazes from activity, "A-Maze-Ing Water" on page 27 in Chapter 4, paper, pencils, schematic sketch of wastewater flow from the home to the septic system or sewage treatment plant, chalkboard and chalk or newsprint and marker for brainstorming.

Water Cycle Relay

ACTIVITY: Participate in a relay that simulates the water cycle.
GOALS: Understand the water cycle and the important role of the sun's energy in driving the water cycle. Understand that cooperation helps us to accomplish things when we work in groups.
AGE: Younger Children and Older Children
PROCEDURE: Describe the water cycle. Stress the role of the sun in evaporating the water that eventually forms clouds and in creating the wind that moves the clouds by causing the unequal heating of the Earth's surface and atmosphere. (See the "Discussion" in Chapter 9 for a detailed description of what causes the wind.) Have someone try to pick up the full bucket of water to see how heavy it would be to carry. Then point out that by cooperating and each taking a little water, the task will be made easier.

Divide the group into two or three smaller groups and have them line up single file at the lakes (full buckets of water) and facing the clouds (empty buckets about 20 feet [6.1 meters] away). Pass out one cup, or other small container, to each child. Give them their directions:

"In order to evaporate and rise up to form clouds, the water must have the sun's heat. Imagine that each person has the sun's energy. When it is your turn, take a cup (or other small container) of water and run up to the clouds. The object is to *not* spill any water. Pour water into the bucket when you get there. When you have poured your water in, *then* the next person can bring his or her water up to the clouds. When all groups have formed new lines at the clouds, you should all squat."

At this point, in case some water was spilled on the

way up to the clouds, you will need to add about one quart (.94 liter) of water to each "cloud" bucket so that there will be enough to go around for the return journey back to the lakes. Here are the directions for round two:

"In round two you will 'rain' into the lake by taking water from the clouds into your cup. Once you have reached the lake and poured your 'rain' into it, put the cup down so the next 'rainstorm' can come down. When the whole cloud is rained out (when you have all emptied your cups into the 'lake'), you should all squat down and the game is over. The water cycle is complete."

MATERIALS: One full bucket of water and one empty bucket for each group in the relay; a can, cup or empty milk or juice carton for each child; signs to mark off lake and cloud areas; open space for running; extra supply of water.

Extending the Experience

• Create a puppet show, play or story about a drop of water that travels through the entire water cycle. Include conversations that the drop of water has with plants, animals, rocks and other parts of the environments it meets on its journey.

• Write a story about life as a frog, turtle, aquatic insect or other freshwater animal.

• *Where Does the Water Go?* Place pans of water out to evaporate. Put one in direct sunlight and the other in a dark, cool place. Discuss how the one exposed to direct sunlight evaporated more quickly due to the sun's heat energy.

• *Here It Is.* Put ice in a bottle and observe how water condenses from the air onto the sides of the bottle.

• List some common plants and animals found in a stream or pond (algae, fish, frogs, insects, etc.) and make a food web out of them. (See Chapter 7, page 50 for information about food webs.)

• Research, list and discuss the problems associated with drought and the different solutions that are used by people who live in water-scarce regions.

As they went together they kept sinking the ground. The earth quaked and quaked and water flowed over it as Kingfisher and Earthquake poured it from their abalone shells.

CHAPTER 11

How Thunder and Earthquake Made Ocean

(Yurok—California)

Thunder lived at Sumig. One day he said, "How shall the people live if there is just prairie there? Let us place the ocean there." He said to Earthquake, "I want to have water there, there so that the people may live. Otherwise they will have nothing to live on." He said to Earthquake, "What do you think?"

Earthquake thought. "That is true," he said. "There should be water there. Far off I see it. I see the water. It is at Opis. There are salmon there and water."

"Go," said Thunder. "Go with Kingfisher, the one who sits there by the water. Go and get water at Opis. Get the water that is to come here."

Then the two of them went. Kingfisher and Earthquake went to see the water. They went to get the water at Opis. They had two abalone shells that Thunder had given to them. "Take these shells," Thunder had said. "Collect the water in them."

First Kingfisher and Earthquake went to the north end of the world. There Earthquake looked around. "This will be easy," he said. "It will be easy for me to sink this land." Then Earthquake ran around. He ran around and the ground sank. It sank there at the north end of the world.

Then Kingfisher and Earthquake started for Opis. They went to the place at the end of the water. They made the ground sink behind them as they went. At Opis they saw all kinds of seals and salmon. They saw all the kinds of animals and fish that could be eaten there in the water at Opis. Then they took water in the abalone shells.

"Now we will go to the south end of the world," said Earthquake. "We will go there and look at the water. Thunder, who is at Sumig, will help us by breaking down the trees. The water will extend all the way to the south end of the world. There will be salmon and fish of all kinds and seals in the water."

Now Kingfisher and Earthquake came back to Sumig. They saw that Thunder had broken down the trees. Together the three of them went north. As they went together they kept sinking the ground. The Earth quaked and quaked and water flowed over it as Kingfisher and Earthquake poured it from their abalone shells. Kingfisher emptied his shell and it filled the ocean halfway to the north end of the world. Earthquake emptied his shell and it filled the ocean the rest of the way.

As they filled in the ocean, the creatures which would be food swarmed into the water. The seals came as if they were thrown in in handfuls. Into the water they came, swimming toward shore. Earthquake sank the land deeper to make gullies and the whales came swimming through the gullies where that water was deep enough for them to travel. The salmon came running through the water.

Sedna grasped the side of the boat. "Let go," Aja shouted at her. "The fulmars will kill me if I do not give you to the sea."

Now all the land animals, the deer and elk, the foxes and mink, the bear and others had gone inland. Now the water creatures were there. Now Thunder and Kingfisher and Earthquake looked at the ocean. "This is enough," they said. "Now the people will have enough to live on. Everything that is needed is in the water."

So it is that the prairie became ocean. It is so because Thunder wished it so. It is so because Earthquake wished it so. All kinds of creatures are in the ocean before us because Thunder and Earthquake wished the people to live.

✦ Sedna, the Woman Under the Sea ✦
(Inuit—Arctic Regions)

Long ago an Inung man and his daughter, Sedna, lived together along the ocean. Their life was not easy, for the fishing was often not good and the hunting was often poor. Still, Sedna grew up to be a strong and handsome young woman and many Inung men came to ask her to marry. No one, though, was good enough for her. She was too proud to accept any of them. One day, just at the time when the long days were beginning and the ice was breaking for spring, a handsome man came to Sedna. He wore clothing of grey and white and Sedna could see that he was not like other men. He was a sea-bird, the fulmar, taking the shape of a man to woo her and he sang to her this song:

> Come with me, come with me
> to the land of the birds
> where there never is hunger,
> you shall rest on soft bearskins.
>
> Come with me, come with me
> to my beautiful tent,
> my fellow birds will bring you
> all that your heart desires.
>
> Come with me, come with me
> and our feathers will clothe you,
> your lamp will be filled with oil,
> your pot will be filled with meat.

His song was so lovely and his promises so enticing that Sedna could not resist him. She agreed to go with him, off across the wide sea. Their journey to his land was a long and hard one. When they reached the place where the fulmar lived, Sedna saw that he had deceived her. His tent was not beautiful and covered with soft skins. It was made of fishskins and full of holes so that wind and snow blew in. Her bed was not made of soft bearskins, but of hard walrus hide. There was no oil for her lamp, for there were no lamps at all, and her food was nothing but raw fish. Too late, Sedna realized the mistake she had made and she sang this song:

> Aja, my father, if only you knew
> how wretched I am, you would come to me.
> Aja, my father, we would hurry away
> in your boat across the wide sea.
>
> The birds do not look kindly
> on me, for I am a stranger.
> Cold winds blow about my bed
> and I have little food.
>
> Aja, my father, come and take me back home.

So she sang each day as a year passed. Now the ice broke again and Aja decided he would go and visit his daughter. In his swift boat he crossed the wide sea and came to the fulmar's country. He found his daughter, cold and hungry, in a small tent made only of fishskins. She greeted him with joy, begging him to take her back home. Just then, the fulmar returned from fishing. Aja was so angry that he struck the fulmar with his knife and killed him. Then he placed Sedna in his boat and began to paddle swiftly back across the sea.

Soon the other fulmars came back from fishing. They found the body of Sedna's husband and they began to cry. To this day you can still hear the fulmars mourning and crying as they fly over the sea. They decided to find the one who had killed their brother and they began to fly in great circles over the sea, searching him out.

Before long, they saw the boat of Aja. They saw Sedna was with him and knew that he was the one who was the murderer. Then, using their magical powers, the fulmars made a great storm begin. The waves lifted high above the small boat and Aja became very afraid. He had seen the birds and knew that they were causing the storm to punish him for the death of Sedna's husband.

"You fulmars," he cried, "look! I give you back this girl. Do not kill me."

Then he pushed his daughter out of the boat. But Sedna grasped the side of the boat.

"Let go," Aja shouted at her. "The fulmars will kill me if I do not give you to the sea."

But Sedna still held on to the side of the boat. Then, taking his sharp knife, Aja cut off the tips of her fingers. The ends of her fingers fell into the water and became the whales. Sedna still grasped the side of the boat and now her father cut off the middle joints of her fingers. Those, too, fell into the water and were transformed into seals.

The fulmars, who saw what Aja did, thought it certain that Sedna would drown. They were satisfied and flew away. As soon as they departed, the storm ended and Aja pulled his daughter back into the boat.

Now, though, Sedna hated her father. When they had reached shore and her father had gone to sleep in his tent, she called to her dogs, who would do whatever she said. "Gnaw off the hands and feet of my father," she said. And the dogs did as she said. When this happened, Aja cursed his daughter. The Earth opened beneath them and all of them fell deep down to the land of Adlivun, which is beneath the land and the sea.

To this day, that is where Sedna lives. Because the whales and the seals were made from her fingers, she can call them and tell them where to go. So it is that when the people wish to hunt, they have their *angakok*, the shaman, descend in his dream-trance to the land under the sea where Sedna lives. He combs out Sedna's long, tangled hair, for without fingers she is unable to do it herself. Then he can ask her to send the whales and seals back to the places where the people can hunt them. Thanks to the blessings of Sedna, who is always generous to those who remember to ask her help in the right way, the people no longer go hungry.

In the first story, "How Thunder and Earthquake Made Ocean," Thunder says that for people to live, they need more than the prairie, they need the ocean too. Earthquake agrees and says he sees water with salmon living in it far away. There is a sense here of how important it is to have a diversity of communities and life forms to ensure survival of people and other living things.

Kingfisher and Earthquake cooperate to create the oceans from prairie by gathering water at Opis and sinking the land. Thunder breaks down the trees. Then they pour the water out of their vessels made of abalone shells. The ocean creatures come to live in the waters as food for people: seals, whales and other animals.

In the second story, "Sedna, the Woman under the Sea," the whales and seals form from the first and second joints of Sedna's fingers. Sedna gets into trouble because she is too proud to take a husband until the fulmar finally comes disguised as a man and lures her away with his beautiful music and promises of a good life. Finally, at the end of the story, we learn of the importance of the whales and seals as food, and how the angakok *or* shaman *can influence Sedna to assure successful hunting of these animals.*

Discussion

Science tells us that oceans formed over four billion years ago when the Earth was young. The hot, molten rocks of the Earth's crust gave off great volumes of water vapor. Clouds formed and rain fell for centuries as the Earth's surface cooled. Salts and other elements washed from the land and into the oceans, which gradually filled with water.

Today 71 percent of the Earth's surface is covered by salty oceans that average 2.3 miles (3.7 kilometers) deep. These oceans are all connected, but we refer to the Atlantic, Pacific, Indian, Arctic and Antarctic Oceans. Sodium and chlorine, the ingredients of common table salt, make up 84 percent of the salt in ocean water, along with over 100 other kinds of elements. The concentration of salts in ocean water is about 35 parts per thousand, or 3.5 pounds (1.6 kilograms) of salt in every 100 pounds (45.4 kilograms) of ocean water.[1] Salt lowers the freezing point of sea water to 28.4°F (-2°C) or below.

In its fluid state ocean water is seldom still. *Waves* and *currents* describe two ways that ocean water is constantly moving. The waves that lap at the shore as

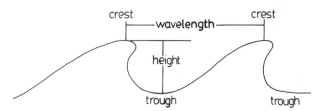

Figure 11-1. Parts of a wave.

you stand and gaze out to sea are usually driven by the wind. Waves are larger when there is, or has recently been, a strong, constant wind blowing over a large open span of water. The distance across an open stretch of water is called the *fetch*. Each ocean wave has the distinctive parts of all forms of waves: a *crest* or high point, a *trough* or low point, the *height* from trough to crest and the *wavelength* from one crest or trough to the next (Figure 11-1). As a wave passes, it causes water molecules to move up and down in a circular motion, but not in a forward direction horizontally.

Major ocean currents in the northern hemisphere travel in a clockwise direction while those south of the

Figure 11-2. The flukes of a humpback whale emerging from the depths give us a hint of the fascinating life beneath the waves.

equator circulate counterclockwise. This is due to the *Coriolis effect*. (See Chapter 9, page 71 for a description of the Coriolis effect.)

The ocean provides a stable environment for *pelagic* plants and animals, those that live in the open water. These range from the tiniest plants and animals called *plankton*, which are microscopic or nearly so, to the blue whale, which at 100 feet (30.5 meters) long is one of the largest animals that has ever lived on Earth. All of these organisms must get food, oxygen and water to live. Green plants use sunlight to produce food energy and oxygen in the process of photosynthesis. (See Chapter 7, page 50 for a detailed look at photosynthesis.) Planktonic plants, called *phytoplankton*, are the base of the ocean food web, and they are the major source of oxygen for the ocean and the Earth's atmosphere. Phytoplankton feeds many forms of *zooplankton*, which are tiny aquatic animals that are in turn an important food source for larger oceanic animals. The whale shark, for instance, which is the largest fish in the world, subsists on zooplankton, as do baleen whales like the blue whale and humpback whale.

As these stories tell us, the whales, seals and other ocean animals are a major source of food for some Native people today, as they have been throughout their history. However, many of the ocean animals that have meant survival to the Native people of the north country have been hunted to scarcity, and some to the brink of extinction. The final activity in this chapter explores some contemporary issues concerning ocean animals as food for Native people.

Questions

1. How do Earthquake and Kingfisher create deep places for the ocean waters? Where do they get the water and what do they carry it in? Where do the seals and whales come from?

2. How does Thunder help out in creating the ocean from the prairie?

3. What is an ocean? What is the scientific explanation for how the oceans formed?

4. Have you tasted ocean water? What is it like?

5. What are waves? How do waves form? Does water move forward when a wave passes?

6. What are currents? Does water move forward in a current?

7. In these stories, the seals and whales are important sources of food. Have you ever eaten seafood? Do you know which ocean animals you are eating when you eat them?

8. In the second story, Sedna is too proud to marry any of the men who come to court her. What finally happens when the fulmar lures her away with his music and great promises? What does it mean to be too proud?

Activities
Pelagic Charades

ACTIVITY: Pantomime and guess the identity of some easily recognizable ocean animals. Practice cooperating in a small group working toward a common goal.
GOALS: Understand some traits of familiar marine animals. Appreciate how a small group can work together to complete a task.
AGE: Younger Children and Older Children
PROCEDURE: Have the children work alone or in groups of two or three. Hand out one animal card to each child or group. Explain that the cards are to be kept secret. Demonstrate how to pantomime a creature by presenting a familiar one, such as a shark. Tell them they can use one or two props if really necessary, like a shark's dorsal (back) fin. Give them about 10 minutes to prepare their acts and help them to visualize the way they will create their animals. Have each child or group take turns pantomiming that animal while the other groups try to guess what animal it is.

With young children, it will help if you display the pictures/drawings on all of the cards together as the children try to guess which animals the others are pantomiming.
MATERIALS: Cards with the name of an animal and some of its common behavior patterns on one side and an accurate drawing or picture of the animal on the other side (for example, a lobster, seal, shark, whale, sea turtle, stork, starfish, crab, octopus, clam, snail or jellyfish); material to use as visual aids such as paper, cardboard, tape, modeling clay, string, balloons, crayons and natural materials.

Ocean Life: The Large and the Small of It

ACTIVITY: Compare the actual sizes of some ocean animals by measuring, marking and observing those sizes on the ground.
GOAL: Realize that ocean animals show enormous variation in size.
AGE: Younger Children and Older Children

PROCEDURE: Beforehand: Go outside and, using the measuring tape, mark out on the ground linear distances showing the relative sizes of the ocean animals listed in the accompanying chart.

Take the children outside to the place where the animal sizes are marked on the ground. Stand one child at the end of each line to create a visual comparison of these relative sizes. When all sizes are marked, go around to each line and state which animal is represented by each line and hold up a picture or drawing of that animal.

Review with the children the size chart that compares ocean animals. Discuss how these animals can grow to be so large because they live underwater where their weight is supported (buoyed) by seawater. Here are some animals and their sizes:

starfish - 8 inches (20.3 centimeters)
American lobster - 2 feet (.6 meters)
elephant - 18 feet (5.5 meters) (This example is included as a graphic reference to a familiar large animal.)
common octopus - to 30 feet (9.1 meters)
bottlenose dolphin - 13 feet (4.0 meters)
humpback whale - 60 feet (18.3 meters)
swordfish - 15 feet (4.6 meters)
whale shark - 60 feet (18.3 meters)
leatherback turtle - 8 feet (2.4 meters)
blue whale - 100 feet (30.5 meters) (this, one of the largest animals that has ever lived on Earth, is now nearly extinct due to overkill by whale hunters.)
plankton - microscopic

MATERIALS: Copy of chart giving relative sizes of ocean animals, long tape measure, pictures or drawings of each animal.

Making Waves and Other Current Events

ACTIVITY: Create a living wave using coordinated arm motions. Circulate as a group to form a current.
GOALS: Understand how the water molecules within a wave move as the wave passes. Understand how large volumes of water move as currents. Practice motor skills

and coordination.

AGE: Younger Children and Older Children

PROCEDURE: Arrange the children shoulder to shoulder in a half-circle and have them stand holding hands with arms outstretched. Explain that a wave is made of rising and falling water molecules that appear to be going forward but which really move very little, except for going up and down in a circular motion. Tell them that you are going to shake the arm of a person on the end of the line and begin the wave moving along the line. When each child feels the wave raise and lower one arm, he or she should raise and lower the other arm to move the "wave" along the line. In this way, the wave of rising and falling arms will travel across the line. Do this several times until the children get a smooth, rhythmic wave going. Now explain that the waves you have just created move much like water moves along an ocean wave—up and down in sequence but not forward.[2] Draw a diagram of a wave and discuss the various parts.

Now get on one side of the line and lead the children around. Tell them that they are still supposed to be water and that this slow, steady movement is called a current. Large volumes of water move in this way. Start a wave as the line of children (current) is moving to help them see how active ocean water really is.

MATERIALS: Marker and newsprint or chalkboard and chalk.

Saltwater Taste and Freeze

ACTIVITY: Create water as salty as the oceans. Taste this salt water and compare its freezing properties to those of fresh water. Watch how the salt is left behind when the salt water evaporates.

GOALS: Understand that ocean water is salty and that the salt causes it to have a lower freezing point than fresh water.

AGE: Younger Children and Older Children

PROCEDURE: Begin this activity early in the day to allow enough time for the water to freeze.

Pass out one cup or glass to each child and fill each of these with 4 ounces (118.3 cubic centimeters or milliliters) of warm water. Now drop 5/6 teaspoon (4.1 cubic centimeters or milliliters) of salt into each child's container of water and have the children stir the solution until the salt is dissolved. Have them taste (but not drink) the solution, which is roughly equal in salinity to ocean water. Tell them that on a larger-scale comparison, ocean water contains about 3.5 pounds (1.6 kilograms)

of salt in every 100 pounds or 45.4 kilograms (around 12 gallons or 45.4 liters) of water.

Pour some of this salt water into an ice cube tray and fill another identical tray with the remaining fresh water. Be sure that the water in both ice cube trays is the same temperature to begin with. Put these trays in the freezer and observe which one freezes first. Salt water freezes at a lower temperature (28.4°F [-2°C]) than fresh water, so the freshwater ice cubes will freeze first.

Use the rest of the salt water to demonstrate how evaporation leaves the salt behind. Put the water into a broad glass plate and set it near a window for several days until it has evaporated. Salt deposits will be left on the plate.

MATERIALS: Enough cups or glasses to provide one for each child, salt, pitchers of warm water, teaspoon, wooden coffee stirrers, ice cube trays, freezer, two thermometers, broad glass plate.

People of the Sea

ACTIVITY: Compile research reports about marine animals that are used as food by Inuit people of the cold regions. Create a scene of an Inuit village. Learn how the Inuit have been affected by the depletion of the animals that make up their food supplies. Role-play a meeting between the different people involved in the issues surrounding the hunting and welfare of these animals.

GOALS: Understand the close ties between the natural resources of the oceans and the music, art, spiritual beliefs and survival of ocean-dependent cultures such as the Inuit (from whom the story "Sedna, the Woman Under the Sea," comes). Understand how the intensity of commercial hunting and fishing, along with efficient modern hunting techniques, have depleted marine animal populations and threatened the survival of ocean-based cultures. Learn about the life history of a marine animal who is important to these people. Identify with a particular point of view in a role-playing exercise.

AGE: Older Children

PROCEDURE: Assign research study projects of specific animals who live in the water near the Inuit people of the North American Arctic and sub-Arctic regions and who provide food for the Inuit. Children should also understand the importance of plankton as the base of the food chain that feeds the marine animals. Have the children learn everything they can about these animals and the people who depend on them for their survival.

Use a wall space to create a scene showing land and sea. The children will create accurate pictures on the mural of their animals and of a village of Inuit people. Or they could create a table-top, three-dimensional village.

Explain that there has been a long and difficult period of adjustment for Native people who depend on the sea for food, materials and spiritual meaning. Modern commercial whaling, fishing and the hunting of seals have depleted these resources in some cases to such low levels that even the hunting by Natives now threatens the animals' well-being and sometimes even their survival. In addition, Native people are frequently using modern hunting techniques. These weapons are far more efficient than traditional weapons, a situation which results in further depletion of marine animal populations. Government restrictions on hunting also pose a problem for the physical and cultural survival of Native people.

Have the children follow up on their research by taking the roles of the Native people, government officials, conservationists and the animals themselves. Role-play a forum to discuss the issues and possible solutions to these problems.

MATERIALS: References, paper, pencils, wall space for a mural, large paper sheets to cover the wall space, stapler, construction paper, tempera paints, paint brushes, water, scissors, markers, crayons.

Extending the Experience

• Visit a seafood store and buy enough of several different kinds of fish to make a fish lunch or dinner. Make a list of the sea animals you have seen in the store. Prepare the meal and eat up! Then study about the animals you have eaten and those you have seen at the seafood market. Learn about them and report on how they live in the sea.

• Keep a saltwater aquarium and put some local species of sponges, sea stars, urchins, fish and other marine life inside (if you live near the ocean), or get some tropical ocean fish from a pet shop and keep them for study and observation. This activity requires time, money and skill to properly equip the aquarium and care for the animals in this mini-ocean environment. Consult a local pet store for tips and references to help with this project.

• Visit a dock along the shore and get some fresh fish. Many fish brought in by the boats are still alive, which gives the children a chance to see them close up.

• Find someone who will take the children out on one of the boats for a day and make an ocean excursion.

• Take a deep-sea fishing trip. Collect plankton in a plankton net and take it back for examination under a microscope. Catch fish with a rod and reel and learn about them.

• Make a life-sized seal, whale or dolphin out of dyed sheets stuffed with newspaper and hang it from the classroom ceiling. Think big! Create internal organs at the same scale as the seal or dolphin and place the organs accurately inside the animal. Slip them in and out through a zipper or velcro strip sewn into its abdomen. This is a great anatomy lesson.

• Use balloons to represent the world. Draw in the continents and oceans with markers for an ocean geography lesson.

• Visit an aquarium or a natural history museum with an ocean exhibit.

Notes

1. In volume, 100 pounds (45.4 kilograms) of water is equal to around 12 gallons, or 45.4 liters.

2. In reality the molecules of water move up and down in a circular pattern as a wave passes, returning to the same horizontal location from which they began.

At last Raven came to the house of a very old woman who was the one who held the tide-line in her hand. As long as she held onto it the tide would stay high.

CHAPTER 12

⋄ How Raven Made the Tides ⋄

(Tsimshian—Pacific Northwest)

A long time ago, the old people say, the tide did not come in or go out. The ocean would stay very high up on the shore for a long time and the clams and the seaweed and the other good things to eat would be hidden under the deep water. The people were often hungry.

"This is not the way it should be," said Raven. Then he put on his blanket of black feathers and flew along the coast, following the line of the tide. At last he came to the house of a very old woman who was the one who held the tide-line in her hand. As long as she held onto it the tide would stay high.

Raven walked into the old woman's house. There she sat, the tide-line held firmly in her hand. Raven sat down across from her.

"Ah," he said, "Those clams were good to eat."

"What clams?" said the old woman.

But Raven did not answer her. Instead he patted his stomach and said, "Ah, it was so easy to pick them up that I have eaten as much as I can eat."

"That can't be so," said the old woman, trying to look past Raven to see out her door, but Raven blocked the entrance. So she stood up and leaned past him to look out. Then Raven pushed her so that she fell through the door, and as she fell he threw dust into her eyes so that she was blinded. She let go of the tide-line then and the tide rushed out, leaving all kinds of clams and crabs and other good things to eat exposed.

Raven went out and began to gather clams. He gathered as much as he could carry and ate until he could eat no more. All along the beach others were gathering the good food and thanking Raven for what he had done. Finally he came back to the place where the old woman still was.

"Raven," she said, "I know it is you. Heal my eyes so that I can see again."

"I will heal you," Raven said, "but only if you promise to let go of the tide-line twice a day. The people cannot wait so long to gather food from the beaches."

"I will do it," said the old woman. Then Raven washed out her eyes and she could see again. So it is that the tide comes in and goes out every day because Raven made the old woman let go of the tide-line.

Raven knows that low tide must come for the people to gather clams, crabs, seaweed and other food from the beaches. He tricks the old woman and she lets go of the tide-line. Then he bargains with her and she agrees to let the tide go out twice a day.

Discussion

The tidal zone is ever-changing and alive with fascinating plants and animals. Tides do for the seashore what seasons do for the weather—they renew it and give it a new face each time we look. For child and adult alike, the endless shapes, smells, textures and sounds along the shore are full of delights.

The tidal environment and the plants and animals that live there are the subjects of this chapter: the rhythms of waves breaking on the shore; sounds of the seashore; filter feeding and the diversity, survival adaptations and ecological roles of plants and animals of the tidal zone. The final activity fosters a personal relationship with the seashore through close observation and a written response to the experience.

Tides are the result of the pull exerted on the oceans by the gravity of the sun and moon (Figure 12-1). Since the moon is so close to the Earth, its gravitational pull is over twice that of the sun. As ocean water is drawn

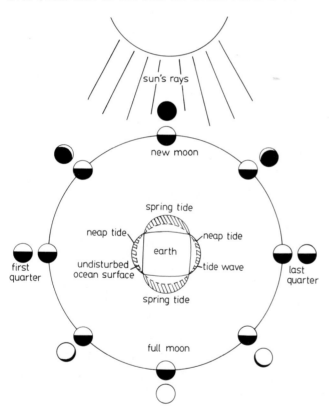

Figure 12-1. Tides and the effects of the gravitational pull of the sun and moon. The gravitational pull of the sun and moon causes the ocean surface to "bulge" outward, resulting in tidal fluctuations. At first quarter and last quarter the gravitational pull on the ocean is weaker because the sun and moon are at angles to one another in relation to the Earth, and the two forces tend to cancel each other out.

toward the sun and moon it builds in places, rising along the shore to form *high tide. Low tide* results when these rises in the sea subside. When the sun, Earth and moon are in a line, during the new and full moons, the pull on the oceans is greatest, which causes our most extreme high and low tides, called *spring tides.* Between these periods, when the moon is in its quarter phases, the pull of the sun and moon are at angles and working partially against one another. This is when we have the lower *neap tides.* The Gulf Coast of North America experiences one high tide each day (actually over a period of 24 hours and 50 minutes), the East Coast has two high tides and two low tides each day and the Pacific Coast has two tidal cycles but with very different extremes of high and low. The range between high and low tide varies from several inches or centimeters along some shores to over 50 feet (15.2 meters) in the Bay of Fundy between Nova Scotia and New Brunswick, Canada.

Tidal habitats are as diverse as the life found there: rocky shores, sandy beaches, mangrove swamps, salt marshes, and swaying beds of sea grasses and seaweed. The plants and animals along the shore are an *ecological community;* they live interdependently in a particular place and share the available food energy and other resources. Here a clam buried in the sand or mud squirting a jet of water from its syphon, there a hermit crab scurrying across a sandy beach with its home made from an abandoned shell. In still pools, barnacles wave their feathery legs from white, cone-shaped houses as they search for plankton and other food adrift on the shifting tides. Sandpipers bob for marine worms hidden in the mud of intertidal flats, while a mummichog swims through salt marsh streams in search of mosquito larvae meals. Life in the tidal zone can satisfy the most curious mind.

Questions

1. Why does Raven want the tide to go out? Is it a good thing that he succeeds in getting the tide to go out?
2. What causes the tides? Is there a tidal cycle in your area? If so, how many high and low tides are there each day?
3. What are some of the plants and animals that live in the tidal zone?
4. Have you ever been to the seashore? What did you find there?

Activities

If there is any place that brings out our instinct to collect and gather objects, it is the seashore. Be sure to bring along some containers for collecting precious stones, shells and other interesting flotsam and jetsam.

your right hand into your left hand. This will help you to remember the number of sounds you hear and what those sounds are."

Give the children about three or four minutes of silence and then have them open their eyes. Ask them to describe and imitate the sounds they heard and try to figure out what made the sounds.

Design variations of this activity for sights, smells, textures, shapes and tastes along the shore.
MATERIALS: Handfuls of small shells or pebbles.

Tide Tack Toe

ACTIVITY: Play a scavenger hunt/matching game while collecting plants and animals in the tide zone. Visit the homes of those plants and animals. Learn about how they live and their ecological roles.
GOALS: Learn about the diversity of tidal plants and animals, their ecological roles, their survival adaptations and how they form a community that uses the available resources.
AGE: Younger Children and Older Children
PROCEDURE: Collect the specimens and place one in each square of the blanket grid. Be sure to include plants and animals that are common and to keep them in containers that provide water and shelter so that they remain healthy while being used in this activity. Be careful not to require the children to enter ecologically sensitive areas, such as sand dunes, in order to collect the things found on the blanket.

Before the activity begins, ask the children how they should treat the plants and animals as they collect them. Emphasize being gentle and careful not to hurt the creatures, who will later be returned to their homes. Give each child a collecting pail. Have them find and bring back to the blanket the plant or animal specimens that match the specimens you have placed on each of the grid squares.

When the collecting is done, visit sites where the specimens were found. At each of the sites discuss how that plant or animal lives in that habitat and what its ecological role is (producer, consumer, decomposer, etc.). Ask questions to get the children to think for themselves. Take a moment to have the group thank each plant or animal as it is returned to its home after each site visit.
MATERIALS: Collecting pails; sandy area marked with a "tick tack toe" type of grid or large blanket so marked with rope or tape; specimens of living things from the tidal zone, and/or plant and animal parts such as old

Figure 12-2. *Dramatic tidal fluctuations of up to 50 feet (15.2 meters) have sculpted bizarre and beautiful shapes along the shore in the Bay of Fundy between Nova Scotia and New Brunswick, Canada.*

Seashore Symphony

ACTIVITY: Listen closely to the sounds of the seashore.
GOAL: Appreciate that there are many different sounds along the seashore that can be heard by listening closely.
AGE: Younger Children and Older Children
PROCEDURE: Travel to the seashore and have each child pick up a handful of small shells or pebbles from the tide zone.[1] Once you reach the water, gather the group into a circle and give them these instructions:

"The seashore is a symphony of sounds made by wind, waves, plants and animals living here. Let's listen carefully by closing our eyes and concentrating on the sounds around us. To begin with, hold all of your shells or pebbles in your right hand. Then, every time you hear a different sound, place one of the shells or pebbles from skate egg cases, pieces of seaweed, shells, shed skins or bones found along the shore; containers that provide water and shelter to store the specimens in at the grid.

Filter Feeders

ACTIVITY: Observe some animals filter feeding.
GOAL: Understand how filter feeders get their food.
AGE: Younger Children and Older Children
PROCEDURE: Visit the shore. Find a place in the shallows where clams are feeding, or a rocky zone where beds of mussels or encrustations of barnacles are filtering food from the water. Explain how shellfish feed by taking water in and filtering out small particles of food. Or watch some barnacles closely to see them reaching out of their calcified homes with feathery arms that trap food and pull it into their mouths. If you do not have access to the shore, you can explain how these creatures feed while using pictures or illustrations to demonstrate.
MATERIALS: Filter-feeding animals to observe along the shore or pictures or illustrations of them.

Waves Ahoy!

ACTIVITY: Create the sounds of an imaginary wave breaking on the shore.
GOAL: Appreciate the rhythms and sounds of a wave as it approaches and breaks on the shore and then returns to the sea.
AGE: Younger Children and Older Children
PROCEDURE: Pass out one piece of paper to each child. You are going to create the sound of a wave breaking on the shore. Use the same general procedure as described for "Rain Making" in Chapter 10, pages 85–86, panning across the front of the group as you conduct each different action.

Tell the children they will hear a wave approach closer and closer from a distance. The wave will thunder as it breaks on the shore and will grate the sand, pebbles and shells as it slips back into the sea. Practice each one of these noisemakers with the children first and then lead each action in sequence to create a wave. (1) Tap the pads of the fingers of one hand onto the palm of the other hand (the wave heard far off). (2) Crumple paper, gently at first and then louder and louder (the wave approaching the shore). (3) Slap your hands on a desk or table and stomp your feet for about 5 seconds (the

wave crashes). (4) Quietly tap the tips of your fingernails on a desk or table (the wave slides over the sand, stones and shells as it flows back into the surf).
MATERIALS: One sheet of scrap paper for each child.

Seashore Solitude

ACTIVITY: Sit quietly alone along the seashore and observe the events in that environment. Collect an object, bring it with you and use it later to write a poem that recalls your seaside experience.
GOALS: Develop a strong, positive feeling for the tidal zone and a small, special part of it. Deepen the seashore experience with words that express feelings for that place and an object collected there. Enhance observational skills.
AGE: Older Children
PROCEDURE: Everyone will walk the shore for a distance and each person will collect one object that catches her or his fancy. Then each person will go off for ten or more minutes to sit alone with the seashore and the object. Tell the children you will call them back with the cry of a seagull or other animal. Ask them to sit still and watch closely for events happening all around them: a bird catching an insect, a crab flitting by, a seed on the wind. After they have gathered, once again allow time for sharing experiences. Have the children bring their object with them to use for a later activity and to remind them of the seashore.

Continue this experience at the seashore or later at home by having the children pull out their natural object to write a poem about it and their seashore experience. A haiku (See Chapter 10, page 90, for details about writing haikus) would be appropriate, or they could write a cinquain. A cinquain has five lines:

1. gives the title or subject in two syllables
2. describes the subject using four syllables
3. brings the subject to life with six syllables
4. describes emotions in eight syllables
5. gives the subject again using two syllables but a different word

Here is an example:

seashore
awesome power
crashing and grinding shore
smooth rocks shattered and broken shells
sandy

MATERIALS: Natural objects, paper, clipboards, pencils.

Extending the Experience

• Hold a fiddler crab race, or use another common, fast-moving animal from your area. Have each child catch a fiddler crab. Put the crabs into the center of a circle. The first crab to cross the edge of the circle wins.

• Collect driftwood and use it for craft projects.

• Gather shells to use for making jewelry or a shell mobile.

• Make sand castles.

• Press different kinds of seaweed between sheets of newspaper and let them dry. Make a collage of the seaweed.

• Play "Tide Tag." Watch the shore for the occasional wave that comes up higher on the beach than most waves are reaching. Make a line in the sand about 50 feet (15.2 meters) long, parallel to the shore and just within reach of this wave. Then make two lines at each end of and perpndicular to the first line reaching down into the water. This forms a box with lines on three sides and the ocean on the fourth side. The children have to stay within the box. They have to keep from getting "tagged" by the breaking waves and they cannot cross any of the lines. See how long they can keep their feet dry!

• Run a magnet through sand to collect iron filings. Since the iron is nearly impossible to remove completely from a magnet, you may want to put the magnet into a plastic bag for this activity.

• Make a matching game with tidal plants and animals on one side and their special adaptations on the other. Represent each adaptation with a common tool. For example, a crab's claw matches a pair of pliers.

Notes

1. Beware of bare feet and the danger of rusty cans, broken glass and other sharp objects.

✦ SKY ✦

"Take Coyote out of the sky," they said. "He is making too much noise with all of his shouting."

CHAPTER 13

⋅ How Coyote Was the Moon ⋅

(Kalispel—Idaho)

A long time ago there was no moon. The people got tired of going around at night in the dark. There had been a moon before, but someone stole it. So they gathered together and talked about it.

"We need to have a moon," they said. "Who will be the moon?"

"I will do it," said Yellow Fox. They placed him in the sky. But he shone so brightly that he made things hot at night. Thus they had to take him down.

Then the people went to Coyote. "Would you like to be the moon? Do you think you could do a better job?"

"I sure would," Coyote said. Then he smiled. He knew that if he became the moon he could look down and see everything that was happening on Earth.

They placed Coyote up in the sky. He did not make the nights too hot and bright. For a time the people were pleased.

"Coyote is doing a good job as the moon," they agreed.

But Coyote, up there in the sky, could see everything that was happening on Earth. He could see whenever someone did something they were not supposed to do and he just couldn't keep quiet.

"Hey," he would shout, so loudly everyone on Earth could hear him, "that man is stealing meat from the drying racks." He would look down over people's shoulders as they played games in the moonlight. "Hey," he would shout, "that person there is cheating at the moccasin game."

Finally, all the people who wished to do things in secret got together. "Take Coyote out of the sky," they said. "He is making too much noise with all of his shouting."

So Coyote was taken out of the sky. Someone else became the moon. Coyote could no longer see what everyone on Earth was doing, but that hasn't stopped him from still trying to snoop into everyone else's business ever since.

As usual, Coyote gets into trouble in this story when he becomes the moon. He keeps yelling down people's secrets so that everyone on Earth can hear him. Finally, he is taken down from the sky and someone else becomes the moon. Coyote now snoops around on Earth.

(Coyote also appears in Chapter 5, "Four Worlds: The Dine [Navajo] Story of Creation" and in Chapter 8, "Old Man Coyote and the Rock.")

Discussion

This story gets the children thinking about the moon in a general way. The rest of the chapter explores in depth the moon and its relationship to the Earth.

What is the moon like? If you could experience the moon it would be strange, beautiful and deadly. There is no air pressure on the moon and its gravity is so weak it cannot hold an atmosphere in place. There is no air to transmit sound waves. If someone sneaked up behind you and yelled, you would not hear a thing! In the heat of a lunar day, the temperature can rise to above the boiling point of water at sea level (212°F or 100°C). At night the thermometer would plummet to below -200°F (-128.9°C). No sign of life or water has ever been found on the moon.

The moon's diameter is about 2,160 miles (3,476 kilometers), compared to the Earth's diameter of 7,913 miles (12,735 kilometers). Mercury, the smallest planet in our solar system, has a diameter that is only about 1,000 miles (1,609 kilometers) larger than the moon's. Earth has a volume 49 times as large as that of the moon and, on the average, the Earth is about 238,856 miles (384,405 kilometers) from the moon. Gravity on the moon is only one sixth that found on Earth. It takes the moon 29.5 days to revolve around the Earth and a 12-month lunar year is 354.4 days long.

Some scientists theorize that the moon formed separately from the Earth, while other scientists think it formed from a piece of Earth that broke away. The moon's surface is thought to have changed little since it formed 4.6 billion years ago. In fact, some of the rock

Figure 13-1. Most of the lunar surface shown in this picture is on the far side of the moon.

pieces and lunar dust brought back from the Sea of Tranquility by the Apollo 11 moon walk on July 20, 1969 were found to be 4.6 billion years old, which is as old as the solar system itself. The oldest known rocks on Earth are around 3.6 billion years old.

The lunar rocks form a dramatic surface covered with large flat plains or *maria*, circular *craters* up to 160 miles (257 kilometers) across (Clavius crater) and up to 5 or 6 miles (8.0 or 9.7 kilometers) deep (Newton Crater); *mountains* over 3 miles (4.8 kilometers) high and river-like *rilles* that snake over its surface. The moon is covered with rocks and dust. Many of the moon's craters formed from meteor collisions, and they have lasted billions of years because there is no water or air on the moon to cause erosion. The moon lacks the protective atmosphere we have on Earth, so meteors crash into it and form new craters. The large, dark maria or seas (which are actually dry) are thought to have been caused by lava filling in where meteors blasted craters. The lava created flat surfaces much as water fills in lakes and oceans on the Earth.

In the sky, the moon appears to change from being "full" to "new" and then to full again, with all of the crescent stages or quarter phases in between. Actually, what we are seeing are varying portions of the light and dark sides of the moon, one-half of which is always illuminated by sunlight and the other half of which is always in shadow (Figure 13-3, page 114). During the partial phases of the moon, we can often see a very faint image of the part of the moon that is in the shadow, which is actually illuminated by sunlight that reflects off the Earth on to the moon. This light is called *earthshine*.

When the Earth occasionally passes directly between the sun and moon, casting a shadow onto the moon's surface, we experience a *lunar eclipse* (Figure 13-2a). A *solar eclipse* occurs when the moon passes directly between the sun and Earth, casting its shadow onto the Earth.[1] (Figures 13-2b [illustration] and 14-1 [photo of a total eclipse of the sun]).

Caution: Do not look directly at a solar eclipse! Severe eye burns and blindness can result during certain phases of the eclipse. One way to view an eclipse is to remove the eyepiece from a telescope and point the telescope at the eclipse. (*Do not look through the eyepiece to position the telescope!*) Then hold a piece of white, nonreflective poster board in the focal plane near the opening where the eyepiece was. Adjust the distance of the poster board from the telescope until the image of the eclipse is in clear focus on the poster board.

In addition, there are sun filters available for telescope eyepieces which allow for direct viewing of an eclipse. These filters should be used only under the

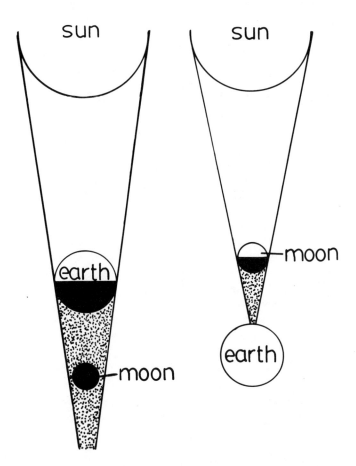

Figure 13-2a. Lunar eclipse.   Figure 13-2b. Solar eclipse.

direct supervision of an expert astronomist, because they will not protect your eyes if used incorrectly or if they are damaged in use. *You should never look directly through the telescope eyepiece, or through binoculars, at an unfiltered image of the eclipse.*

Questions

1.   Why do the people take Coyote out of the sky? How does Coyote benefit by poking into everyone's business?
2.   What does it look like on the surface of the moon? Is it hot or cold? Wet or dry? Does anything live there?
3.   How big is the moon and how far away is it?
4.   How many days does it take for the moon to experience a complete cycle from full moon to new moon and back again to full moon?
5.   How old do you *think* the moon is? How old *is* the moon?
6.   What do you think the surface of the moon is like?
7.   Why does the moon seem to change its shape when we see it at different times in the night sky?

Activities
Reading the Moon

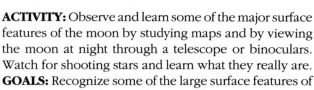

ACTIVITY: Observe and learn some of the major surface features of the moon by studying maps and by viewing the moon at night through a telescope or binoculars. Watch for shooting stars and learn what they really are.
GOALS: Recognize some of the large surface features of the moon and understand how they formed. Understand the true nature of meteors or "shooting stars."
AGE: Younger Children and Older Children
PROCEDURE: *This activity is best when conducted on a night when the moon is in clear view and at least two-thirds full.*

Take the children out on a clear, moonlit night and view the moon through binoculars and/or a telescope. Using a flashlight, a map of the moon and photographs of the moon's surface, point out some of the features on the moon, such as the craters and maria. Find some lunar mountain ranges and look for the river-like rilles. (Use the "Discussion" earlier in this chapter describing the physical appearance and origin of the features of the lunar landscape.)

Watch for meteors in the night sky, which can be seen by a patient eye on almost any clear night. *Meteors* are solid particles or objects from space that enter the Earth's atmosphere. The surface of the Earth is protected by the atmosphere, which causes meteors to burn up from friction as they are pulled down to the Earth by gravity, thus causing a streak of light that lingers briefly across the night sky. This is where the terms "falling star" and "shooting star" come from. A meteor that survives its journey through the Earth's atmosphere and crashes to the ground is called a *meteorite.*

Note: As a follow-up to this activity, have younger children make a moon with detailed surface features by looking at pictures of the moon and, from these images, creating their own moon by building up papier-mâché around a balloon and painting it when it is dry. Have older children create a mural showing profiles of the different lunar formations.
MATERIALS: Binoculars and/or telescope, flashlight, map of the moon, photos of the moon. Materials for the follow-up to this activity: pictures of the lunar surface, balloons, wheat paste, water, newspaper strips, tempera paints, paintbrushes, construction paper, stapler, pencils, crayons, scissors, tape, glue.

Moon Walker

ACTIVITY: Watch a demonstration that shows the relative sizes of the Earth and the moon, the distance between them and the causes of the phases of the moon.

GOALS: Understand the relative sizes of the Earth and moon and the distance between them. Visualize that the backside of the moon is always in a shadow and that the side facing the sun is always illuminated. Understand that the angle at which we view the light and dark sides of the moon causes it to appear "full" sometimes, "new" at others, and the various phases in between.

AGE: Older Children

PROCEDURE: Make a hole from top to bottom through the styrofoam ball along the edge of the black and white zones. This can be done by gradually pushing the sharp end of the pencil through the ball using a firm, twisting motion (Figure 13-3). Be sure the ball turns freely on the pencil. This ball represents the moon. Drive the wooden stake into the ground in the center of the open area, then tape the "Earth" (blue balloon) on top of it. Tie one end of the long string loosely around the stake so it will turn on the stake without winding onto it. Use the short string to tie the other end of the long piece onto the two ends of the pencil sticking through the moon as shown in the diagram (Figure 13-3).

Explain that the size of the moon and Earth are accurate compared to one another, but that they are scaled down to 1 inch = 945 miles (1 centimeter = 599 kilometers). The distance between the Earth and moon, as represented at the same scale by the connecting string, is 238,856 miles (384,405 kilometers). Then say that at this scale, the sun would have to be 75 feet (23 meters) in diameter to represent its actual diameter of 850,000 miles (1,367,956-kilometers), and that it would be about 1.6 miles (2.6 kilometers) away in this activity! The purpose of the model of the sun you are using here is strictly to show the direction from which it is shining onto the Earth and moon.

Have the children sit near the Earth at the center stake. Walk the moon around the Earth while keeping the light side toward the sun and the dark side (shadow) facing away from it. You will have to turn the moon on the pencil as you walk. From the Earth, the children will see that the moon looks full when it is farthest from the sun, new when it is closest to the sun, and appears as the various crescent and quarter stages when it is in between these two positions.

MATERIALS: Styrofoam ball 2.3 inches (5.8 centimeters) in diameter which is painted white on one side and black on the other; tempera paints; brushes; water; drill and bit; large, round, blue balloon blown up to 8.4

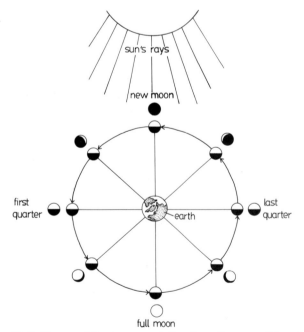

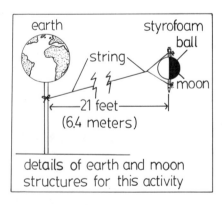

Figure 13-3. Phases of the moon and directions for assembling the props for Moon Walker. The inner circle of moons shows the position of the moon during the various crescent stages and quarter phases of the lunar cycle. The outer circle of moons shows the corresponding appearance of the moon at each of these times as seen from Earth.

inches (21.3 centimeters) in diameter with the continents drawn on in green; green felt-tipped marker; heavy string 21 feet (6.4 meters) long, plus an extra 1-foot (.3-meter) piece; pencil; large yellow ball or round piece of yellow paper to represent the sun; open area of at least 50 feet (15.2 meters) in diameter; round wooden stake 3 feet (.9 meter) long, such as a piece of broom handle; masking tape.

Hot Moon, Cold Moon

ACTIVITY: Watch and participate in demonstrations that show the extreme heat and cold of lunar days and nights.

GOAL: Understand that the surface of the moon normally experiences extreme temperature changes from day to night.

AGE: Younger Children and Older Children

PROCEDURE: Explain that the moon's surface temperatures range from the boiling point of water at sea level (212°F or 100°C) during the day to below -200°F (-128.9°C) at night. Boil the water and tell the children that on a hot lunar day the water would boil all by itself without the help of a stove!

Using the metal tongs or gloves, hold up a piece of dry ice and explain that the dry ice is made of the same compound (carbon dioxide) that our breath is largely composed of when we exhale. The surface of the moon at night is much colder than the dry ice, which is -109.3°F (-78.5°C). Nighttime on the moon is cold enough to cause the water vapor and some of the gases contained in our breath to freeze solid.

Remove the lid from the cooler that contains the dry ice. Have the children take turns putting on the safety goggles or glasses and exhaling gently but steadily into the cooler. Their breath will form dense white clouds as it is cooled by the ice. Caution the children not to blow too hard because small flecks of dry ice could be carried up on the clouds that form.

Caution: Always handle dry ice with gloves or tongs. Frostbite can result from direct contact with the skin.

MATERIALS: Stove, pan of water, cooler holding about 3 pounds (1.4 kilograms) of dry ice chunks, gloves or metal tongs for handling the dry ice, at least one pair of safety goggles or glasses with clear lenses.

Extending the Experience

• Make a scale model of the planets, moons and sun in our solar system and hang them from the ceiling. Calculate the relative sizes and distances for this model as a math project.

• Map or create a bulletin-board model of a part of the moon's surface and get to know its beautiful features and the names of the maria, mountain ranges, craters and river-like depressions called rilles.

• Look up the forthcoming astronomical events for your area in the most recent edition of *The Astronomical Almanac.*[2] Share these events with the children and study the astronomical causes of these occurrences (eclipses, meteor showers, etc.).

Notes

1. See Chapter 12, page 104 for information about the effect of the moon on tides.

2. To order write: Superintendent of Documents, U.S. Government Printing Office, Washington, D.C., 20402. Published annually.

"Grandson," said the squirrel, *"don't kill me. I can give you some good advice."*

CHAPTER 14

How Fisher Went to the Skyland: The Origin of the Big Dipper

(Anishinabe—Great Lakes Region)

Fisher was a great hunter. He was not big, but he was known for his determination and was regarded as one with great power. Fisher's son wanted to be a great hunter also. One day the son went out to try to catch something. It was not easy, for the snow was very deep and it was very cold everywhere. In those days it was always winter on the Earth and there was no such thing as warm weather. The son hunted a long time with no luck. Finally, though, he saw a squirrel. As quietly as he could he sneaked up and then pounced, catching the squirrel between his paws. Before he could kill it, though, the squirrel spoke to him.

"Grandson," said the squirrel. "don't kill me. I can give you some good advice."

"Speak then," said the young fisher.

"I see that you are shivering from the cold. If you do what I tell you, we may all enjoy warm weather. Then it will be easy for all of us to find food and not starve as we are doing now."

"Tell me what to do, Grandfather," the young fisher said, letting the squirrel go.

The squirrel climbed quickly up onto a high branch and then spoke again. "Go home and say nothing. Just sit down in your lodge and begin to weep. Your mother will ask you what is wrong, but you must not answer her. If she tries to comfort you or give you food, you must refuse it. When your father comes home, he will ask you why you are weeping. Then you can speak. Tell him the winds are too cold and the snow is too deep. Tell him that he must bring warm weather to the Earth."

So the young fisher went home. He sat in the corner of the lodge and cried. His mother asked what was wrong, but he did not answer. She offered him food, but he pushed it away. When his father returned and saw his only son weeping, he went to his side.

"What is wrong, son?" Fisher said.

Then the young fisher said what the squirrel had told him to say.

"I am weeping because the wind is too cold and the snow is too deep. We are all starving because of the winter. I want you to use your powers to bring the warm weather."

"The thing you are asking of me is hard to do," said Fisher, "but you are right. I will do all I can to grant your wish."

Then Fisher had a great feast. He invited all of his friends and told them what he planned to do.

"I am going to go to the place where the skyland is closest to the Earth," he said. "There in the skyland the people have all the warm weather. I intend to go there to bring some of that warm weather back. Then the snow will go away and we will have plenty to eat."

Gitchee Manitou placed Fisher high up in the sky among the stars.

All of Fisher's friends were pleased and offered to go with him. So when Fisher set out, he took the strongest of his friends along. Those friends were Otter, Lynx and Wolverine.

The four of them traveled for a long time through the snow. They went toward the mountains, higher and higher each day. Fisher had with him a pack filled with dried venison and they slept at night buried under the snow. At last, after many, many days, they came to the highest mountain and climbed to its top. Then Fisher took a pipe and tobacco out of his pouch.

"We must offer our smoke to the Four Directions," Fisher said. The four of them smoked and sent their prayers to Gitchee Manitou, asking for success.

The sky was very close above them, but they had to find some way to break through into the land above. "We must jump up," said Fisher. "Who will go first?"

"I will try," said Otter. He leaped up and struck the sky but did not break through. Instead he fell back and slid on his belly all the way to the bottom of the mountain. To this day all otters slide like that in the snow.

"Now it is my turn," said Lynx. He jumped too, striking hard against the sky and falling back unconscious. Fisher tried then, but even he did not have enough power.

"Now it is your turn," said Fisher to Wolverine. "You are the strongest of us all."

Wolverine leaped. He struck hard against the sky and fell back, but he did not give up. He leaped again and again until he had made a crack in the sky. Once more he leaped and finally broke through. Fisher jumped through the hole in the sky after him.

The skyland was a beautiful place. It was warm and sunny, and there were plants and flowers of all kinds growing. They could hear the singing of birds all around them, but they could see no people. They went farther and found many long lodges. When they looked inside, they found that there were cages in the lodges. Each cage held a different bird.

"These will make for fine hunting," Fisher said. "Let us set them free."

Quickly Wolverine and Fisher chewed through the rawhide that bound the cages together and freed the birds. The birds all flew down through the hole in the sky. So there are many kinds of birds in the world today.

Wolverine and Fisher now began to make the hole in the skyland bigger. The warmth of the skyland began to fall through the hole and the land below began to grow warmer. The snow began to melt and the grass and plants beneath the snow began to turn green.

But the sky people came out when they saw what was happening. They ran toward Wolverine and Fisher, shouting loudly.

"Thieves," they shouted. "Stop taking our warm weather!"

Wolverine jumped back through the hole to escape, but Fisher kept making the hole bigger. He knew that if he didn't make it big enough, the sky people would quickly close the hole again and it would be winter again in the land below. He chewed the hole larger and larger. Finally, just when the sky people were very close, he stopped.

The hole was big enough for enough warm weather for half of the year to escape through, but it was not big enough for enough warm weather to last all the time. That is why the winter still comes back every year. Fisher knew that the sky people might try to close the hole in the sky. He had to take their attention away from it and so he taunted them.

"I am Fisher, the great hunter," he said. "You cannot catch me." Then he ran to the tallest tree in the skyland. All the sky people ran after him. Just as they were about to grab him, he leaped up into the tree and climbed to the highest branches, where no one could follow.

At first the sky people did not know what to do. Then they began to shoot arrows at him. But Fisher wasn't hurt, for he had a special power. There was only one place on his tail where an arrow could kill him. Finally, though, the sky people guessed where his magic was and shot at that place. An arrow struck the fatal spot. Fisher turned over on his back and began to fall.

But Fisher never struck the Earth. Gitchee Manitou took pity on him because he had kept his promise and done something to help all the people. Gitchee Manitou placed Fisher high up in the sky among the stars.

If you look up into the sky, you can still see him, even though some people call that pattern of stars The Big Dipper. Every year he crosses the sky. When the arrow strikes him, he rolls over onto his back in the winter sky. But when the winter is almost ended, he faithfully turns to his feet and starts out once more on his long journey to bring the warm weather back to the Earth.

In this story, Wolverine and Fisher make the hole in skyland big enough for the warm weather to come through for half of the year. Fisher is shot by the sky people with an arrow that strikes his vulnerable tail spot. Gitchee Manitou places Fisher in the sky as a reward for the great sacrifice he makes for the people.

(Gitchee Manitou also appears in Chapter 10, "Koluscap and the Water Monster," and in Chapter 17, "Manabozho and the Maple Trees.")

Discussion

The themes of determination, sacrifice and cooperation are an important part of this story. The story is also about seasons, which are the main topic of Chapter 15.

"How Fisher Went to the Skyland" is an unusual story because myths throughout the world describe the Big Dipper as a Great Bear. In life, the *fisher* is a fox-sized animal that is closely related to weasels. It plays and hunts using fox-like movements. The fisher's fur varies from greyish brown or reddish above to black and dark brown below, although the belly is sometimes dappled with white. Legs, belly and tail are usually black. Despite its name, the fisher dislikes water and hunts not fish but squirrels and other small animals.

The Great Bear, Ursa Major, is the most well-known of all the *constellations*, which are associated groups of stars that cover certain areas in the sky. The Big Dipper is only a portion of the constellation of the Great Bear, while the seven stars of the Little Dipper outline the entire constellation called the Little Bear, Ursa Minor. Even though stars appear to create images as we view them overhead, they are often very distant from one another. The stars of the Pleiades are an exception, all being about 400 *light-years* away.[1] There are 88 constellations and 41 of them can be seen from the northern hemisphere. Some constellations, like the Big Dipper, Little Dipper, Cassiopeia, Cepheus and Draco, are *circumpolar:* they are located close to the North Star and are visible all year long (Figure 14–2, page 122). Other constellations are more prominent at different seasons. Some major constellations of the Northern Hemisphere and the times of year they are visible are:

Spring	Summer	Fall	Winter
	northern skies:	*northern skies:*	
Leo	Aquila	Pegasus	Taurus
Bootes	Cygnus	Andromeda	Canis Major
Virgo	Lyra	Perseus	Canis Minor
Corvus		Triangulum	Gemini
Crater			Orion
Cancer	*southern skies:*	*southern skies:*	Auriga
	Sagittarius	Pisces	
	Libra	Aries	
	Scorpius	Aquarius	
		Capricornus	
	near the zenith:		
	Hercules		
	Corona Borealis		
	Sagitta		
	Delphinus		
	Ophiucus		

A portion of our galaxy, the *Milky Way*, is seen as a pale band of stars in the night sky. There are more than 100 billion stars in the Milky Way, along with planets and other heavenly bodies. Our *solar system* consists of the sun, nine major planets and their moons and all other satellites of the sun such as comets and asteroids. Some stars are much brighter than others and are said to have a greater *magnitude*. Higher numbers denote dimmer stars. A star of magnitude 1 is 2.5 times brighter than a star of magnitude 2, and so on. Extremely bright objects, such as the moon (magnitude -12.5) are given negative numbers.

Our own sun is a star 850,000 miles (1,367,956 kilometers) in diameter and 93,000,000 miles (149,670,480 kilometers) away from the Earth. The *sun* is a fiery ball—a continuous nuclear reaction in which heat and light are released as hydrogen is being converted into helium. The sun's light travels through space for 8 minutes and 20 seconds before it reaches the Earth. Our home star is 107 times larger in diameter than the Earth, and its surface temperature is 10,000°F or 5,538°C. Still, it is not a very big star. If a red giant, like Antares in the constellation Scorpius, were brought close to the Earth, it would more than fill up the space between the Earth and sun. The next closest star to Earth is very far off. Alpha Centauri (which is not visible in the northern hemisphere) is four light years away. The light being created by Alpha Centauri as you read this sentence will not reach the Earth until four years from now. (See Chapter 7 for more information and activities about the sun.)

Planets can be distinguished from stars because they move in relation to the stars and each other.

Figure 14-1. *The immense energy of the sun is evident in the glow of the expansive solar corona, the outermost part of the sun's atmosphere that can be seen here reaching hundreds of thousands of miles into space beyond the edge of where the moon covers the solar disc. The corona is characterized by low density and an extremely high temperature of around 3,600,032°F (2,000,000°C). Since it is only as bright as the light of the full moon, the corona is normally masked by the intense light of the sun. This photograph was taken in Green River, Wyoming, during a total eclipse of the sun on 8 June 1918. The black disc covering the sun is the dark side of the moon as it passed between the Earth and the sun.*

"Planet" is Greek for "a wanderer." Planets also shine more steadily and twinkle less than stars. Through a telescope a planet shows as a disc while stars are just points.

When you take your group outside on a starry night,

the *zenith*, the highest point in the sky directly over-head, makes a good reference point, as do the stars of the Big Dipper. The *meridian* is the imaginary line that runs from the northernmost point on the horizon through the zenith and down to the southernmost point on the horizon. The *ecliptic* is another common reference, which is the path of the sun through the constellations during the year. On its journey along the ecliptic, the sun passes through the band of twelve constellations known as the *zodiac.*

You can refer to stars by using a powerful flashlight as a pointer, but discourage children from bringing flashlights because it takes the eyes about thirty minutes to fully readjust to the dark once they have been exposed for a time to the glare of a flashlight. Watch for *meteors*, which are sometimes called "shooting stars" or "falling stars." Meteors are solid particles or objects from space that are pulled downward by Earth's gravity. They appear as tracks of light across the sky that leave a brief, glowing streak when they burn up upon encountering the friction of the Earth's atmosphere.

Questions

1.   In "How Fisher Went to the Skyland," why does Fisher decide to bring the warm weather? Who does he take along on the journey to skyland? What do Fisher and his friends do first when they get to the top of the tallest mountain?
2.   Wolverine and Fisher work together to open a hole in skyland. Fisher makes a great sacrifice when he stays behind to chew a bigger hole as the sky people are coming. What does he sacrifice?
3.   What is a constellation? How many are there? How many constellations can we see from the northern hemisphere?
4.   The five constellations we can see year-round are very close to the north star. What are these five called? Name three constellations that can be seen for each of the four seasons. Find them on a star map.
5.   What is a star? A galaxy? Which galaxy is our solar system found in?
6.   How far away is our star, the sun? What is the sun made of?
7.   What is the zenith? The meridian? The ecliptic? The zodiac?

Activities
Creating Constellations

ACTIVITY: Make a map of the circumpolar constellations by gluing "stars" (dried beans and grains) onto a cardboard "sky."

GOALS: Understand how the stars within each of the five circumpolar constellations are arranged, and how these constellations are situated relative to each other. Understand what a circumpolar constellation is.

AGE: Younger Children

PROCEDURE: Transpose the map (Figure 14-2a) onto a large piece of paper or a chalkboard and post it where it is clearly visible. Discuss the definition of a circumpolar constellation. Introduce the five circumpolar constellations and tell the story about how Fisher becomes the Big Dipper. Point out that the Big Dipper is only a part

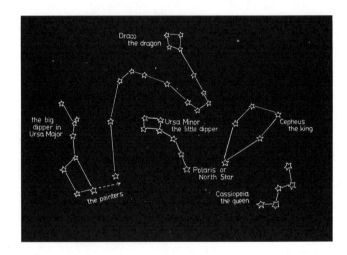

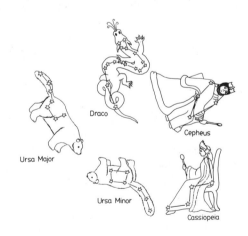

Figures 14-2a and 14-2b. a) The circumpolar constellations are located close to the north star. b) The images of the circumpolar constellations as they are imagined in the night sky.

of the constellation of the Great Bear, Ursa Major. Have the children glue the black paper onto the cardboard and draw in the stars for the Big Dipper. (With very young children you may need to premark the star locations.) These stars can be represented by gluing rice where each star is marked. The children will later use a different kind of dried pea, bean or cereal grain for each constellation, with all of the stars in any specific constellation being marked with the same kind of pea, bean or grain. When they have completed the Big Dipper, tell a story about one of the other four constellations and have them glue on another kind of dried object for those stars. Do this until all five of the constellations are on their cardboard "skies." When you discuss the Little Dipper, mention that it is also known as the Little Bear or Ursa Minor.

Since these constellations are visible year round, they are a great place for the children to start learning the stars.

MATERIALS: Marker and newsprint or chalkboard and chalk; tacks; tape; rice; four different kinds of dried peas, beans or cereal grains; glue; black construction paper; cardboard; pencils; map of the circumpolar constellations (Big Dipper, Little Dipper, Cassiopeia, Cepheus, Draco) (Figure 14-2).

From the Milky Way to the Zodiac

ACTIVITY: Listen to a discussion about the solar system, Milky Way galaxy, circumpolar constellations and the major reference points to use when viewing the stars and other heavenly bodies and locating constellations. Make a model of the relationship between the sun, Earth and constellations to demonstrate the zodiac.

GOALS: Understand that our sun is a star. Understand the common and important terms and reference points used in stargazing, such as zodiac, meridian and circumpolar constellations. Visualize how the Earth's location and movement cause us to see different stars and constellations during the year. Understand that Earth is part of our solar system, and that the solar system is part of the Milky Way galaxy.

AGE: Older Children

PROCEDURE: Using the information from the "Discussion," and appropriate pictures and illustrations from reference books, explain that the Earth and moon are revolving around the sun in our solar system, along with nine other planets, their moons and all other satellites of the sun such as comets and asteroids. Our solar system is part of the Milky Way galaxy. Discuss the composition

of our sun, its properties and the concept of magnitude among stars.

Now explain that five constellations are circumpolar and can be seen year-round, while others are best looked for during certain seasons as the Earth revolves around the sun. Use the list of constellations provided in the "Discussion." The *ecliptic* is the path the sun takes among the stars as a result of our motion around the sun. The *zodiac* is the band of 12 constellations that the sun passes through as it moves along the ecliptic.

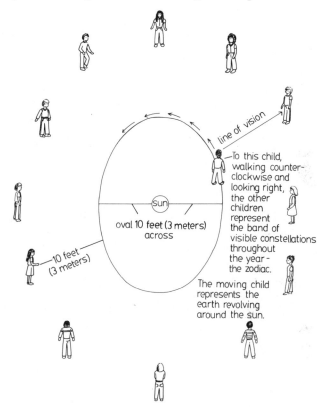

Figure 14-3. From the Milky Way to the Zodiac.

Take the children outside to demonstrate the zodiac. Mark a large oval or ellipse on the ground about 10 feet (3 meters) in diameter and stand someone in the center to represent the sun. This ellipse represents the Earth's path as it revolves around the sun. Now space 12 objects (or children if you have a large group) around the ellipse about 10 feet (3 meters) out from its edge as shown in Figure 14-3.

These objects (children) represent stars and constellations. Have a child become the Earth and walk counterclockwise around the inner ellipse while looking over her/his right shoulder at the "constellations" on the outside. On the way, as the Earth revolves around the sun, certain constellations are visible during each season. That band of constellations she/he sees represents the zodiac. The band is broken up into twelve sections called the *signs of the zodiac.*

MATERIALS: Information from the "Discussion" section of this chapter, reference books, something to mark the ground with such as chalk, string or a stick to scratch a mark in the dirt, measuring tape.

Stargazing

ACTIVITY: Look at some constellations, learn how to find them in the sky and listen to some related myths and legends. Look for meteors (shooting stars) and learn what they are.

GOALS: Understand how to locate the major constellations in the seasonal skies. Know the difference between a star and a planet, the origin of meteors (shooting stars) and how to spot a satellite. Have fun with starry myths and legends.

AGE: Younger Children and Older Children

PROCEDURE: Familiarize yourself with the constellations that are visible at that time of year, the terms and pointers given in the "Discussion" section of this chapter and some stories about these constellations.

You may want to take the group out before dark and lead some of the activities described earlier in this chapter. Once you are outside and the stars are beginning to show clearly, begin with the story of how Fisher became the constellation we now call the Big Dipper, which is really a portion of the constellation called the Great Bear or Ursa Major. This constellation will be a reference point. Describe and point out, using your flashlight beam, the zenith and the stars of the Big Dipper, which will help in locating other things for the group. Then, using the pointer stars of the Big Dipper as a reference, point out the North Star and outline the stars of the Little Dipper, which is also known as the Little Bear, Ursa Minor. Another good reference is the *meridian.* Trace this in the sky from the northernmost point on the horizon, through the zenith and across to the southernmost point on the horizon. Continue alternating between discussions of the constellations and stories. The binoculars can be passed around as you point out some major features of the moon if it is out. However, a moonless night, or one where a crescent phase of the moon is present, is best for stargazing because a bright moon obscures the stars.

Tell the group to watch for meteors or "shooting stars," which will appear suddenly as streaks of light in the sky. The answers to many of the questions you will encounter about meteors and other subjects are found in the "Discussion." You may also see a faint, planet-like light moving steadily across the sky and taking no more than six minutes to travel from horizon to horizon. This is a satellite which is visible because it reflects sunlight.

MATERIALS: "Discussion" section from this chapter, flashlight, books containing stories and myths of the constellations present at that time of year, reference books, star maps, Figure 14-2, several pairs of binoculars, insect repellant (if necessary).

A Stroll to the Sun

ACTIVITY: Walk between scale models of the Earth and sun, placed at an accurately measured distance from one another, all at the scale of 1 inch = 64,000 miles (1 centimeter = 40,567 kilometers).

GOALS: Appreciate the relative sizes of the sun and Earth, as well as the great distance between them.

AGE: Younger Children and Older Children

PROCEDURE: Explain that the Earth is 7,913 miles (12,735 kilometers) in diameter, that the sun is 850,000 miles (1,367,956 kilometers) in diameter and that the distance between them is 93,000,000 miles (149,670,480 kilometers). In order to imagine these sizes and this distance in relation to one another, you are going to set up an Earth and a sun at the proper relative distance and a scale of 1 inch = 64,000 miles (1 centimeter = 40,567 kilometers). The Earth will be the 1/8-inch (about 1/3-centimeter) sphere, the sun the 13-1/4-inch (33-2/3-centimeter) yellow ball and the distance between them will be 121 feet (37 meters). Measure out the distance, then have one child hold the Earth up at one end of the line and another hold the sun at the other end. Tell the children they will be walking twice 93,000,000 miles (149,670,480 kilometers) and have them stroll from the Earth to the sun and back again. Mention that the sun is not a large star and that the diameter of the giant red star Antares, of the constellation Scorpius, would reach all the way from the Earth to beyond the sun, filling the entire space in between.

MATERIALS: Small sphere of 1/8-inch or about 1/3-centimeter diameter (such as a kernel of popcorn or an unground piece of black pepper), yellow ball 13.25 inches (33.66 centimeters) in diameter, long measuring tape, open area at least 130 feet (39.6 meters) long.

Speedy Sunbeams

ACTIVITY: Calculate a light-year and the time it takes sunlight to reach the Earth. Use a timer to demonstrate the elapsed time between when light leaves the sun and arrives on Earth.

GOALS: Understand the speed of light, the meaning of "light-year" and the amount of time it takes for sunlight to reach the Earth.

AGE: Older Children

PROCEDURE: Tell the children that light travels at the speed of 186,000 miles (299,341 kilometers) each second. Have them calculate the distance traveled by light per minute (x60), per hour (x60), per day (x24) and per year (x365).[2] This last distance is called a *light-year*.

Now give the children the distance between the Earth and sun, which is 93,000,000 miles (149,670,480 kilometers). Have them calculate the time it will take for sunlight to reach the Earth.

93,000,000 miles	(149,670,480 kilometers)
11,160,000 miles/minute	(17,960,457 kilometers/minute)

=8.33 minutes or 8 minutes and 20 seconds

Take the minute timer and tell the children you are going to set it to time some sunlight on its journey to the Earth. Lead the children in saying, "On your mark, get set, Sunshine!" and set the timer for 8 minutes and 20 seconds. Continue your activities and the clock will go off, giving the children a sense of what these big figures mean.

MATERIALS: marker and newsprint or chalk and chalkboard, pencils, paper, minute timer or alarm clock.

Extending the Experience

•   Use a telescope to observe the intricate details of the moon, Saturn's rings, the red spot on Jupiter and other secrets of the sky.

•   Discuss the connection between Fisher and the sacrifices we all need to make for the benefit of other people and the Earth. See Chapter 6, page 46 for an activity on this theme.

•   Research forthcoming celestial events in your area in *The Astronomical Almanac*, United States Naval Observatory.[3] Study and observe these events with the children.

Notes

1. Light travels 186,000 miles (299,341 kilometers) each second, or nearly 6 trillion (6,000,000,000,000) miles (nearly 9.5 trillion kilometers) in one year. This distance is called a light-year.

2. These calculations are all cumulative. Keep multiplying the answers by the following multiplier.

3. To order write: Superintendent of Documents, U.S. Government Printing Office, Washington, D.C. 20402. Published annually.

✦ SEASONS ✦

He sat inside his lodge in front of a fire which gave off no heat, though a strange flickering light came from it.

CHAPTER 15

⟡ Spring Defeats Winter ⟡

(Seneca—Northeast Woodlands)

When the world was new, long ago, an old man was wandering around. This old man had long, white hair and wherever he stepped the ground grew hard as stone. When he breathed the rivers stopped flowing and the ponds became solid. The birds and animals fled before him and plants dried up and died as the leaves shriveled and fell from the trees.

Finally this old man found a place where he could set up his lodge. He made the walls of ice and covered it over with snow. He sat inside his lodge in front of a fire which gave off no heat, though a strange flickering light came from it. His only friend was the North Wind, who sat beside the fire with him and laughed as they spoke of things they did to make the world a cold, hard place. They sat and smoked their pipes through the long, white nights.

One morning, though, as the two dozed by their fire, they felt that something was wrong. The air was harder to breathe and when they looked outside, they saw strange things happening. The snowdrifts were growing smaller. Cracks were forming in the ice on the ponds.

"Henh!" said the North Wind. "I can stay no longer." He went out of the lodge and flew through the air toward the north, not stopping until he again reached a place where snow and ice were deep and there was no hint of warmth. But the old man did not stir. He knew his magic was strong. He had built his lodge to last.

Now, there came a knocking at his door. Someone was striking against the ice so hard that pieces were falling away from his blows.

"Go away!" the old man shouted. "No one can enter my lodge."

Even as he said it, the door of the lodge broke and fell to the ground. A young man with a smile on his face stood there. Without a word he stepped into the lodge and sat on the other side of the fire from the old man. He held a green stick in his hand and with it he stirred the fire. As he stirred the fire it began to grow warm. The old man felt sweat begin to run down his face.

"Who are you?" said the old man. "Why have you broken my door? No one can come in here but my friend, North Wind. If you do not leave, I will freeze you with my breath." Then the old man tried to blow his chilly breath at the young stranger, but only a thin mist came from his lips.

The young man laughed. "Old Man," he said, "let me stay here and warm myself by your fire."

The old man grew angry. "I am the one who makes the birds and the animals flee. Wherever I step the ground turns into flint. I make the snow and ice. I am mightier than you." As he spoke, though, the old man felt more sweat run off his brow, and the young

The old man opened his mouth to speak, but no words came out. He grew smaller and smaller and the sweat poured from his brow as he melted away.

man continued to smile.

"Listen," the stranger said, "I am young and strong. You cannot frighten me. Surely you know who I am. Do you not feel how warm my breath is? Wherever I breathe the plants grow and the flowers bloom. Where I step the grasses sprout and snow melts away. The birds and the animals come to me. See how long my hair is? Your hair is falling out now, Old Man. Wherever I travel I bring the sunshine and you cannot stay. Do you not know me, Old Man? Do you not hear my companion, the Fawn? She is the South Wind. She is blowing on your lodge. It is your time to leave."

The old man opened his mouth to speak, but no words came out. He grew smaller and smaller and the sweat poured from his brow as he melted away. Then he was gone. The walls of his lodge of ice and snow fell in. Where his cold fire had burned, white flowers now bloomed. Once again, the Young Man, Spring, had defeated the Old Man, Winter.

When reading "Spring Defeats Winter," it is easy to imagine why Old Man Winter sits confidently in his lodge as Young Man Spring enters. When the cold winter wind blows snow into drifts and ice encrusts the ponds and rivers, the chilling grip over the land seems complete. Still, spring comes. Flowers bloom. Plants grow. Snow melts and birds return from the south. In this story, Young Man Spring and the Fawn, the South Wind, prevail over Old Man Winter. Yet in time Old Man Winter will win out, and the story goes on forever.

Discussion

We who live in the temperate regions tend to think of four distinct seasons—spring, summer, fall and winter—but many climates show extremes that are sometimes more and sometimes less exaggerated than our own. Some climates are entirely different. Tropical seasons may be marked by a wet half of the year followed by a dry half. The length of tropical days and nights is remarkably similar all year. In polar regions the frost never leaves the ground. The light of polar days lasts 24 hours during the summer and the sun barely disappears as it skirts the horizon, if it sets at all.

While they are remarkably different throughout the world, *seasons* occur because the Earth's axis is tilted 23.5° to the plane of its orbit as it revolves around the sun. This tilt causes the north pole to be tilted closest to the sun during the *summer solstice* on June 21, and farthest away during the *winter solstice* on December 21 (Figure 15-1). On June 21 the sun's rays strike the Earth's surface more directly in the northern hemisphere than any other time of year, causing the summer heating north of the equator. The winter solstice finds the sun's rays meeting the Earth at small angles. This spreads the sun's energy out over a larger surface area of ground and is the source of Old Man Winter's strength. During the *vernal equinox* (March 21) and the *autumnal equinox* (September 23), the sun is directly above the equator and day and night are of equal length in all parts of the Earth.

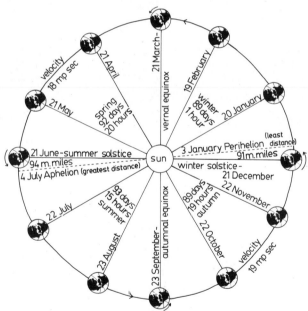

Figure 15-1. The seasons of the northern hemisphere are plotted on Earth's orbit around the sun. The Earth's summer swing peaks at around 4 July. At that time the Earth is roughly three million miles farther from the sun than it is during the winter (3 January).

This sequence of events is further complicated because the Earth's orbit around the sun is elliptical: we are closest to the sun (*perihelion*) on January 2 or 3 and farthest away (*aphelion*) on July 4. As a result, the seasons are unequal in length, with summer being longest, followed by spring, fall and winter, which is our shortest season. Summer is more than four days longer than winter in the northern hemisphere. When it is closest to the sun, the Earth receives 7 percent more sunlight than when farthest away. For this reason, the winters of the northern hemisphere are slightly moderated from those south of the equator, while summers are a bit cooler. In January the Earth's speed of 19 miles or 30.6 kilometers per second is 1 mile (1.6 kilometers) per second faster than it is in July, when the Earth travels at 18 miles or 29 kilometers per second.

Figure 15-2. The life cycles of plants and animals are adapted to the seasons.

Along with the dramatic seasonal changes in weather, there comes a procession of responses in the plants and animals all around us. Spring buds unfurl into bright green, young leaves and flowers bloom. Bees and other insects buzz, hop and drift through the moist air. Winter coats begin to shed their thick insulating underhairs. Birds return from their southern getaways and mating instincts and activities reach a frenzy. As summer's hazy, hot weather settles in, the rhythms of life settle down and reach a more even stride. With fall's shorter days and cool temperatures the pace quickens, not to get ready for new life but to prepare for either a long sleep, a perilous journey to the south, or active life during the endurance test of cold winds and long nights. Leaves fall, heartbeats slow down, tails curl around noses for warmth, wings turn southward, seeds rest and doors close tight. All life, in its own way, lives the Earth's sleep and awaits the spring's certain awakening.

The activities in this chapter explore the causes of

seasons, seasonal changes in weather and plant responses to those changes. Animal adaptations to winter, such as migration and hibernation, are the subject of Chapter 19, "How Turtle Flew South for the Winter."

Questions

1. When you heard or read the story, did you want Old Man Winter to melt from Young Man Spring's warmth? Do you like the cold or hot season better?
2. Do all parts of the world have four seasons? What are the seasons like in the tropics? The polar regions?
3. What causes the seasons?
4. How do the seasons affect people? Plants? Animals?

Activities
Season Suite

ACTIVITY: Act out the seasonal cycle of a wildflower from seed to flower to seed again.
GOALS: Understand how plants respond to the seasonal changes of day length, moisture levels and temperatures. Understand that each year plants complete a cycle of life and death, wakefulness and sleep.
AGE: Younger Children
PROCEDURE: Introduce the activity by asking the children to identify and describe each of the four seasons. Ask, "What changes come during each season?" Discuss temperature, day length, rainfall and other seasonal changes.

Now tell them they are going to go through a whole growing season as a wildflower. You could specify a certain kind of wildflower, such as morning glory, but be sure it is an annual. The flower in this narrative/play completes its whole life cycle from seed to seed in one season, which makes it an annual.

Before the play begins, each child will make a flower hat from the construction paper. This should be a flower built onto the top and front of a ring of paper that is just the right size to be worn as a hat. Each child will keep this hat nearby during the play. Also, one child will need to make a bee outfit with wings, antennae and three pairs of legs. This child also needs a paintbrush and flour (pollen) to pollinate the "flowers." This bee, along with the children dressed as the sun, wind and rain, will wait for their cues as you narrate the play. Read the play through once and rehearse it so that the children will know what to do and when to do it. Then, stand up front and lead the children through their moves as they become plants that complete one year's growing cycle.

(Children begin all curled up on the floor as unsprouted seeds. Then they follow your cues as you narrate.)

Season Suite

You are a seed resting in the soil. Winter is moving north and the soil around you feels warm and wet. Slowly you begin to unfold. Your root goes down into the soil and your sprout pushes upward. In a few days your leaves begin to unfold (their arms stretch out) and they poke up out of the dark soil into the bright, warm sun (the sun walks briskly across the room among the flowers). You grow taller and taller. You can feel the sap flowing through your veins. Your green leaves stretch wider and higher toward the sun (arms and fingers reaching higher).

As spring turns into summer, a bud forms on your head and finally opens into a beautiful flower (put flower hats on). Feel the long, hot days of summer (pause here as the sun walks *slowly* across the room) and imagine the patter of rain upon your leaves and flower petals (pause as the rain cloud walks through the flowers and lightly sprays them with water, while the wind follows behind blowing the cloud along). On some cool mornings there are beads of dew on your leaves and petals glistening in the sun.

One day a bee buzzes over and she is covered with pollen from other flowers. She sips nectar and gets pollen from your flower and she leaves pollen from another flower to help your seeds grow. (Bee buzzes around to each flower using the paintbrush to dust pollen [flour] onto each flower's head.)

The days grow short during the fall (sun walks briskly across the room) and one morning you find that frost has frozen your leaves and you are all shriveled up (they take off the flower hats and fold arms). But now you have seeds where you had none before. (Go around and place seeds in their hands.) One day a cold, hard wind blows (wind blows through the plants) and your seeds shake loose and fall to the soil (they let the seeds drop to the floor or ground). There is not much left of you now and the days are very short (sun *runs* through the flowers). You are a dead, dried-up brown stalk when the first snow comes (cloud comes through throwing shredded paper or white confetti for snow). But in the soil near your withered roots are resting the seeds that will make new life when the long days, warm weather and rainstorms come again in the springtime.

MATERIALS: Dried beans for seeds; construction paper; glue; masking tape; small paintbrushes with small containers of flour; one child dressed as a bee; one child dressed as the sun with a huge, yellow cardboard disc with rays coming out of it for a sun suit; one child dressed in white as a large cloud with rain for the flowers (spray bottle with water in it); one child dressed as the wind with long-flowing streamers attached to her/his clothes; white confetti or shredded paper.

Friend for All Seasons

ACTIVITY: Observe a plant closely through several seasons. Record the seasonal changes and the plant's responses to those changes. Share the experience with the children through stories, pictures or other media.

GOALS: Understand the seasonal changes in day length, rainfall, temperature and the responses of a plant to those changes. Understand that each year plants complete a cycle of life and death, growth and dormancy. Appreciate how plants and other parts of the Earth can become meaningful to us if we spend time with them and learn about them.

AGE: Younger Children and Older Children

PROCEDURE: The children will choose a plant outdoors and adopt it as their "friend for all seasons." Have them visit that plant at least two times during each season to record in pictures (drawings or photographs), words (stories, poems, descriptions) and sculpture (such as clay) that plant's experiences and changes. For each visit they should bring something for their plant, such as a leaf to feed the soil near its roots. They can talk to the plant, make friends with it!

Have them use all of their senses. How do the plant's shape, smell, texture (feeling) and appearance change? How does the weather change? Have older children take more exacting records such as temperature, day length, windspeed, rainfall and cloud cover during each season. Have them look very closely at these differences on a small scale, for instance, by measuring relative temperatures above and below winter snow cover as well as on the soil surface and several inches deep.

At the end of the activity, have the children compile their whole experience into a booklet and write one final story, or draw pictures, describing the seasonal changes and which experiences meant the most to them during the seasons. Have them share these reports and stories with the group.

MATERIALS: Paper, pencils, cameras and film, modeling clay, crayons, thermometers, hand lenses, anemometer (wind speed gauge), rain gauge, cloud charts, other supplies as needed, seasonal clothing, stapler.

Seasons on Earth: Our Tilted Planet

ACTIVITY: Demonstrate how seasons are caused by the different angles at which sunlight strikes the Earth during the year.
GOAL: Understand what causes the seasons.
AGE: Older Children
PROCEDURE: Explain why the seasons occur, using the information from the "Discussion" section. Be sure to explain about the summer and winter solstices and the vernal and autumnal equinoxes. Also, discuss the tremendous speed at which the Earth revolves around the sun in an elliptical orbit, being sometimes closest to it (perihelion), farthest away (aphelion) and all of the stages in between.

Then lead the following activity to help the children visualize how sunlight strikes with different levels of intensity, depending on the tilt of the Earth in relation to the sun and the resulting angle at which the sun's light meets the Earth's surface.

Mark a set of ten parallel lines on the ground about 2 feet (.6 meters) apart. These will represent the path of the sun's incoming energy, which is measured in *photons*. Now make an arc at one end of these lines as shown in Figure 15-3a. This arc is a portion of the Earth's

surface during the summer. Have the children walk along these lines to represent ten photons coming from the sun to the Earth. Measure along the arc the distance between each photon and the total distance from one end of the photon field to the other. In this case (summer), 10 photons give their energy to, for example, 23 feet (7 meters) of the Earth's surface. Explain that this is just an exercise and that the number of photons and the surface area they cover are not accurate. The figures given in this activity are only used to demonstrate seasonal changes in sunlight intensity.

Now change the Earth's arc as shown to create a smaller angle in relation to the path of the photons, as in Figure 15-3b. Have the children walk the photon path again and measure along the arc the space between photons and the width of the overall photon field. This time (winter) the 10 photons fall over, for example, 28 feet (8.5 meters) of the Earth's surface. Much less solar energy falls over each unit of the Earth's surface. This is why winter is colder than summer.
MATERIALS: "Discussion" section from this chapter; diagram of the sun and Earth to explain the causes of the seasons; Figure 15-1; globe; measuring tape; means for marking lines on the ground, such as chalk, a stick to scratch the soil or tape.

Extending the Experience

• Take clippings of different plants while they are dormant outside. Put them in water and observe which ones will leaf out or bloom indoors. The ones that do respond are usually more sensitive to temperature changes, while those that do not are more responsive to day length changes and will not be as affected by the warmth indoors. Use a sunlamp to expose these last types of plant clippings to longer "days" to induce blooming. This activity works best when the dormant plants have already experienced several months of short days and cold temperatures outdoors.

• Gather colorful leaves during the fall, or any time of year. Have everyone choose one leaf and look at it closely for a few minutes. Throw these into a pile and stir them up while everyone's eyes are closed. Now have the children try to pick out their own leaf. Later, press the leaves between newspaper and they will dry with their colors intact. Make a leaf mobile.

• In winter, catch, observe and draw snowfleas. This is a kind of insect known as a springtail. Snowfleas are often so numerous that they look like ground pepper sprinkled over the snow.

• Make snow ice cream by mixing snow (fresh and uncontaminated), sugar and vanilla.

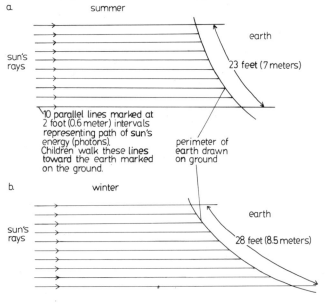

Figure 15-3. Seasons on Earth: Our Tilted Planet.

✦ PLANTS AND ANIMALS ✦

She rubbed her hand along the side of her body, and dried corn poured out to fill the basket. Now the boy grew afraid.

Chapter 16

⋄ The Coming of Corn ⋄

(Cherokee—North Carolina)

Long ago, when the world was new, an old woman lived with her grandson in the shadow of the big mountain. They lived happily together until the boy was seven years old. Then his Grandmother gave him his first bow and arrow. He went out to hunt for game and brought back a small bird.

"Ah," said the Grandmother, "You are going to be a great hunter. We must have a feast." She went out to the small storehouse behind their cabin. She came back with dried corn in her basket and made a fine-tasting soup with the small bird and the corn.

From that point on the boy hunted. Each day he brought back something and each day the Grandmother took some corn from the storage house to make soup. One day, though, the boy peeked into the storehouse. It was empty! But that evening, when he returned with game to cook, she went out again and brought back a basket filled with dry corn.

"This is strange," the boy said to himself. "I must find out what is happening."

The next day, when he brought back his game, he waited until his Grandmother had gone out for her basket of corn and followed her. He watched her go into the storehouse with the empty basket. He looked through a crack between the logs and saw a very strange thing. The storehouse was empty, but his grandmother was leaning over the basket. She rubbed her hand along the side of her body, and dried corn poured out to fill the basket. Now the boy grew afraid. Perhaps she was a witch! He crept back to the house to wait. When his Grandmother returned, though, she saw the look on his face.

"Grandson," she said, "you followed me to the shed and saw what I did there."

"Yes, Grandmother," the boy answered.

The old woman shook her head sadly. "Grandson," she said, "then I must get ready to leave you. Now that you know my secret I can no longer live with you as I did before. Before the sun rises tomorrow I shall be dead. You must do as I tell you, and you will be able to feed yourself and the people when I have gone."

The old woman looked very weary and the boy started to move toward her, but she motioned him away. "You cannot help now, Grandson. Simply do as I tell you. When I have died, clear away a patch of ground on the south side of our lodge, that place where the sun shines longest and brightest. The earth there must be made completely bare. Drag my body over that ground seven times and then bury me in that earth. Keep the ground clear. If you do as I say, you shall see me again and you will be able to feed the people." Then the old woman grew silent and closed her eyes. Before the morning came, she was dead.

Her grandson did as he was told. He cleared away the space at the south side of the cabin. It was hard work, for there were trees and tangled vines, but at last the earth was bare. He dragged his Grandmother's body, and wherever a drop of her blood fell a small plant grew up. He kept the ground clear around the small plants, and as they grew taller it seemed he could hear his Grandmother's voice whispering in the leaves. Time passed and the plants grew very tall, as tall as a person, and the long tassels at the top of each plant reminded the boy of his grandmother's long hair. At last, ears of corn formed on each plant and his Grandmother's promise had come true. Now, though she had gone from the Earth as she had once been, she would be with the people forever as the corn plant, to feed them.

Grandmother brings both joy and sadness in this story. She is giving in every way. In life she gives the boy the bow and arrow to hunt with and the corn to eat. When the boy discovers her secret, Grandmother dies and gives her greatest gift: corn to feed the people through the generations. But the boy has to help the corn to grow. The land has to be cleared to prepare for the "seeds," his Grandmother's drops of blood. Then he has to keep the earth clear around the small plants and care for them.

Discussion

The images in this story are symbolic. The relationship between the Grandmother and the Boy can be seen as a metaphor for the relationship between the planter and the crop; through personal sacrifice and work, the planter sows the seeds that bring forth new plant life to feed the people.

No matter how food crops have changed over the thousands of years that people have grown them, they were all first cultivated from native plants in the wild. Many of the most important food plants used worldwide today are native to North America. (See Chapter 4, page 27 for more information on native food plants.)

Farming these crops requires knowledge of the plants' needs: soil, rain, warmth and sunlight. The soil must be prepared and cared for. Farmers use different approaches for growing crops. One common distinction is between "chemical" and "organic" methods of fertilizing the plants and controlling insect damage and other crop losses. The last activity in this chapter studies different methods of fertilizing the soil and the relationship between these methods and the nutrient cycle.

Soil is a key in the giving and receiving cycle between the planter and crop: it is the fertile bed from which new life springs time and again.[1] However, the soil is not an infinite source of new life that can give, give and then give some more. Soil is part of a circle. It, too, must receive to keep giving.

The dead plants and animals, called *detritus*, return to the soil to feed it. Fresh plant and animal remains are eaten by insects, mites, worms and many other organisms, who break these remains down mechanically and leave them partially decomposed as excrement. These remains are consumed by the *decomposers*: chiefly bacteria and fungi, which break them down further into

Figure 16-1. Fungi, such as this mushroom called the shaggy mane, are important decomposers of dead plant and animal remains.

proteins, fats, carbohydrates, ash and other compounds. Nutrients are released for plant growth through leaching from detritus, excretion and on death of the decomposers, in a process called *mineralization.*

This process, called *decomposition*, is vital to the *nutrient cycle*, which is one of the essential circles of life on Earth—the circle of life and death. (See Chapter 22 for more about life and death.) It is this important event in the thin skin of topsoil on Earth that makes continuing life possible for the plants that use the sunlight to grow and the animals who eat them. (See Chapter 7 for information and activities about the sun as the source of energy for plants and animals.)

Questions

1.   How do you feel when Grandmother has to die in the story? What are the gifts she gives while alive? When she dies?
2.   The boy has to prepare the soil and care for the young corn plants. When we grow food, what are the steps we need to take to grow and care for the seeds and plants?
3.   Where do our food plants come from: corn, beans, apples, squash, rice, wheat, potatoes and others?
4.   Can the soil keep giving more food without anything being given back? What does the soil need? How does soil get "fed" to continue the circle of giving and receiving?
5.   What are some different kinds of farming practices, and how do they work to keep the soil fed to grow food crops for the future?

Activities
The Planter, the Crop and the Soil

ACTIVITY: Establish and cultivate a vegetable garden to grow some favorite vegetables. Grow these crops, from seed through harvest, and then preserve them. Give special attention to caring for the soil and plants.
GOALS: Realize where food comes from. Understand the balance between the planter and the crop, and the need to give labor and nutrients to the soil in order to keep receiving food. Learn the basics of soil care and vegetable gardening.
AGE: Younger Children and Older Children
PROCEDURE: Establish and fence off a garden space in your yard or on the learning center grounds. If this is not possible, you can grow a garden in window boxes or in rooftop planters. Be sure that the soil in the planter is

well-drained by layering it over several inches of sand. Prepare the seedbed ahead of time by tilling the soil and adding fertilizer in the form of manure or compost. Do this during the fall season before planting, if possible, to allow the manure to begin decomposing so it will most benefit the young plants. Add some lime if the soil is too acid. The local branches of the governmental Soil Conservation Service or Department of Agriculture will often provide free soil testing for pH levels and nutritional balance.

Make a list of your children's favorite vegetables and fruits, and narrow these down to around ten or so different kinds that are most popular. Do not neglect perennials such as asparagus and blackberries, which can be enjoyed for years to come. Keep in mind that constant weeding and long-term care are required for perennials.

Figure 16-2. Sowing peas during the early growing season.

Be sure the chosen food crops will grow under the conditions at hand (light levels, soil type, temperature, length of growing season, etc.). Some crops, for instance, need much longer growing seasons than others. Lima beans and melons are harder to grow to maturity in Canada and in the northern extremes of the United States because the growing season is so short.

The seeds of some crops, such as peas, can be planted directly in the spring garden as soon as the soil has dried out enough to be worked. Other crops, like tomatoes and peppers, are best when started as seeds in flats and transplanted into the garden beds when the seedlings are several inches tall. You will need to start them in a cold frame or indoors, so be sure to expose them gradually to the outdoor climate to prevent shock when they are transplanted. Do this by putting the seedlings outside for short periods of time each day at first. Then gradually increase the length of this exposure time as field planting approaches.

Throughout this experience, have the children keep close track of weather and care for the plants accordingly, such as watering plants during dry periods and covering them during early frosts. (See Chapter 9 about wind and weather.) Set up a schedule where children will keep the plants watered, weeded, pruned, well fed and free of pests. Vigorous plants that are well cared for and provided with balanced nutrition will have fewer problems with diseases as well as other pests because the plants' natural resistance will be high. With intensive growing like this, you can remove by hand any pests that do appear. This is also a good means for learning about insect life cycles. The idea is to experience growing food, not to produce crops for commercial market, so you can afford a few blemishes on the vegetables and lower yields due to the fact that this is a learning experience.

Encourage the children to develop a relationship with the plants. Research shows that plants do respond to positive energy such as talking to them kindly and playing soothing music. This will seem strange at first, but after a while you will all enjoy it, including the plants! It is important to conduct the gardening lesson as a natural, nurturing and expanding experience. Have the children occasionally place manure or other fertilizer along the sides of the rows of crops to feed the plants. Emphasize that in doing this the children are giving back to the soil.

Harvest the crops, then clean, process and preserve the vegetables and fruits. Turn the unused portions of the plants back into the soil or haul them to a compost heap. Then lightly spread manure and plant a winter cover crop, such as winter rye, to protect the soil when it is exposed during the cold months.

MATERIALS: Paper, pencils, garden space, shovels, hoes, rakes, spades, seeds for food crops, seed flats, cold frame, source of water, watering cans or hose, fertilizer (manure or compost), fencing and fence posts to keep animals from eating seeds, fence staples, hammer, mulch to cover and protect soil, seeds for cover crops (such as winter rye) when the soil is fallow (unprotected by the food crop), weather reports, gardening reference books, agricultural lime (if needed), window boxes or planters, soil, sand, freezer, knives and other necessary equipment for processing and preserving the crops.

Nutrient Cyclers

ACTIVITY: (A) Visit a woodlot and study decomposition and the plants and animals that are causing things to decay. Collect decaying leaves and create a bulletin board display of the nutrient cycle. (B) Play a game that "cycles" nutrients among the players in the "nutrient cycler."

GOALS: Understand that nutrients are used for plant growth. Understand that when plants and animals die, they are decomposed by the soil organisms and nutrients are thus released for further plant growth. Be familiar with the meaning of *nutrient cycle* and the plants and animals involved in the process of decomposition.

AGE: Younger Children and Older Children

PROCEDURE A: *Recycling the Forest Floor.* Take a trip out to a wooded area. Any grove of trees is fine as long as there are leaves decaying in the soil. Walk into the woodlot with the children and then suddenly say, "Look, soil is forming all over. Come quick and see!"

"Look," you say, "all of these leaves are turning into soil. Can you see it happening?" Have the children use

Figure 16-3. All of these leaves are turning into soil. Can you see it happening?

the hand lenses to look closely at the leaves as they gently peel leaf layers off the top of the soil. The farther down they go, the more decomposed the leaves will be.

Have the children explore what is causing the leaves to turn from leaves into soil. Help them to discover the white threads of fungi, which are one of the few living things that can break down cellulose in wood and leaves. There will be worms, mites, many kinds of larvae, spiders, centipedes and millipedes and many more. Refer to these organisms as you describe the process of *decomposition* (see "Discussion" section). Then, with the children, collect some leaves in various stages of decomposition.

Younger children will create a "Nutrient Cycler" bulletin board or mural by making, out of construction paper, a large circle with an arrow pointing in one direction. Have them place the leaves in sequence onto part of the circle, with the arrow pointing from whole leaves to those that are the most decomposed. The children will draw pictures of the soil organisms they found and put these pictures on the mural, indicating that the organisms are eating the leaves and, in some cases, each other. At the spot on the circle where the leaves are thoroughly decomposed, have the children create some plants growing from the newly formed "soil." Further along on the circle, show some of these plants dying and leaves falling from trees and shrubs to start the cycle over again.

PROCEDURE B: *Cycle Circle Game.* Older children will play this game in teams of about six or more. Make name tags out of cardboard that list the cycle circle players (see "Materials") and have the children hang the name tags around their necks.

To start the game, sit the children down in a circle with everyone facing the center, review the nutrient cycle and name the players. State that during the game the "nutrients" will keep getting cycled among the players. To play the game, one player (the nutrient "cycler") will take the "nutrients" (the leaf) and walk around the outside of the circle. At some point this "cycler" will drop the "nutrients" behind a seated player and will then run around the circle. The seated player will pick up the "nutrients," run after the cycler and try to tag him or her. The cycler tries to get back to the spot where that player was seated without getting tagged. If the cycler gets tagged, then he or she remains the cycler, takes back the "nutrients" and begins the game again. If the cycler succeeds in getting back to that spot and sits in the circle before getting tagged, then the other player becomes the cycler, keeps the "nutrients" and starts the *Cycle Circle Game* over again.

MATERIALS: (A) hand lenses, wooded area, bags to collect leaves in, wall space or bulletin board, construction paper, crayons, stapler and staples, pencils, scissors, paste, leaves in various stages of decomposition from the field trip. (B) open space for playing the game; a leaf; string; cardboard; felt-tipped marking pen to make name tags with names of things that are part of the nutrient cycle: leaf, worm, mite, fungus, bacterium, nematode (small roundworm), centipede, plant roots, beetle, springtail, others you may have found on the field trip.

Farming and the Nutrient Cycle

ACTIVITY: Explore farming techniques that rely on chemical fertilizers and those that rely on organic nutrients to enrich the soil. Compare and contrast the benefits and drawbacks of these methods. Use a role-playing experience to examine the relevant issues.

GOALS: Understand that there are different ways of providing soil nutrients while farming, and that some of these methods more closely approximate the natural nutrient cycle than others. Understand the distinction between chemical fertilizer and organic fertilizer.

AGE: Older Children

PROCEDURE: If possible, visit several farms or gardens where people use different approaches to nutrient cycling. Some farms and gardens recycle nutrients from the land by using manure and plant compost for fertilizers. Others use synthetic chemical fertilizers as a nutrient supply. If taking a field trip is not possible, have the children study these different types of farming from other sources, such as books, magazines, news reports and visits from farmers.

In their reports, the children will compare and contrast the different types of farming and draw conclusions about the ability of the various methods for maintaining soil health and fertility longterm. Hold a brainstorming session and list the pros and cons for these different farming methods as related to the nutrient cycle.

Assign roles to the children, allowing them to choose a role that they prefer, if possible, and hold a forum to bring out the issues. The roles could be: agribusiness farmer, "environmental" or "organic" farmer, the soil, soil organisms, crop plants, farmer's family, consumers of the crops, etc. Several children can play the same role. Discuss the issues that arise and try to reach a consensus on the farming method(s) that best support soil health and nutrient cycling in the long run. Explore the ecological, economic and social costs, benefits and trade-offs of the different methods.

MATERIALS: Three or more farms using different farming practices ranging from approaches that are chemical-intensive to "environmental" or "organic" methods, information and pictures about these various methods, references and articles on different kinds of farming, paper, pencils, felt-tipped marking pens and newsprint or chalkboard and chalk.

Extending the Experience

• Make a list of some of our most commonly used modern farm plants and research where they came from and which Native people originally used them. Set up a bulletin board with pictures of modern crops and their predecessors from the wild, as well as the Native people who eat them today and have eaten them in the past.

• Set up a recycling program. Put out collecting containers for glass, aluminum, bimetal cans, paper and organic waste. Compost and return the organic material to the soil via the garden. Collect the other materials and periodically bring them to a recycling station in your area. If you do not have a recycling station nearby, you may want to start one.

• Follow up the stories and activities of this chapter with an exploration of Chapter 22, "The Origin of Death."

• Share a popcorn feast! Popcorn is a gift from Native Americans.

Notes

1. See Chapter 8 for information and activities about soil formation and the composition of soil.

They were all just lying on their backs with their mouths open, letting the maple syrup drip into their mouths.

CHAPTER 17

❖ Manabozho and the Maple Trees ❖

(Anishinabe—Great Lakes Region)

A long time ago, when the world was new, Gitchee Manitou made things so that life was very easy for the people. There was plenty of game and the weather was always good and the maple trees were filled with thick sweet syrup. Whenever anyone wanted to get maple syrup from the trees, all they had to do was break off a twig and collect it as it dripped out.

One day, Manabozho went walking around. "I think I'll go see how my friends the Anishinabe are doing," he said. So he went to a village of Indian people. But there was no one around. So Manabozho looked for the people. They were not fishing in the streams or the lake. They were not working in the fields hoeing their crops. They were not gathering berries. Finally he found them. They were in the grove of maple trees near the village. They were all just lying on their backs with their mouths open, letting the maple syrup drip into their mouths.

"This will not do," Manabozho said. "My people are all going to be fat and lazy if they keep on living this way."

So Manabozho went down to the river. He took with him a big basket he had made of birch bark. With this basket he brought back many buckets of water. He went to the top of the maple trees and poured the water in so that it thinned out the syrup. Now thick maple syrup no longer dripped out of the broken twigs. Now what came out was thin and watery and just barely sweet to the taste.

"This is how it will be from now on," Manabozho said. "No longer will syrup drip from the maple trees. Now there will be only this watery sap. When people want to make maple syrup they will have to gather many buckets full of the sap in a birch bark basket like mine. They will have to gather wood and make fires so they can heat stones to drop into the baskets. They will have to boil the water with the heated stones for a long time to make even a little maple syrup. Then my people will no longer grow fat and lazy. Then they will appreciate this maple syrup Gitchee Manitou made available to them. Not only that, this sap will drip only from the trees at a certain time of the year. Then it will not keep people from hunting and fishing and gathering and hoeing in the fields. This is how it is going to be," Manabozho said.

And that is how it is to this day.

Manabozho sees that the relationship between the maple trees and people is not good. The people are taking the easy path and letting the trees feed them while they neglect their hunting, fishing, gathering and farming. So Manabozho thins the sap and makes it flow only during the late winter and early spring. This way it will be appreciated, and the people will have to hunt, fish, gather and grow food to sustain themselves.

(Gitchee Manitou also appears in Chapter 10, "Koluscap and the Water Monster," and in Chapter 14, "How Fisher Went to the Skyland: The Origin of the Big Dipper.")

Discussion

Trees and forests give us maple sap and other gifts such as wood to build with and to burn for heat; beauty, both in the countryside and city; a place to find solitude; shade; noise reduction; clean air (leaves filter out particulate pollution); food for people and animals from nuts, fruits, bark, roots and other parts of the trees; erosion protection as the roots hold the soil in place and so keep the waters clean and preserve the soil; and oxygen from photosynthesis occurring in the leaves.

The major themes of this chapter are the basic parts of trees and their functions, the forest community, plant succession (secondary succession) and change in the developing forest.

The sweet maple sap that Manabozho thins in this story is a combination of water and minerals brought up from the roots of the tree, along with sugars made in the leaves. Let's look at the parts of a tree to see how they function to move the sap and keep the tree alive, growing and healthy:

Roots anchor the tree. They branch underground and eventually form into small rootlets with miles of fine *root hairs* that take up minerals and water from the soil. There is great power in a growing root. A growing root that is 4 inches (10.2 centimeters) in diameter and 3 feet (.9 meter) long can raise 50 tons (45.4 metric tons).

Leaves (broad leaves and "needles") use sunlight to create food for the tree via photosynthesis (See Chapter 7, page 50 for details about photosynthesis). Evapora-tion from leaf surfaces, called *transpiration*, accounts for the loss of up to 99 percent of the water absorbed by roots. *Deciduous* trees drop all of their leaves each year. *Evergreens* have green leaves all year because their leaves last several growing seasons. Evergreen trees grow some new leaves each year but they lose only the oldest ones, which are usually two to four years old when they fall.

Trunks provide support and act as pipelines to carry water and nutrients to the parts of the tree. Figure 17-1 shows the major trunk layers, whose functions are described below, moving from the outside to the inside:

• *Outer bark* is what we see covering the trunk and branches. It protects the tree from disease, fire and injury.

• *Inner bark* or *phloem* carries sap—which is rich in sugars made in the leaves as well as minerals—down from the leaves to the branches, trunk and roots. Phloem can also bring stored sugar up from the roots when it is needed.

• *Cambium* is a layer that is about two cells thick. Each year it grows new phloem to the outside, sapwood to the inside, and new cambium. Branches, trunks and roots grow in thickness as a result of cambium growth.

• *Xylem* makes up the bulk of the tree trunk. Just inside the cambium is the new xylem called *sapwood*, which carries minerals and water up from the roots to the rest of the tree. Some vessels in the sapwood can move stored water and nutrients horizontally to other parts of the tree. To the inside of sapwood is old xylem called *heartwood*, which mainly provides support for the tree. Heartwood is older, dead sapwood that is usually darker and can no longer carry minerals and water up from the roots. Since it is dead, heartwood can rot away to leave a hollow tree with a sleeve of living wood on the outside.

The yearly cycle of tree growth forms distinct layers of xylem that appear in cross section as *annual rings*. The inner, lighter colored part of each annual ring, called *springwood*, forms during the spring when water is usually abundant and thus growth is rapid. Spring-wood has larger pores and is less dense than the darker *summerwood*, which forms later in the growing season when water is often in short supply, causing the tree to grow more slowly. Annual rings can be counted to determine the approximate age of a tree.

There are distinct layers formed by the soil and plants of the forest. Most animals are specific in their habitat preference in the forest apartment house. Seventy percent of all arthropods—insects, mites, spiders,

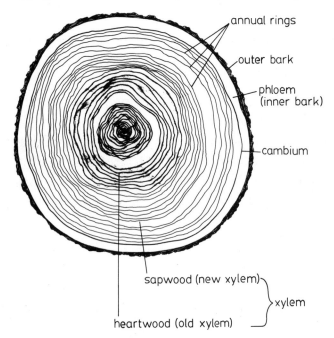

annual rings

outer bark

phloem (inner bark)

cambium

sapwood (new xylem) } xylem
heartwood (old xylem)

Figure 17-1. Cross section of a tree trunk showing the different parts.

crustaceans and their relatives—live in only one layer of the forest throughout their lives. Downy woodpeckers, hairy woodpeckers and red-bellied woodpeckers do not compete directly for food and nesting holes because they use different parts of the forest trees to nest and feed in. Chickadees, woodpeckers, certain ducks, squirrels and other animals nest in tree cavities. The main layers of the forest high rise are: the soil layer, where decomposition occurs (see Chapter 16) and where 95 percent of all insects live at one point in their life cycle; the forest floor, where soil and air meet amid a mass of rotting leaves and branches; the shrub and herb layer of flowers, ferns, shrubs and young trees; the tree trunks and lower canopy, where wood and branches are the dominant habitats; and the crowns that form the canopy, where leaves catch sunlight, create new growth, release oxygen and provide shelter and shade in the forest below.

When you stand on the floor of an ancient forest there is a timeless, cathedral-like feeling. Yet even forests are not forever; nature's way is one of *change*. The actions of people, insects, diseases, storms and fires can weaken and kill trees—sometimes over very large areas. When the trees are dead and the sun once again beams down onto the soil, a process known as *secondary succession* or *plant succession* begins. (See Chapter 8 about soil formation or *primary succession*.)

Plant succession occurs in abandoned farmland or where drought, insect blight or some other agent of change has wiped out a community of forest trees. Seeds that need lots of sunlight, and so have been lying dormant in the soil of the forest floor, now begin to sprout. Other seeds will arrive borne on the wind, in the water, in bird and mammal droppings or as hitchhikers on animal feathers and fur. In temperate regions daisy, dandelion, mustard and many grasses are common young field plants. Milkweed, goldenrod, mullein and others may show up later. Then woody plants begin to sprout: blackberry, rose, spiraea, white pine, red cedar, aspen and wild cherry are common.

The many levels of the forest high rise are being built. Leaves cast heavy shade on the ground. The soil becomes cooler, richer, moister and spongier because plant roots plow through it, and dead plant remains and other organic matter accumulate. Successional plants change the environment as they grow, and eventually their own seeds no longer thrive in the understory. With these changes, the seeds of forest trees, shrubs and flowers begin to flourish: pine, spruce, fir and hemlock; oak and hickory; birch, beech and maple; blueberry; trillium; wood aster; and more. The kind of forest community that will develop depends on climate, soil

Figure 17-2. The waxy white stems of "Indian pipe" can be found growing in the moist soil of the forest floor. This is one of the few flowering plants that is a saprophyte, living on the remains of dead plants and animals.

type, elevation, slope and past land-use practices, among other factors. The mature forest is sometimes called a *climax community*, but a disturbance can set succession back to an earlier stage at any time.

As the plants change the animals respond. Bobolinks, meadowlarks, savannah sparrows and goldfinches are found in fields. Shrubs are the homes of field sparrows, towhees, yellow warblers and yellowthroats. The deep, rich whistle of the oriole joins chorus with the calls of tanagers, jays and the melodious thrushes when the branches of a thick forest canopy arch overhead.

Questions

1. Why does Manabozho think people should have to hunt, fish, gather and grow their own food? Do you think it is a good idea that he should thin the maple sap so it has to be boiled to become sweet syrup? Why or why not?

2. Besides maple sugar and syrup, what are some other things the trees give us? What do they give the

plants and animals that live in the forest?

3. What are the major parts of a tree? What functions do they serve in keeping the tree alive and helping it to grow?

4. Think of the forest as being made of layers. What are the bottom layers? Middle layers? Top layers? Name some plants and animals that live in these layers in a forest near your home.

5. If someone cut down all of the trees in a forest, what would the clearing look like in five years? Ten years? Thirty years? One hundred years? What is secondary (plant) succession? What are some other agents, besides people, that could kill forest trees?

Activities[1]
Tree Parts and Their Functions

ACTIVITY: (A) Construct a small "tree," including all of the major parts of a tree, and use that model tree to demonstrate how tree parts work. (B) Visit some living trees and use cross sections of trees to study the different parts of a tree and their functions.

GOAL: Understand the basic parts of a tree and how they help the tree to live and grow.

AGE: Younger Children and Older Children

PROCEDURE A: *Trees for the Making.* Give each child a diagram of the tree parts. Have him or her construct a small "tree" including all of the parts it will need to live. When the projects are done, have each child share his or her tree and describe it to the rest of the group. Ask them to point out how the sap flows from the leaves and roots to the rest of the tree, and where the tree's food is made from sunlight (leaves). Have them point out which parts of the tree are alive and where the dead heartwood is found. Ask how their homemade tree is different from a living tree.

PROCEDURE B: *Tree Walk.* Take the children outside to visit some trees. Use information from the "Discussion" to describe the parts of a tree—leaves, trunk and roots—and their respective functions. Pass out one of the small cross sections of a branch and a hand lens to each child. Use the diagram of the tree trunk (Figure 17-1) and the large cross section of a trunk to explain the parts of the trunk and their roles in keeping the tree alive. Have each child find the parts of the tree trunk on her or his cross section of a branch as you are describing the parts on the larger cross section of tree trunk.

MATERIALS: (A) diagrams of tree parts (one for each child), cardboard tubes (such as empty paper-towel tubes), pencils, tape, construction paper, glue or paste,

scissors, crayons, watercolor paints, brushes, water, pipe cleaners, string, natural plant parts (acorns, leaves, etc.). (B) "Discussion" information; one large cross section of a tree clearly showing the outer bark, inner bark, cambium, sapwood and heartwood; one small cross section of a branch with these parts visible for each child; diagram of tree parts; Figure 17-1; hand lenses.

Field to Forest

ACTIVITY: (A) Create miniature landscapes showing different stages of plant succession as depicted in photographs. (B) Crawl from field to forest to take note of how conditions change as a field grows up to forest. (C) Take measurements and make observations of plants and animals in areas at different stages of plant succession.

GOALS: Understand that change is a natural part of the environment. Learn about plant succession. Understand the environmental changes that occur during plant succession and some of the plants and animals associated with the different stages of plant succession.

AGE: Younger Children and Older Children

PROCEDURE A: *Succession Snapshots.* (Younger children) Beforehand: Take photographs of environments showing four stages of plant succession: open field with flowers and grasses; old field with shrubs and young trees; young forest with a mix of field trees and mature forest trees; mature forest (Figure 17-3).

Divide the children into pairs and have each pair create a scene that resembles one of the photographs. Assign each photograph to at least one pair. Lay down a piece of green or brown cloth for each pair to use as

Figure 17-3. Field to forest: secondary or plant succession. The changes in time as an open field grows to mature forest can be seen in this illustration. Natural or human disturbances can create new clearings in the forest and plant succession will begin again.

a landscape base and put some objects under each cloth to create small hills. Have the children place pebbles on top to represent rocks. Flowers, trees and shrubs can be created for the landscapes by standing up natural plant materials in the clay, such as plant twigs and wildflower parts. Do not forget to put animals into the scene. (See "Discussion" section for some ideas on which animals to include in the different stages of succession.) Discuss the sequence of scenes in chronological order and the idea of change through time.

PROCEDURE B: *Time Creep.* (Younger Children and Older Children) Take the children to an area where there is a good sequence of successional growth that spans in a short distance (100 feet [30.5 meters] or less) from open field to mature forest. Ask the children to describe how the conditions of light, heat, moisture levels and density of plant growth change as a field grows up. Now have them get down on all fours and crawl from field to forest, imagining they are moving forward in time and the field is growing up. (See the activities listed at the end of this chapter for more ideas on this theme.)

PROCEDURE C: *Succession Samples.* (Older Children) Take the children to four different places outdoors, each representing a different stage of plant succession from field to forest. Have the children sample the plants, locate available animals (insects, birds, etc.) and signs of animals in the four areas and record their findings on paper. Have them take soil samples and temperatures of both the air and the soil surface. When the children are done, gather them together and have them explain and demonstrate their findings. Have the children describe the adaptations among the plants and animals found (seed dispersal mechanisms, food preferences, etc.) that make those organisms well-suited to the environment in which they live.

MATERIALS: (A) camera and film, photographs of areas showing four chronological stages of plant succession, pieces of green or brown cloth, objects to place under the pieces of cloth to create hills, plant parts, crayons, modeling clay, pencils, construction paper, toothpicks, pipe cleaners, pebbles, scissors, glue, paste. (B) outdoor area with plant growth representing stages of plant succession from open field to forest. (C) outdoor area as described in Procedure C, field guides, hand lenses, paper, pencils, clipboards, thermometers, bags and containers for collecting, spades.

Extending the Experience

• Study the Native American cultures of local woodland environments to learn how they used trees and worked the wood with their tools.

• Make a poem about a tree. Each child will think of an adjective or two while looking at the tree from a different perspective than the others (close up, far away, lying down, standing . . .). Now have the children put all of their words together and make a poem out of them. Have them write the poem in the shape of a tree.

• Use Chapter 5 as an extension to this chapter, leading from understanding trees to taking a stewardship role toward trees and forests.

• Read about methods for tapping maple trees and set some taps to collect sap. Most of the water can be boiled out of the maple sap over an outdoor fire. Carefully finish the boiling over a stove when the sap gets close to the syrup stage. Remember that it takes about 40 gallons (151 liters) of sap to make 1 gallon (3.8 liters) of syrup.

• Visit a working sugarbush and experience a maple-sugaring operation firsthand.

• Look at the branching patterns of trees: opposite, alternate and whorled. Use field guides to identify some common trees in your area. Have the children keep a field sketchbook of tree characteristics and natural history: branching patterns; leaf shapes; crown shapes; bark textures; animals and plants living in, on and around the trees; site characteristics (shade, moisture, temperature, slope, soil); and so on.

• Create a safe sensory-awareness blindfold walk by running a rope as a handrail between trees. Make sure the path is fairly level and free of low branches. String the rope through different kinds of habitats such as from a shady pine grove into a sunny field. As the blindfolded children move silently along this rope, they will use their senses of smell, touch and hearing to imagine what the area they are entering looks like. Once they arrive at the end of their rope, have them lie on their backs and look straight up—*then* have them remove their blindfolds.

• Have the children create a mural of a forest showing the forest layers (see "Discussion") from soil to tree crowns. Have each child use references to research a forest plant or animal and to identify which forest layer it lives in. Have them illustrate that plant or animal and place it on the mural while reporting about it to the rest of the children. Later, take a field trip to see the layers in a nearby forest and to observe the life there.

Notes
1. See Chapter 5 for activities on caring for trees and forests.

"That is easy," said Kokopilau, taking the arrow and passing it quickly under his wing covers so that it seemed the arrow had pierced him and come out the other side.

CHAPTER 18

⋄ Kokopilau, the Hump-Backed Flute Player ⋄

(Hopi—Southwest)

After the Hopi people had come out of the sipapu into the Fourth World, they were told by Masaw, the ruler of this world, that they must migrate to the four directions before they could come to the place where they would finally settle. So their travels began.

There are many stories of these migrations. More than one of them tells of Kokopilau, an insect person who accompanied them. Carvings which depict Kokopilau can be found in rocks from South America to Canada, and the Hopi people say this is proof of how far they traveled. You can see Kokopilau's long antennae branching out from his head in many of those rock drawings, for Kokopilau was a locust or a grasshopper. He was also a flute player and a trickster of sorts, as the following story shows.

Near the start of their migrations, the Hopi people climbed to the top of a mountain. On top of that mountain was a great Eagle.

"I am the one who guards this place," said the Eagle. "I have lived here since this Fourth World was created. Anyone who would pass into this land must pass my test."

Then Kokopilau stepped forward. "We wish to live in this land," he said. "I am ready to be tested."

At that the Eagle drew forth an arrow. "You must be able to do as I do," he said. Then the Eagle pierced himself with the arrow and drew it with great effort out the other side without hurting himself.

"That is easy," said Kokopilau, taking the arrow and passing it quickly under his wing covers so that it seemed the arrow had pierced him and come out the other side.

"I see that you have great power, indeed," said the Eagle. "You have my permission to lead your people into this new land. You may also use my feathers for your prayer sticks whenever you wish to speak with the Creator. As I am the one who flies the highest and closest to the Sun, your prayers will be taken up to the Creator quickly." So it was that ever since then, the Eagle's feathers have been placed on the *pahos*, or prayer sticks, of the Hopi people.

Then Kokopilau led the people into the new land. As he played his flute, the land and the winds became warm. In the hump on his back he carried seeds of useful plants. Thus the corn and beans and squash and flowers began to grow as the people traveled with the Hump-backed Flute Player across the beautiful new Fourth World in those early days.

Kokopilau seems like a cross between a magician, the Pied Piper and Johnny Appleseed. First, the Eagle presents a feat that Kokopilau must perform in order for him and the people to enter the Fourth World. He meets the Eagle's challenge and appears to pass the arrow through his own body. Next Kokopilau plays his flute to lead the people into the Fourth World. Finally, in the hump on his back, he brings the seeds of useful plants: corn, beans, squash and flowers.

Discussion

This story shows the importance of insects in Hopi beliefs, especially Kokopilau, who is a locust or grasshopper. As the story ends, Kokopilau brings the seeds of the most important Hopi food plants. It may seem strange to us that a locust, which is usually considered a pest insect that sometimes ravages crops, appears in such a positive light in this Hopi tale. The story teaches us that all animals have a rightful place in the ecosystem. The Hopi did not curse Kokopilau for the destructiveness of locusts. Instead they sought, through their beliefs, to achieve harmony with this part of their environment.

This chapter explores the unique designs of insects and flowers. It focuses on how these designs aid in the transfer of pollen from male to female flower parts to produce seeds and fruit.

Insects have been around for 350 million years, and they live in virtually every kind of habitat in the world. If the total number of all kinds of animals in the world were added up, insects would make up two-thirds of this number. The average size of all of the animals in the world is about that of a housefly. Many people shudder at this thought, because they think of harmful or painful insects that bite, sting, spread disease and ravage crops. But insects also provide food for many fish, birds, mammals and people; help to keep the nutrient cycle going by cleaning up the remains of dead plants and animals (see Chapter 16); produce honey, beeswax and silk; and give us some of the most colorful and diverse of all of nature's sights, sounds and shapes. Insects have also been used in medicine and research. Most well-known of all is that they help to pollinate countless flowers every year.

Insects are grouped in a category of animals called *arthropods,* which also includes spiders, mites, centipedes, millipedes and crustaceans such as crabs, lobsters and crayfish. All these animals have jointed legs and a hard body covering. Insects are distinctive in that they have three body parts—a *head, thorax* and *abdomen* (Figure 18-1). Three pairs of legs and (when present) one or two pairs of wings are attached to the

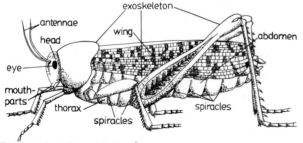

Figure 18-1. Basic parts of an insect.

thorax. Eyes, antennae and mouthparts are located on the head. The antennae are used for smelling and feeling. Some insects even taste with their feet. An insect's skeleton is on the outside of its body (*exoskeleton*), and it breaths through openings called *spiracles* which are located on its thorax and abdomen. A series of tubes (*tracheae*) leads from the spiracles to supply oxygen to the insect. Insect blood does not play the oxygen-carrying role that it does in many animals.

Some insects change dramatically as they mature, undergoing *complete metamorphosis* from an *egg* to a *larva* (caterpillar stage in moths and butterflies), *pupa* and *adult.* Other insects, like grasshoppers, hatch directly into small, adult-like *nymphs* which keep shedding their exoskeletons as they grow until they become adults. This kind of insect development is called *simple* or *gradual metamorphosis.* Insects are the only animals without backbones that have wings, although not all insects are winged.

Figure 18-2. This cecropia moth has emerged from its cocoon after completing the miraculous transformation from a caterpillar.

Many insects and flowers have become totally dependent on each other. Bees visit flowers in search of nectar and pollen for food. In the process, the bees move some of the *pollen* from the male *stamens* to the female *pistils* and so fertilize the waiting embryos. Seeds are formed. Flowers have special shapes, colors, patterns, scents, pollen and nectar to attract specific insects, while insects have acute senses, efficient body parts and shapes as well as specialized behaviors that help them to find and extract the pollen and nectar.

The relationship between insects and flowers makes it possible for Kokopilau and his insect relatives to bring us the seeds of the plants we need to live. If it were not for beneficial insects, many of our modern food plants would go unpollinated and no seeds would be produced. Imagine a world without these plants: most orchard fruits such as apples, plums, pears, cherries, citrus; nuts; melons; squash (including pumpkins); raspberries; blackberries; strawberries; cranberries; blueberries; onions and carrots. These are just some of the useful plants that insects play a crucial role in pollinating.

Questions

1. How does Kokopilau trick the Eagle to get into the Fourth World? What does he give to the people as they travel in the Fourth World?
2. What kind of insect is Kokopilau?
3. What makes an insect an insect? What are the main body parts of an insect?
4. How do insects help people? In what ways are they harmful?
5. What is pollination? How does it work?
6. Name four plants that are useful to people and that would not be able to make seeds without help from insects.

Activities
Creating Kokopilau

ACTIVITY: Create a model of Kokopilau that accurately shows all of the basic parts of an insect. Discuss the functions of an insect's parts.
GOALS: Understand the basic anatomy of insects and their bodily functions. Have fun creating the story character Kokopilau.
AGE: Younger Children and Older Children
PROCEDURE: Use the insect diagram to explain the parts of an insect and their functions: head (with eyes, antennae, mouthparts), thorax (with three pairs of legs, two pairs of spiracles and optional wings), abdomen (with several pairs of spiracles) and the exoskeleton. (See Figure 18-1.)

Reread the story of Kokopilau and have the children close their eyes to imagine what Kokopilau looks like. Make a list of all the insect parts needed to make a true insect and place it where the children can see it. Now have them create their own Kokopilau while being sure to include all parts of an insect. They can add the flute or anything that they imagined Kokopilau to have in the story.

MATERIALS: Diagram of a basic insect showing its parts (Figure 18-1), story of "Kokopilau, the Hump-Backed Flute Player," felt-tipped marking pen and newsprint or chalkboard and chalk, balloons or clay for the body, pencils, sticks or toothpicks, construction paper, scissors, paste, tape, string, crayons, felt-tipped marking pens of assorted colors, cardboard, pipe cleaners, natural plant materials for body parts.

Busy as a Bee

ACTIVITY: Observe flowers, insects that are pollinating flowers, male and female flower parts and the process of pollination. Pollinate a flower using a paintbrush. Return to the flower later in the growing season to look at the seeds that have formed.
GOALS: Understand the need for pollen transfer for seed formation. Understand the parts of a flower and how they function during pollination. Understand the role of insects in pollination.
AGE: Younger Children and Older Children
PROCEDURE: Explain pollination using the diagram of how insects transfer pollen from male to female flower parts (Figure 18-3).

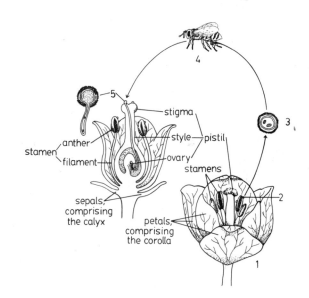

Figure 18-3. The route taken by the pollen and the role of pollinating insects. (1) The flower with its pistil, stamens and visually striking petals. The ripe anther (2) releases the pollen (3). An insect (4) transports it to the stigma of another flower of the same species. Having arrived on the correct stigma (5), the pollen grain germinates; the pollen tube grows down to the ovary, where the ovum is produced and fertilized.

Go outside to a field or other area where there is a lot of insect activity among the flowers. A vegetable farm or garden is an excellent place where the children can see insects working on food crops. Large blooms like those on squash plants are suitable because the male and female parts are conspicuous. Have each child find a flower and sit 3 feet (.9 meter) from it. He or she will observe the flower for about ten minutes, looking carefully for bees and other insects that visit the flower and record those findings in words or pictures. Then, gather the children together and have them share what they found happening at the flowers and which kinds of insects were visiting there. Which flower colors are most frequently visited?

Now point out the male and female parts of the flowers they were watching. Demonstrate how pollen is exchanged. Have the children return to their flowers and use the small paintbrushes to dab some pollen from the male stamens onto the female pistils.

Mark some of the flowers they have visited by placing small stones nearby or by tying pieces of cloth onto the plant stems. Return to the site periodically during the growing season to look at the seeds that have formed. As a follow-up, have the children draw pictures or write stories imagining that they are insects roaming from flower to flower gathering nectar and pollen.

MATERIALS: Figure 18-3; flowers to observe on which the male and female parts are conspicuous; small paint-brushes; diagram of flower showing male and female parts; paper; clipboards or cardboard backing; pencils; crayons; small stones or pieces of cloth.

Extending the Experience

• Invent a flower with a pollination strategy, along with the seeds it will produce. Invent an insect to help pollinate this flower. Draw pictures or construct models of the flower and insect.

• Hold a feast in honor of the insects with a meal prepared from foods that are gifts from the pollinating insects. (See the list of foods given in the "Discussion".)

• Research and report on how pesticide use affects pollinating insects, such as honeybees in orchards.

• Keep a cocoon or chrysalis and watch for the moth or butterfly to emerge.

• Read *Charlotte's Web*. Spiders are not insects, but this story evokes strong empathic feelings in the children for "crawly" creatures that are often scorned.

• Visit an observation beehive and learn about the workings of its complex society.

• Hold a scavenger hunt to look for insects.

• Develop a Kokopilau nature trail with a focus on insect and plant interactions.

• Compare the structure of insects from different habitats: pond, field, forest, desert, etc.

They flapped their wings hard and lifted Turtle off the ground. Soon they were high in the sky and headed toward the south.

CHAPTER 19

✦ How Turtle Flew South for the Winter ✦

(Dakota [Sioux]—Midwest)

It was the time of year when the leaves start to fall from the aspens. Turtle was walking around when he saw many birds gathering together in the trees. They were making a lot of noise and Turtle was curious.

"Hey," Turtle said, "What is happening?"

"Don't you know?" the birds said. "We're getting ready to fly to the south for the winter."

"Why are you going to do that?" Turtle said.

"Don't you know anything?" the birds said. "Soon it's going to be very cold here and the snow will fall. There won't be much food to eat. Down south it will be warm. Summer lives there all of the time and there's plenty of food."

As soon as they mentioned the food, Turtle became even more interested. "Can I come with you?" he said.

"You have to fly to go south," said the birds. "You are a turtle and you can't fly."

But Turtle would not give up. "Isn't there some way you could take me along?" He begged and pleaded. Finally the birds agreed just to get him to stop asking.

"Look here," the birds said, "can you hold onto a stick hard with your mouth?"

"That's no problem at all," Turtle said. "Once I grab onto something no one can make me let go until I am ready."

"Good," said the birds. "Then you hold on hard to this stick. These two birds here will each grab one end of it in their claws. That way they can carry you along. But remember, you have to keep your mouth shut!"

"That's easy," said Turtle. "Now let's go south where Summer keeps all that food." Turtle grabbed onto the middle of the stick and two big birds came and grabbed each end. They flapped their wings hard and lifted Turtle off the ground. Soon they were high in the sky and headed toward the south.

Turtle had never been so high off the ground before, but he liked it. He could look down and see how small everything looked. But before they had gone too far, he began to wonder where they were. He wondered what the lake was down below him and what those hills were. He wondered how far they had come and how far they would have to go to get to the south where Summer lived. He wanted to ask the two birds who were carrying him, but he couldn't talk with his mouth closed.

Turtle rolled his eyes. But the two birds just kept on flying.

Then Turtle tried waving his legs at them, but they acted as if they didn't even notice. Now Turtle was getting upset. If they were going to take him south, then the least they could do was tell him where they were now!

"Mmmph," Turtle said, trying to get their attention. It didn't work. Finally Turtle lost his temper.

"Why don't you listen to . . . " but that was all he said, for as soon as he opened his mouth to speak, he had to let go of the stick and he started to fall. Down and down he fell, a long long way. He was so frightened that he pulled his legs and his head in to protect himself! When he hit the ground he hit so hard that his shell cracked. He was lucky that he hadn't been killed, but he ached all over. He ached so much that he crawled into a nearby pond, swam down to the bottom and dug into the mud to get as far away from the sky as he possibly could. Then he fell asleep and he slept all through the winter and didn't wake up until the spring.

So it is that today only the birds fly south to the land where summer lives while turtles, who all have cracked shells now, sleep through the winter.

The birds tell Turtle that he cannot migrate with them because turtles do not fly, but Turtle will not take "no" for an answer. At last the birds figure out a way that Turtle can join them. He leaves with the birds by biting onto a stick that two birds are carrying between them in their claws. But Turtle becomes curious and impatient about where they are flying to. He starts to talk, then falls and cracks his shell. Hurt from the fall, Turtle crawls into the mud of a pond and sleeps through the winter.

Discussion

Turtle's experience is used here as an introduction to the study of fall and winter conditions in the wild and the major adaptive strategies found among animals for surviving the cold season: becoming dormant, migrating or remaining active. Activities emphasize observing animals through the seasons. The last activity explores one of the lessons Turtle learns—that patience is important when trying to accomplish something.

As the birds in this story explain, winter is snowy and cold and food is scarce. Day length also grows shorter. Animals must adapt to these changes by either staying active and surviving the winter, hiding in a sheltered area, hibernating during the stressful months, wintering as an egg or other resting stage or migrating to warmer climes.[1] Some animals, like the fox and hare, grow thicker coats to keep warm while they are active all winter. Many insects, like crickets and grasshoppers, overwinter as eggs. Others, like ants, amass deep in the soil. Honeybees cluster above ground in hollow trees to concentrate and contain their collective body heat. This story is about those who migrate and those who become dormant to escape having to be active when ice and snow lay over the land.

The shortening days and dropping temperatures of fall cause many birds to eat more to accumulate fat for their long *migration*. Other animals, such as the caribou and monarch butterfly, also migrate, but here we will look closely at birds. Most songbirds migrate at night under the protective cover of darkness, while many geese, hawks and cormorants move during the day.

Cold and stormy weather will often slow the springtime migration northward and trigger the fall journey to the south.

The arctic tern flies over 20,000 miles (32,187 kilometers) round-trip from its breeding grounds in the Arctic to its southern wintering grounds in the Antarctic Ocean, and back again. Bobolinks, birds that breed in open fields in the northern half of the United States and southern Canada, overwinter in Argentina, South America. How do birds find their way on long flights? Birds use one or more of these cues for getting their bearings: sunlight, stars, the moon, landmarks (mountains, coastlines, rivers, lakes) and the magnetic force of the Earth. Along the way these birds face many hazards: storms bringing rain, ice, snow and lightning; predators such as hawks and hunters; tall buildings and windows; power lines and towers; airplanes and jets; and pollution, such as oil spills.

Many animals stay behind and seek refuge from the short, cold days when food is scarce. *Hibernation* is one way of surviving this period of stress. During hibernation animals become dormant; there is a marked drop in the rate of metabolism and growth, including heartbeat, respiration and circulation. To varying degrees, body temperature also drops during hibernation. Some animals enter a period of deep hibernation which often lasts for the entire winter.

Cold-blooded animals have to hibernate to survive because they depend on the environment as their source of body heat and they cannot regulate temperature independently from that of their surroundings. Snakes

Figure 19-1. The brown thrasher breeds during the summer east of the Rocky Mountains throughout the United States and southern Canada. It migrates to wintering grounds located primarily in the southern United States and down along the Gulf Coast.

seek out burrows in the ground, while many turtles and frogs take refuge in the mud at the bottom of ponds, where they enter a state of deep hibernation that includes a nearly complete cessation of bodily processes.

Some *warm-blooded* animals, who can produce their own body heat internally and regulate body temperature independently of the environment, also enter deep hibernation, during which the body temperature drops considerably. Animals in deep hibernation can lower their body temperature for a long period of time, only to raise it when conditions are again favorable. These animals include the groundhog (woodchuck), the meadow jumping mouse, the poorwill (a bird of southwestern North America and Central America) and many bats, whose body temperatures while hibernating have been recorded as low as 2°C (35.6°F).[2] A groundhog's heartbeat slows from 90 beats per minute when active to 10 beats per minute when hibernating.

Other animals, such as the chipmunk, bear, raccoon, skunk and many squirrels, undergo a partial hibernation that is sometimes known as *torpor*. It is a winter sleep, but not a deep hibernation, during which body temperatures often drop less than among deep hibernators. The body temperatures of hibernating bears, for instance, have been recorded at 35°C (95°F), yet their respiration rate drops to two to three times per minute.[3]

These dramatic adaptations among dormant animals, which help them to survive the cold winter months, are also found among other animals as a response to environmental extremes. Certain bats in temperate regions undergo partial dormancy in summer during their restful daytime periods. This process is called *diurnation*. *Estivation* is a dormancy similar to hibernation, during which an animal retreats from the heat of summer and experiences a lower body temperature and reduced rates of growth and metabolism. Desert animals, such as the spadefoot toad in the Colorado Desert of California, often estivate. Many salamanders burrow under debris or into the ground to estivate during hot, dry summer periods, when food and water are scarce. The resourceful adaptations of animals enable them to survive the extremes of weather that are found in every region of the Earth.

Questions

1.   Turtle is a turtle but he wants to fly south with the birds. What happens to him when he tries to do something he is not meant to do?
2.   Turtle gets very impatient to know where the birds are taking him. What happens when he cannot wait and he opens his mouth to ask where they are going?
3.   Why do many birds fly south for the winter? What is migration? Do any other animals migrate?
4.   What kinds of dangers do migrating birds face on their journeys?
5.   What tells a bird that it is time to migrate? How does the bird prepare for the long flight?
6.   How does a migrating bird find its way? Do birds migrate during the day or night?
7.   Besides migrating, what are some other ways that animals survive the winter?
8.   What is hibernation? How does an animal change when it is hibernating? Name some animals that hibernate.
9.   What is torpor? How does it differ from deep hibernation?
10. What is the difference between a warm-blooded animal and a cold-blooded animal?

Activities

Winter Is Coming

ACTIVITY: Listen to a fantasy and imagine being an animal living in the wild as winter is coming. Discuss how to survive harsh winter conditions.
GOALS: Understand what the fall and winter conditions are like for a wild animal. Understand the major adaptive strategies used by animals to survive the winter months.
AGE: Younger Children and Older Children
PROCEDURE: Tell the children they are going to imagine that winter is coming. Have them close their eyes, relax their muscles, clear their minds and listen carefully to this brief fantasy. First, each child must imagine that he or she is a mammal or a migrating bird (a mammal if you plan to lead into a study of dormancy, a bird if migration is to be your lesson). You can adapt this fantasy to describe the climate of your local fall and winter.

Winter Is Coming

It is fall and all around you leaves are turning bright colors and dropping to the ground. The sun is rising later and setting earlier every day and the morning air is cold. Fog forms over the ponds, lakes and rivers as the sun rises. The mist disappears when the sun climbs high in the sky. You have a great need to eat as many berries, insects and nuts as you can find, and you are storing fat as you eat. Can you feel your body growing larger?

As each day goes by, the nights grow longer and colder. White frost crystals cover the plants, turning many of them brown and lifeless. Food is running low, yet you are using more food to keep warm. Ponds and lakes are freezing over and you have to travel farther each day to get water. Winter is coming fast! Soon the snow will blow, food will be hard to find and much of the water around you will become ice.

You are a wild creature and winter is coming. What are you going to do to survive?

Now discuss the ways that animals survive the winter: adapting and staying active; entering a period of deep hibernation or torpor; living as a resting stage like an egg; migrating; or waiting it out in a sheltered area, like honeybees in a tree or ants underground. Discuss dormancy and migration and describe these coping strategies. Use the activities in the rest of this chapter to expand the children's experiences and understanding.
MATERIALS: Copy of "Winter Is Coming" fantasy.

Snoozing Away the Winter

ACTIVITY: Study the heartbeat of a hibernating woodchuck. Keep a record, using a mural, of when the animals in and around a local pond begin to hibernate in the fall and when they become active again in the spring.
GOALS: Understand two types of dormancy—deep hibernation and torpor—and the changes animals undergo when they become dormant. Learn about the seasonal rhythms of animals at a nearby pond.
AGE: Younger Children and Older Children
PROCEDURE: Explain about deep hibernation and torpor and the changes in metabolism and heartbeat that occur in dormant animals. Using a watch with a seconds indicator, have the children measure their number of heartbeats per minute. You will need to show them where they can feel a pulse. Now tell them that a groundhog normally has 90 heartbeats each minute and only ten when it is hibernating. To illustrate this, begin timing a minute and beat out one heartbeat every six seconds while everyone listens quietly as the minute goes by.

Visit a nearby pond. Draw a sketch of the pond and record all of the animals you see there. (See Chapter 10 for more pond activities.) Now create a mural on a wall or bulletin board showing the pond and its immediate surroundings. Plot all of your sightings on the mural. Write the date next to each sighting. Do this several times during the fall and/or spring. Patterns will appear showing when certain animals begin and complete their dormancy (frogs, turtles, salamanders, snakes, etc.).

MATERIALS: Watch with a seconds indicator, binoculars, paper, pencils, clipboards, scissors, tempera paints, construction paper, crayons, stapler, pond, calendar, paintbrushes, water.

Migration: By Day and By Night

ACTIVITY: (A) Make a poster board model of a migrating bird and of Turtle from the story. (B) "Fly" the bird and Turtle along a migration route while avoiding the dangers along the way.

GOALS: Understand the natural signs that migrating songbirds use to navigate and consider how perilous their journey is.

AGE: Younger Children

PROCEDURE A: *Birds to Fly.* Use the materials listed under "A" to make two-sided birds (Figure 19-2). Have the children follow these steps: Choose a specific bird to make by looking at the bird pictures. Cut out the two halves of the bird and the tailpiece from poster board that is the same color as the bird you are making. Or you could color the poster board with crayons. Sandwich the popsicle stick in between the halves, sticking out of the bird's lower breast. Attach the stick with tape and glue.

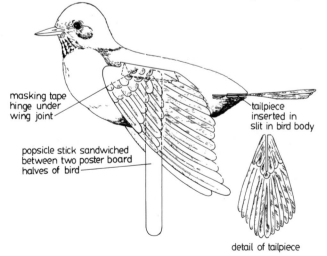

masking tape hinge under wing joint

tailpiece inserted in slit in bird body

popsicle stick sandwiched between two poster board halves of bird

detail of tailpiece

Figure 19-2. Diagram showing bird assembly for Birds to Fly.

Now glue the two halves of the bird together. Color in the details of your bird using the pictures of birds as models. Make the wings out of poster board and glue or tape a piece of heavy cardboard onto the tip of each wing. This extra weight creates a better flapping motion. Hinge the wings onto the body with pieces of masking tape. Cut matching slits in the tail and rear body and slip the tail on.

When the children move the birds up and down, the wings will flap. Using similar methods, have the children work in pairs to make the Turtle from the story to accompany them on their migration journey.

PROCEDURE B: *Migration Trail.* Beforehand: Set up a migration route about 40 feet (12.2 meters) long by 20 feet (6.1 meters) wide. Arrange the course so there are trees or chairs along the way. Some trees or chairs will be marked with stars to show the migration route the children must follow, while others will be marked with pictures or word descriptions of the hazards en route (see "Discussion"). Mark one end as "north" and the other end as "south."

The children will fly their birds starting at one end (north in the fall and south in the spring) and moving the birds along the marked route while avoiding the hazards along the way. Each pair of "birds" will carry its Turtle along the migration trail. To start the children off, hold the sun up high and slowly bring it down to create a sunset. After sunset the children will follow the stars and avoid the dangers as their birds migrate. Have them complete a yearly cycle, going north to south and back again, or vice versa. Design a daytime version of this activity and have the children fly in a V-shaped formation like many ducks, geese and cormorants.

MATERIALS: (A) colored poster board, scissors, crayons, pencils, pens, one popsicle stick per child, glue, masking tape, pictures of birds that migrate. (B) measuring tape, trees or chairs for obstacles, white poster board to make stars, scissors, signs or pictures identifying hazards en route and the north and south ends of the course, stapler, large yellow ball or paper model of the sun.

Taking Flight: North by South

ACTIVITY: Study the migration habits and routes of a local song bird and locate its summer and winter grounds on a map of North and South America. Observe when the bird leaves in the fall, when it returns in the spring, and mark its seasonal location on the map.

GOALS: Understand that, at each end of their migration

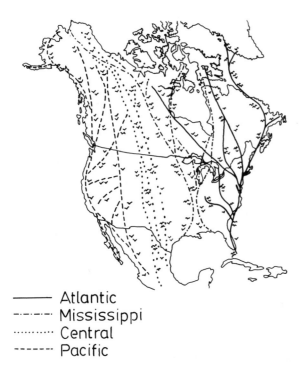

—— Atlantic
-·-·-·- Mississippi
··········· Central
------ Pacific

Figure 19-3. General flight paths along the four major migra-tory flyways used by North American birds. These migration flight paths continue across Central America, the Gulf of Mexico, the West Indies and down into South America.

routes, migrating bird species have regions that they use for summer breeding grounds and for wintering. Under-stand that migrating birds follow certain general routes called *flyways* and that they encounter many dangers along the way.

AGE: Older Children

PROCEDURE: Have children research and report on the migration habits of common songbirds in your area and create or collect pictures of those birds. Using large sheets of paper backed by cardboard, create generalized maps of North and South America. Map the four major North American *flyways* (Pacific, Central, Mississippi and Atlantic) (Figure 19-3). Introduce the hazards faced by migrating birds and have the children draw these on the map along the migration routes. Children will go up to the map and report on the migratory habits of their birds, and will sketch in the route taken using different colors or line patterns to distinguish between migration routes. Then the pictures of birds will be placed in the proper geographic locations and at the correct end of their migration routes for that time of year. Make outdoor observations in the spring and fall to see which birds are in your area and mark them on the mural accordingly, placing them in the south when they have

left in the fall and in the north when they have arrived in the spring.

MATERIALS: Maps of North and South America, map of the four major North American migration flyways (Fig-ure 19-3), magazines with pictures of common song-birds, felt-tipped marking pens, reference books, paper, pencils, crayons, large sheets of blank newsprint, card-board, stapler, glue, binoculars, field guides to common songbirds in your area.

Begin with Who You Are

ACTIVITY: Discuss a dream of something you want to do or someone you want to be and what you need to do to make that dream come true. Set a goal and work toward accomplishing it.

GOALS: Appreciate that we each have certain abilities that help us to accomplish things, including improving those abilities. Understand that patience is important when learning new things in life. Realize that we can better accomplish something if we have a clear goal to work toward.

AGE: Younger Children and Older Children

PROCEDURE: Ask the children why Turtle did not end up flying south with the birds. Emphasize that Turtle thought he could migrate with the birds and ended up crashing to Earth. Discuss how we can all grow and dream and learn to do new things, and sometimes even wonderful things, but that we have to accept who we are and be patient about making changes and accomplish-ing our goals.

Have each child say or write some things that he/she can do well and some things that he/she would like to be able to do. For instance, a child may want to learn how to draw faces well, carve a wooden toy, make clothes for a doll, write a story, learn to play an instrument or become a better basketball player. Have each child work to accomplish his or her goal. Encour-age a healthy attitude for maintaining a balance between accepting reality and reaching for growth and accom-plishments in life.

MATERIALS: Paper, pencils, other supplies as needed for specific projects chosen.

Extending the Experience

• Call a nearby environmental organization to find out about good places to go locally to watch birds. Take a field trip to a good vantage point on a clear, moonlit night in the spring or fall to watch and listen for migrating flocks of songbirds. Or, visit this spot during the day to watch for hawks, geese, cormorants and other daytime migrants.

• Make a bird mobile.

• Make a chart listing common animals in your area that undergo deep hibernation and torpor. Keep a log of sightings of these animals throughout the year. Begin looking for them just before the cold season comes and continue looking for awhile after spring arrives. What can you conclude from your observations about the habits of these animals? Combine this activity with written research reports on the winter habits of these animals to verify your findings.

• Dig holes in the ground at several different depths, such as 1 inch (2.5 centimeters), 1 foot (.3 meter), 2 feet (.6 meter) and 3 feet (.9 meter). Do this during the fall season and bury the end of a remote sensing thermome-

ter in each hole. The thermometers will sense how well the ground above would insulate hibernation burrows, or *hibernacula*, located at the different depths. Keep track of the temperatures at these different depths in the ground during the winter and contrast these with the temperatures of the air above out in the open. What do the findings reveal about the ground as a hibernaculum? Conduct similar observations of winter temperatures in old trees, fallen logs, stone walls and other places where animals hibernate.

Notes
1. See Chapter 15 for plant adaptations to winter.
2. Robert T. Orr, *Vertebrate Biology* (Philadelphia, Pennsylvania: W.B. Saunders Company, 1976), p.348.
3. Orr, p.340.

"Grandmother," he said, "This is not good enough." "Eh, Gluscabi," said Grandmother Woodchuck, "how can I please you? What kind of game bag do you want?"

CHAPTER 20

· Gluscabi and the Game Animals ·

(Abenaki—Northeast Woodlands)

Long ago Gluscabi decided he would do some hunting. He took his bow and arrows and went into the woods.

But all the animals said to each other, "Ah-hah, here comes Gluscabi. He is hunting us. Let us hide from him."

So they hid and Gluscabi could not find them. He was not pleased. He went home to the little lodge near the big water where he lived with Grandmother Woodchuck.

"Grandmother," he said, "Make a game bag[1] for me."

So Grandmother Woodchuck took caribou hair and made him a game bag. She wove it together tight and strong, and it was a fine game bag. But when she gave it to Gluscabi, he looked at it and then threw it down.

"This is not good enough," he said.

So then Grandmother Woodchuck took deer hair. She wove a larger and finer game bag and gave it to him. But Gluscabi looked at it and threw it down.

"This is not good enough, Grandmother," he said.

Now Grandmother Woodchuck took moose hair and wove him a very fine game bag indeed. It was large and strong, and she took porcupine quills which she flattened with her teeth, and she wove a design into the game bag to make it even more attractive. But Gluscabi looked at this game bag, too, and threw it down.

"Grandmother," he said. "This is not good enough."

"Eh, Gluscabi," said Grandmother Woodchuck, "how can I please you? What kind of game bag do you want?"

Then Gluscabi smiled. "Ah, Grandmother," he said, "make one out of woodchuck hair."

So Grandmother Woodchuck pulled all of the hair from her belly. To this day you will see that all woodchucks still have no hair there. Then she wove it into a game bag. Now this game bag was magical. No matter how much you put into it, there would still be room for more. And Gluscabi took this game bag and smiled.

"Oleohneh, Grandmother," he said. "I thank you."

Now Gluscabi went back into the woods and walked until he came to a large clearing. Then he called out as loudly as he could, "All you animals, listen to me. A terrible thing is going to happen. The sun is going to go out. The world is going to end and everything is going to be destroyed."

When the animals heard that, they became frightened. They came to the clearing where Gluscabi stood with his magic game bag.

"Gluscabi," they said, "What can we do? The world is going to be destroyed. How can we survive?"

"All you animals, listen to me. A terrible thing is going to happen. The sun is going to go out. The world is going to end and everything is going to be destroyed."

Gluscabi smiled. "My friends," he said, "just climb into my game bag. Then you will be safe in there when the world is destroyed."

So all of the animals went into his game bag. The rabbits and the squirrels went in, and the game bag stretched to hold them. The raccoons and the foxes went in, and the game bag stretched larger still. The deer went in and the caribou went in. The bears went in and the moose went in, and the game bag stretched to hold them all. Soon all the animals in the world were in Gluscabi's game bag. Then Gluscabi tied the top of the game bag, laughed, slung it over his shoulder and went home.

"Grandmother," he said, "now we no longer have to go out and walk around looking for food. Whenever we want anything to eat we can just reach into my game bag."

Grandmother Woodchuck opened Gluscabi's game bag and looked inside. There were all of the animals in the world.

"Oh, Gluscabi," she said, "why must you always do things this way? You cannot keep all of the game animals in a bag. They will sicken and die. There will be none left for our children and our children's children. It is also right that it should be difficult to hunt them. Then you will grow stronger trying to find them. And the animals will also grow stronger and wiser trying to avoid being caught. Then things will be in the right balance."

"Kaamoji, Grandmother," said Gluscabi, "That is so." So he picked up his game bag and went back to the clearing. He opened it up. "All you animals," he called, "you can come out now. Everything is all right. The world was destroyed, but I put it back together again."

Then all of the animals came out of the magic game bag. They went back into the woods, and they are still there today because Gluscabi heard what his Grandmother Woodchuck had to say.

Once again Gluscabi is too smart for his own good. He gets frustrated with hunting, takes the magical game bag made by Grandmother Woodchuck and tricks all of the animals in the world into being captured. Gluscabi makes a mistake. Grandmother Woodchuck tells Gluscabi that the animals cannot survive in a game bag and that there will be none left for the children of generations to come. The animals cannot live in a game bag because they have the same survival needs as people: food, water, air and shelter. Then Grandmother tells Gluscabi that by hunting the animals, he will grow stronger and wiser and so will the animals. Gluscabi listens and learns from Grandmother Woodchuck's wisdom. He sees she is right and frees the animals.

(Gluscabi also appears in Chapter 3, "The Coming of Gluscabi," Chapter 9, "Gluscabi and the Wind Eagle" and as Koluscap in Chapter 10, "Koluscap and the Water Monster." Grandmother Woodchuck also appears in Chapter 9, "Gluscabi and the Wind Eagle.")

Discussion

In this chapter, Grandmother Woodchuck's wisdom leads to discussion, questions and activities that explore the Earth as a home where humans and animals meet their survival needs. It also examines the relationship between the hunter and hunted.

For Native Americans, hunting was a means of getting food, clothing and other necessities vital to their survival. There were many practices performed before,

during and after each hunt. These rituals grew out of the individual's relationship with the Creator and the spirits in the natural world, including the spirits of plants and animals. Some specific Abenaki rites are described in this chapter during the fantasy, "A Journey with the Abenakis," on page 169.

Today, for many people hunting has become a sport and a supplement to their food supply rather than a means of surviving. Most people hunt because they like

Figure 20-1. The great horned owl is a formidable predator with saucer-like eyes that catch sufficient light to enable it to see even on dimly lit nights. The disc-shaped feather arrangement around its eyes funnels sound to sensitive ears, which are hidden under feathers just behind each eye. The "horns" are made of feathers and are not associated with the ears. These owls have a very poor sense of smell and have even been known to capture and eat skunks!

being outdoors in nature, and they enjoy the challenge of stalking and finding their prey. Many other people consider hunting to be cruel because it involves chasing and killing wild animals. No matter how hunting is viewed, the same skills that are used for hunting are valuable for sharpening senses in the wild. They can help teach us how to stalk and observe animals in their homes.

Hunting is work that takes time, patience and skill. The hunter's senses of sight, hearing, smell, touch and even taste are all needed. Animal trails are marked by *signs*, such as hoof and paw prints (*tracks*), broken twigs, crunched leaves, animal droppings (*scat*) and scents. Whether the hunter is a person or a wild animal like a fox, hawk or mink, the experience of these *predators* makes their senses more keen (Figure 20-1).

As Grandmother Woodchuck tells Gluscabi in the story, the *prey*, such as a rabbit or mouse, may grow wiser and stronger as it tries to keep one step ahead of the predator. Likewise the predator may grow stronger and wiser as it tries to catch the prey. Both predator and prey are often well *camouflaged*, with colors and patterns that blend in with the plants and other parts of their surroundings. The strongest, most alert and fastest prey will usually survive. The hunting animal often catches the weaker and slower individuals. In this way, certain animals are chosen to live and to die. This is called *natural selection*: those animals with the more successful physical ability and behavior survive.

Questions

1. What happens to Gluscabi when he is lazy and greedy and catches all of the animals?
2. What does Gluscabi learn when he listens to Grandmother Woodchuck? Do you think it is a good thing that he follows the lessons he learns from her and frees the

animals from the game bag?

3. Why can the animals not live in a game bag? What do the animals need from nature to live?

4. What does Grandmother Woodchuck mean when she says, "Then things will be in the right balance"? Why would keeping the animals in a game bag and separating them from their needs in nature be bad for children to come?

5. What kind of relationship did Native Americans have with the Creator and the animals that they hunted?

6. What are the reasons that people hunt today?

7. How do you feel about hunting? Do you know any hunters?

8. What is a predator? A prey? What are the skills and senses that the predator and prey use—the predator when it chases the prey and the prey when it flees?

9. What is camouflage? How does it help the predator? The prey?

10. How do the hunter and hunted grow stronger and wiser during the hunt? What is natural selection? Are human hunters part of that process?

Activities
A Journey with the Abenakis

ACTIVITY: Listen to a story in which you will visit an Abenaki village, accompany a group of Abenaki Indians on a deer hunt and learn some Indian beliefs, practices and lessons for living well with the Earth and other people.

GOALS: Learn about Abenaki Indian culture of 1,000 years ago (during the Woodland period) and some Abenaki rituals and lessons that helped them to live in peace and assure survival of the animals that provided them with food, clothing and other needs. Understand that we need to care for the plants, animals and Earth if we are to leave all of these things well for the people who come after us.

AGE: Younger Children and Older Children

PROCEDURE: Beforehand: Cut the strings to length, moisten one end of each string with glue and shape to a point. Let the glue dry. Threading the beads will now be easier.

Have the children lie down on their backs with their eyes closed. Tell them to breath in deeply and slowly, hold the breath for a few seconds and to then breath out. Repeat this a few times and ask them to clear their minds and get ready for a journey to an Abenaki village and a hunting expedition one thousand years ago during the Woodland period.

Read "A Journey with the Abenakis." When you are done, have the children sit up and repeat the four lessons: silence, respect, sharing and circles. Write these lessons where everyone can see them. Now have all of the children say each lesson together as they string one bead at a time. When all the beads are strung, tie the ends of the string together to make necklaces.

A Journey with the Abenakis

Our journey begins in the pine woods. As we walk, the wind sighs through the pine boughs and causes them to wave. Little patches of sunlight shine on the soft pine needles beneath our feet. A twig cracks underfoot. There is a clearing in the distance and gentle curls of smoke rise into the sky. We can smell wood burning as we approach.

In the clearing are some dome-shaped shelters with arched roofs made of bark wrapped over poles. There are holes in the roofs for chimneys and smoke pours out of them. Many lodges are arranged in a big circle that is surrounded by a high log fence. We walk over to one house and feel the lines in the bark on its side. There is a pair of snowshoes leaning on the house.

We turn and walk to a great fire ring in the center of the camp, where a group of men and women are warming themselves by the blazing fire. The women wear their hair long, as do the men. Women are wearing leather skirts and leggings with moccasins attached. A blanket covers each woman's head and flows down over a leather coat. Men wear leggings and a small, skirt-shaped piece of leather. But on each man's head is a hood-like cap with two feathers sticking out of the tip. A bow and arrows are carried by the hunters, along with spears and knives that are laced to their belts.

These people prepare to go on a hunt by burning tobacco, a sacred plant whose smoke carries their prayers up to the "Owner" or Creator, Tabaldak, and the animal spirits. These prayers ask for permission to hunt. They also express the people's respect and appreciation for the lives of the animals they will soon hunt, and offer thanksgiving for the food, clothing and other gifts the animals will give the people. Soon the hunters leave the fire ring, carrying their weapons, and walk through the pine grove.

Some faint deer signs are found and two of the hunters begin to follow the trail very quietly. After a long, slow, tiring search, some animals are heard chewing on the buds of small trees up ahead. The hunters creep closer and look through the branches of a low bush. The animals are deer! And so we learn one of the lessons of survival in nature: SILENCE.

The hunters look carefully at the deer in the herd, recognizing each one individually. Two of the deer are pregnant does who the hunters know are expecting fawns—these two will not be hunted. Finally, the hunters decide on a certain buck as their quarry.

In an instant several arrows are strung and sent whistling through the air. The buck is shot and it falls kicking on the ground, blood flowing from wounds in its side. One deer alone is taken because the others are needed to produce more young to keep the herd alive and because the hunters take only what they need. A second lesson of survival in nature is learned: RESPECT—respect for other life besides people's.

The hunters quickly skin the deer, cut up the meat and lash the pieces onto a pole that is carried between them on their shoulders. When they arrive in camp people are excited to see them with their catch. "A successful hunt," a child cries out. "We will have food to eat!"

The deer is not kept by the hunters and their families; it is cut into smaller pieces and given to all those who need food beginning with those who are the most hungry. Another lesson is learned of how people can survive in the natural world and with one another: SHARING—sharing the gifts of nature.

As the meat is prepared, the people burn some fat on the glowing coals of the cooking fire. The smoke that drifts upward is an offering to Tabaldak. Every part of the deer is used, because to waste any would show disrespect for Tabaldak and the animal spirits and make them angry. Finally, the deer's bones are returned to the land where the animal was killed. This offering of the bones completes the circle of giving and receiving—the Creator and deer giving life through the gifts of food and clothing to the people, and the people completing the circle by giving the deer bones back to show respect, appreciation and thanks. A final lesson is learned for living well with the natural world: CIRCLES.

SILENCE—RESPECT—SHARING—CIRCLES— these are lessons to be remembered each day. If we live by them we will be able to live in peace with other people and in balance with the Earth and all living things.

MATERIALS: Enough 29-inch (73.7-centimeter) pieces of string for each child to have one, white glue, scissors, four wooden beads for each child (beads should have

holes that are at least .16 inch [4 millimeters] in diameter), copy of the fantasy, "A Journey with the Abenakis," newsprint and felt-tipped marking pens or chalkboard and chalk.

Predator and Prey

ACTIVITY: (A) Play a predator-prey game in which the "predator" hunts using only its sense of hearing. (B) Play a camouflage game during which "foxes" hunt for different colored "mice" to see which colors make better camouflage.

GOALS: Understand how important animals' senses of hearing and sight are when they are stalking (predator) and when they are being stalked (prey). Understand camouflage and natural selection.

AGE: Younger Children and Older Children

PROCEDURE A: *Predator and Prey.* Take a small group of children and have them sit in a circle about 10 feet (3 meters) across. Place the "predator" blindfolded in the center of the circle. Have that child choose the kind of predator he or she wants to be and the kind of prey he or she wants to hunt. Point silently to the child you want to become the prey and tell the predator when the prey comes inside the circle. Each prey must go *around* the predator inside of the circle in either direction while both predator and prey are down on hands and knees. He or she must then return to his or her spot in the circle without being tagged by the predator. Children forming the circle should not make distracting noises or the predator will be thrown off the trail. When a predator "catches" its prey by hearing and tagging it, the prey then becomes the predator. If a predator does not catch its prey for two turns, then someone else becomes the predator. Repeat this sequence until all children have had one turn as predator and prey. They will not want to stop!

PROCEDURE B: *Hiders and Seekers.* Divide a small group of children in half. Have one half of the group hide the colored mice secretly in a marked-off area in a field, forest or indoors. Once the "mice" are hidden, take the other half of the group to that spot and tell them that they are foxes hunting mice to eat. Show them what one of the mice looks like. Give them five minutes to "hunt" and see how many mice they can find. Repeat the activity by having the hiders and seekers switch roles.

Discuss why it was easier to find mice of certain colors than it was to find others. Ask what this would mean for the color of an animal trying to hide from a predator. Then ask, "What color would you want to be if you were a prey animal?" Discuss how the placement of the mice helped to hide them. Define camouflage and natural selection, discuss how they are working here and ask the children to think of other examples (see "Discussion").

Note: A variation on this activity is to have the children hide and find other objects of assorted colors indoors, such as colored toothpicks.

MATERIALS: (A) one blindfold. (B) 30 "mice" cut from five different colors of construction paper (six of each color).

Extending the Experience

• Rewrite the deer-hunting story found in "A Journey with the Abenakis" as if you are one of the deer in the herd. Create a story of the hunt from the deer's point of view. Include descriptions of what you imagine the deer sees, hears, smells, feels and thinks during the hunt.

• Pass out photographs and pictures from magazines of predator and prey animals. Have each child "become" that animal and write a story about what it would be like to be in a predator/prey relationship as a wolf, fawn, rabbit, hawk, etc. Have them share these stories.

• Lead a deer walk and practice stalking carefully while being as quiet as possible. (See Chapter 2, page 13, for directions.)

• Use one of these camouflage activities: (A) Play the "Camouflage!" game en route along the trail (see Chapter 2, page 15, for directions). (B) You will need a camera and film for this activity, preferably a setup that produces instant pictures. Point your camera in a certain direction into a field of tall grass. Set the lens for maximum "depth of field" if your camera has that feature. Mark boundaries for the area that will be in focus. Have the children hide within those boundaries. Take a picture of them hiding. Now have the children stand up in the same places they were hiding in and take another picture. It's fun to see these two pictures side-by-side once they are developed. This comparison shows how much can be hidden in tall grass.[2]

Notes
1. A game bag is used by the hunter to carry animals once they are captured.
2. Thanks to the Reverend Greg Marshall of Meriden, New Hampshire, for this idea.

Before long, all of the hunters began to treat the animals with respect and to follow Little Deer's teachings.

CHAPTER 21

⋄ Awi Usdi, the Little Deer ⋄

(Cherokee—North Carolina)

Back when the world was young, the humans and the animal people could speak to each other. At first they lived in peace. The humans hunted the animals only when they needed food or skins to make clothing. Then the humans discovered the bow and arrow. With this new weapon they could kill many animals quickly and with great ease. They began to kill animals when they did not need them for food or clothing. It seemed as if all the animals in the world would soon be exterminated. So the various animals met in council.

When the bears came together and talked about what the humans were doing, they decided they would have to fight back.

"How can we do that?" said one of the bear warriors. "The humans will shoot us with their arrows before we come close to them."

Old Bear, their chief, agreed. "That is true. We must learn how to use the same weapons they use."

Then the bears made a very strong bow and fashioned arrows for it. But whenever they tried to use the bow, their long claws got in the way.

"I will cut off my claws," said one of the bear warriors. He did so and then he was able to use the bow and arrow. His aim was good and he hit the mark every time.

"That is good," said Old Bear. "Now can you climb this tree?"

The bear without claws tried to climb the tree, but he failed.

Old Bear shook his head. "This will not do. Without our claws we cannot climb trees. Without our claws we will not be able to hunt or dig for food. We must give up this idea of using the same weapons the humans use."

So the bears gave up their idea of fighting back against the humans with weapons.

One by one each of the animal groups met. One by one they came to no conclusion. It seemed there was no way to fight back. But the last group to meet was the deer.

Awi Usdi, Little Deer, was their leader. When all were gathered together, he spoke.

"I see what we must do," he said. "We cannot stop the humans from hunting animals. That is the way it was meant to be. However, the humans are not doing things in the right way. If they do not respect us and hunt us only when there is real need, they may kill us all. I shall go now and tell the hunters what they must do. Whenever they wish to kill a deer, they must prepare in a ceremonial way. They must ask me for permission to kill one of us. Then, after they kill a deer, they must show respect to its spirit and ask for pardon. If the hunters do not do this, then I shall track them down. With my magic I will make their limbs crippled. Then they will no longer be able to walk or shoot a bow and arrow."

Then Awi Usdi, Little Deer, did as he said. He went at night and whispered into the ears of the hunters, telling them what they must do. The next morning, when they awoke, some of the hunters thought they had been dreaming and they were not sure that the dream was a true one. Others, though, realized that Little Deer, Awi Usdi, had truly spoken to them. They tried to do as he told them. They hunted for the deer and other animals only when they needed food and clothing. They remembered to prepare in a ceremonial way, to ask permission before killing an animal and to ask pardon when an animal was killed. Some of the hunters, though, paid no attention. They continued to kill animals for no reason. But Awi Usdi, Little Deer, came to them and, using his magic, crippled them with rheumatism. Before long, all of the hunters began to treat the animals with respect and to follow Little Deer's teachings.

So it is that the animals have survived to this day. Because of Awi Usdi, Little Deer, the Indian people show respect. To this day, even though the animals and people no longer can speak to each other as in the old days, the people still show respect and give thanks to the animals they must hunt.

In "Awi Usdi, the Little Deer," the people are overhunting with bows and arrows. Awi Usdi demands respect and says that the people should hunt only what is needed or he will cripple them with his magic. He tells the people to ask for his permission to kill deer, to prepare for the kill in a respectful, ceremonial way and, after the kill has been made, to ask the deer's spirit for pardon.

Discussion

These early hunters learned to manage the deer wisely and to respect them to assure that the deer would be there for seasons to come. Although few people hunt for their survival today, there are many lessons that the beliefs and practices of the Indian hunters can teach us about caring for animals.

In days long ago, the Indians had to be concerned with the numbers of animals they hunted and the kind of habitat the animals had to live in. It is now known that in many areas Indians, by burning, maintained open, brushy clearings and fields to provide good habitat, especially food and cover, for deer and other animals.[1]

Today the threats to animals are much more numerous and complicated than they were back then: destruction of habitat for expanding farmlands, tree harvesting, urbanization and public works projects such as reservoirs; pollution in the form of oil spills, toxic wastes, air pollution and water pollution; introduction of exotic species that compete with native animals for food, shelter and water; animal collection for pets, zoos and research; overhunting; advanced technology that has given us the power to change our world quickly and dramatically; overpopulation of people competing with animals for trees, food, water and other resources. What would the Little Deer, Awi Usdi, say to us today? It would be a long commentary!

Because of these pressures, many animals are now *extinct;* there are no more survivors of these species on Earth. At the present time, human environmental disruptions and outright killing are causing plants and animals to become extinct at the rate of one species each day. Who does not remember the story of the dodo birds that could not fly and were hunted until there were none left? The list of extinct animals is long and growing—such as the passenger pigeon; the great auk; the Carolina parakeet (which was our only native North American parakeet); and the ivory-billed woodpecker, which is thought to be extinct in North America and is now found

Figure 21-1. Peregrine falcons have been absent from most of their former range for over twenty years. They are now returning to some of their former breeding grounds—a result of a ban on the use of DDT and intensive efforts by biologists and conservationists to re-establish peregrines in areas where they had traditionally bred.

only in Cuba in very small numbers. Members of *endangered species* are so rare that they are in immediate danger of being wiped out completely—such as the red wolf, the California condor, the black-footed ferret and the blue whale. If the surviving population of a species is so low that it would be threatened with extinction if it declined further, it is a *threatened species*.

Two of the major human influences on species survival are overhunting and the destruction of habitat. Pollution has also caused many animal populations to decline. Both the peregrine falcon and osprey became exterminated over much of their breeding range when DDT pesticide poisoning caused nesting failures due to undeveloped embryos and abnormally thin eggshells, which resulted in eggs cracking under the weight of the brooding parents. These birds are now making a gradual comeback in some areas with help from concerned biologists and other conservationists.

In many cases, with wise management and knowledge about a certain animal's needs and reproduction rates, people have successfully hunted those animals while leaving sufficient numbers to assure the survival of healthy populations. This level of hunting is called the *sustainable yield*. Other actions needed for wise *wildlife management*, to protect our animal species, are habitat preservation and management to provide adequate food, water and shelter; limits on hunting, and in some cases bans on hunting; pollution clean-up and prevention; human population control; and wise resource use (taking only what we need from the environment).

The following questions and activities explore how hunting pressures affect wildlife populations and the

survival of both predator and prey species; people's responsibility to care for animals, both domesticated and wild; and the plight of threatened and endangered species.

Questions

1. What does the little deer, Awi Usdi, tell the hunters they should do to treat the deer with respect?
2. The story says that the hunters should take only what they need, not what they want. What is the difference between a *need* and a *want*? Do we, today, take more than we need? What are some of our real survival needs? How are these different from our wants?
3. In "The Little Deer," the hunters are overhunting with bows and arrows. What are some ways that we kill animals today? What are some animals that are now threatened with extinction because of overhunting?
4. What happens when we destroy an animal's home?
5. What does extinction mean? What is an endangered species? A threatened species? Name some plants and animals that are in danger of becoming extinct.
6. How can we help animals in our neighborhoods to assure their survival? What can we do for endangered and threatened species?

Activities
Caring for Animals: Inside and Outside

ACTIVITY: (A) Take care of a pet. Discuss stewardship of wild animals and the concepts of endangered and threatened species and extinction. (B) 1. Provide wildlife plantings for food and cover. 2. Put up bird feeders. 3. Erect bird nesting boxes. 4. Create brush piles to provide homes for small wildlife. Visit and discuss dead trees and their importance as animal homes.

GOALS: Appreciate the tasks involved when caring for a pet. Understand that people are responsible for taking care of wildlife and wildlife habitat. Understand that we can all become involved in practical projects to provide for the needs of animals.

AGE: Younger Children and Older Children

PROCEDURE A: *Caring for Animals: Inside.* Involve the children in the decision of what kind of pet to acquire. Give the children responsiblity to feed and water the animal(s), clean the cage(s) and any other necessary tasks. Explain the basic needs of animals (see Chapter 20 for more activities on this theme) and how people, because we are such powerful determiners of what happens in the environment, are responsible for the

BIRDHOUSE SPECIFICATIONS

Species	Entrance diameter (inches)	Entrance above floor (inches)	Floor dimensions (inches)	House depth (inches)	Nest above ground (feet)
Bluebird	1 1/2	6–7	5x5	8–9	4–10
Chickadee, black-capped	1 1/8	6–8	4x4	8–12	5–50
Creeper, brown			crevices in tree trunks		
Duck, wood[1]					
(metal guard[3])	4	18–19	11–12 (dia.)	24	5–15
(wooden guard[3])	3x4 oval	18–19	12x12	24	5–15
Flicker[3]	3	14–16	7x7	16–24	6–20
Flycatcher, great crested	2	6–8	6x6	8–10	8–20
Hawk, sparrow	3	9–12	8x8	12–15	10–30
Martin, purple[2]	2 1/2	2	7x7	7	8–16
Merganser					
common			hollow trees		
hooded			hollow trees and nesting boxes		16–30
Owl					
barn	6	4	10x18	15–18	12–18
saw-whet	2 1/2	8–10	6x6	10–12	12–20
screech	3	9–12	8x8	12–15	10–30
Phoebe	open sides		6x6	6	8–12
Robin	open front		6x8	8	6–15
Sapsucker	1 3/4	12–16	6x6	14–18	12–40
Swallow					
barn	open sides		6x6	6	8–12
tree[2]	1 1/2	1–5	5x5	6	10–15
Titmouse, tufted	1 1/4	6–8	4x4	8–10	4–15
Woodpecker[3]					
downy	1 1/4	6–8	4x4	8–10	6–20
hairy	1 1/2	9–12	6x6	12–16	12–20
red-bellied	2 1/2	10–12	6x6	12–14	12–50
red-headed	2	9–12	6x6	12–15	12–100
Wren					
Bewick's	1 1/4	6–8	4x4	4–6	6–10
Carolina	1 1/4	4–6	4x4	4–6	5–12
house	1–1 1/4	6–8	4x4	4–6	5–10
winter	1–1 1/4	6–8	4x4	4–8	5–10

[1]Wood duck boxes must be predator-proof (especially from raccoons) to be safe. A 4-inch in diameter metal guard or 4x4-inch wooden guard at entrance, or a 4-inch horizontal by 3-inch vertical oval guard may be sufficient.
[2]Also uses gourds for nesting.   [3]Add wood shavings or sawdust to 2- 3-inch deep.

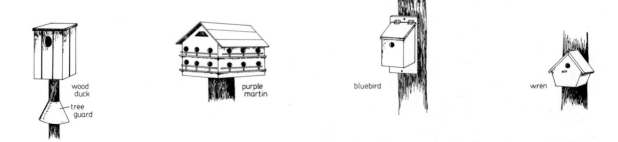

Figure 21-3. Birdhouse specifications. Nesting boxes (birdhouses).

well-being of not only our domestic animals but of all the wild animals and plants in the world. Nature centers can use a domestic or wild animal exhibit as a take-off point for discussion about the outdoor segments of this activity. Use some of the information from the "Discussion" to talk about endangered species, threatened species and extinction as a result of human activities around the world.

PROCEDURE B: *Caring for Animals: Outside.* Explain that habitat management and improvement are ways in which we can help to care for wild animals in our neighborhoods and beyond. Here are some things to do with the children: (1) *Wildlife plantings* are excellent ways to green-up an area while providing valuable food and cover for birds, squirrels, rabbits and other small animals. Some good shrubs and trees that provide food and shelter are shadbush, staghorn and smooth sumac, autumn olive, switchgrass, wild cherries, dogwoods, apples and crabapples, arrowwood, elderberry, blueberry, inkberry, winterberry, azalea, American holly, highbush cranberry and rhododendron. (2) *Bird feeders* are fun ways to get children interested in wildlife. They range from seeds held in a hanging empty milk carton to the elaborate wooden, plastic and metal seed palaces that can be bought. Contact a local environmental organization for ideas about designs you can build or buy. (3) *Bird nesting boxes* can be built to attract many different species. See Figure 21-3, which lists specifications for nesting boxes to house certain species, and which illustrates some sample nesting boxes. (4) *Brush piles* and other small-scale wildlife management projects are good ways to improve the cover availability in a wooded or open area. First, pile loose sticks to a height of about 2 feet (.6 meter), then put down a layer of several inches of broad leaves and/or evergreen needles for insulation and protection from wind and rain. Next add larger sticks on top to hold the pile together. Also, visit some dead standing trees, called *snags*, and point out their value as nest sites for birds and mammals such as chickadees, woodpeckers and flying squirrels. Dead trees are also homes for wood-boring beetles, carpenter ants, termites and other insects, which in turn serve as food for woodpeckers and other animals. Discuss the importance of leaving some dead trees standing when a forest is cut, as well as the need for leaving enough live trees to produce seeds for new forest growth.

These projects are beginnings; they prompt the children to start thinking about their role as stewards of the Earth, which is habitat for other living things besides people.

MATERIALS: (A) cage, bedding, water, food, dispensers for food and water, animal[2], other supplies as needed for that particular pet. (B) 1. seeds or young plants, water, shovels, fertilizer, soil; 2. supplies needed depending on the bird feeder chosen. These supplies can range from a plastic milk jug, knife and string, to supplies similar to those listed next for *Bird Nesting Boxes*. 3. Figure 21-3, pine shelving, dowelling, nails, hammer, pencil, measuring tape, straight edge, drill, hollow log, metal flashing, screws, exterior glue, screw driver, hinges, saw, exterior primer and paint, brushes, paint thinner (water or turpentine depending on whether the paint is water-base or oil-base), sandpaper, shovel, post, etc. 4. small branches, leaves and/or needles, large branches, dead standing trees or "snags."

Helping a Species in Need

ACTIVITY: Research the background of some local threatened and endangered species and get involved in efforts to save one or more of these species. Present your findings to local groups and try to get more people involved in the issues.

GOALS: Understand how to become well-informed and active in helping to assure the survival of a local threatened or endangered species. Understand how to inform others about environmental issues and ways that they can become involved. Obtain skills in researching, writing and speaking while writing a report and presenting it to other people.

AGE: Older Children

PROCEDURE: Review, with the children, the information from the "Discussion." Have the children research the history and current status of a threatened, endangered or in some way imperiled species in your area. For instance, the California condor, grizzly bear, peregrine falcon, Atlantic salmon, bald eagle (lower 48 United States) and Florida manatee. Find out about local groups that are active with research and habitat management projects for those species and have the children conduct interviews with people from those groups to ask them how the children can help.

Have the children present their findings to a group such as a local conservation organization. For these presentations the children will use charts, graphs, models, films and other media to get their message across.

MATERIALS: References, news clippings, "Discussion" from this chapter, information on endangered species from local and/or regional conservation groups, resources as needed for the kind of program children will use to present their findings to other groups.

Extending the Experience

• Research the story of the blue whale and present it to the group as an example of how *not* to care for our wildlife. This is one of the largest animals that has ever lived. (See Chapter 11, page 99, for an activity that helps the children to imagine how big the blue whale is.) A good source of information about the blue whale is *Biological Conservation*,[3] Chapter 5, pages 133-141.

• Get the children involved in local environmental projects that affect wildlife and habitat. Local nature centers and other conservation groups are good places to start.

• Study herbicide use along powerline rights of way. Investigate the kinds of chemicals used and their effects on plants and animals. Have the children write letters to the editors of local papers to raise consciousness about this and other herbicide- and pesticide-use problems.

• Find pictures of extinct animals and have the children write stories about them, draw pictures or make models of them, and report on their natural history and the reasons why they became extinct.

• Study the Federal Endangered Species Act and the Federal Register of Endangered and Threatened Wildlife and note whether any animals in your locality or region are listed as being endangered or threatened.[4] Write to government representatives to express support for this legislation and funding to care for the animals.

• Design a bumper sticker or poster about endangered and threatened species.

• Study the Inuit of northern and central Canada. Their traditional cultures have been closely tied to the hunting of marine animals, caribou and other big game. What has happened to these people? Read *People of the Deer* and *Sea of Slaughter* and discuss these books. Contrast these stories with how the animals and Indians of the United States have been treated over the last 300 years.

Notes

1. Stephen J. Pyne, "Indian Fires," *Natural History*, volume 92, number 2, February 1983 pp. 6-11.

2. See the ground rules on page 14 of Chapter 2 for collecting wild plants and animals.

3. David W. Ehrenfeld, *Biological Conservation* (New York: Holt, Rinehart and Winston, Inc., 1970).

4. In the United States this information is available from:
The Department of the Interior
United States Fish and Wildlife Service
Endangered Species Program
Washington, D.C. 20240

In Canada write to:
Coordinator, Threatened Species and Transboundary Wildlife
Wildlife Research and Interpretation Branch
Canadian Wildlife Service
Environment Canada
Ottawa, Ontario K1A 0E7

LIFE, DEATH, SPIRIT

Old Woman threw the stone into the water. It sank immediately.

CHAPTER 22

✦ The Origin of Death ✦

(Siksika [Blackfeet]—Montana)

When the world was new, Old Man and Old Woman were walking around.

"Let us decide how things will be," Old Man said.

"That is good," said Old Woman. "How shall we do it?"

"Well," Old Man said, "since it was my idea I think I should have the first say in everything."

"That is good," said Old Woman, "just as long as I have the last say."

So they walked around and looked at things. Then Old Man spoke. "I have been thinking about hunting," he said. "The men will be the hunters. Anytime they want to shoot an animal they will call it and it will come to them."

"I agree men should be the hunters," Old Woman said. "But if the animals come when they are called, life will be too easy for the people. The animals should run away when they see the people. Then it will be hard for the men to kill them. That way people will be smarter and stronger."

"You have the last say," Old Man agreed. Then they walked around some more.

After a while, Old Man spoke again. "I have been thinking about what people will look like," he said. "They will have eyes on one side of their face and their mouth on the other. Their mouths will go straight up and down. They will have ten fingers on each hand."

"I agree that people should have their eyes and their mouth on their faces," Old Woman said. "But their eyes will be at the top of their face and their mouth at the bottom and they will be set across. I agree they should have fingers on their hands, but ten on each hand will make them clumsy. They will have five fingers on each hand."

"You have the last say," Old Man agreed.

Now they were walking by the river.

"Let us decide about life and death," Old Man said. "I will do it this way. I will throw this buffalo chip into the river. If it floats, when people die they will come back to life after four days and then live forever."

Old Man threw the buffalo chip into the water. It bobbed up and floated.

"I agree we should decide it this way," Old Woman said. "But I do not think it should be done with a buffalo chip. I will throw this stone into the water instead. If it floats, the people will die for four days and then come back to life and live forever. If it sinks, the people will not come back to life after they die."

Old Woman threw the stone into the water. It sank immediately.

"That is the way it should be," Old Woman said. "If people lived forever, the Earth would be too crowded. There would not be enough food. This way people will feel sorry for each other. There will be sympathy in the world."

Old Man said nothing.

Some time passed. Old Woman had a child. She and Old Man loved the child very much and they were happy. One day, though, the child became sick and died. Then Old Woman went to Old Man.

"Let us have our say again about death," she said.

But Old Man shook his head. "No," he said, "you had the last say."

Questions of life and death are among the oldest ones of all. There is the circle of old and new, of loss and gain that we are part of throughout life. Even the title of this story presents us with a beginning and ending. "The Origin of Death" turned around is "The End of Life."

Old Woman makes death final so that the Earth would not become too crowded for the amount of food available. She sees that death would bring sympathy and compassion among people. When the Old Woman's child dies at the end of the story, she wants to undo the finality of death. But Old Man stands fast and reminds her that it was her say that made death so. As the Old Woman learns, the finality of death is sometimes very hard to accept.

Discussion

These are good lessons for today as the population of the Earth grows faster and faster. We can see the role death plays in keeping a balance on the Earth. In the first activity, a population explosion is simulated which exceeds the Earth's *carrying capacity*, the population size that the Earth's resources are capable of sustaining. The *nutrient cycle* of birth, growth, death, decomposition and new life from the old is a microcosm of how death works in our lives and in the world.[1] The importance of this lesson is evident in those examples where people have removed the natural sources of death from the animal world. Often, when predators are killed off from a community where there is a rough balance between predator and prey, the prey suffers as well. The prey can become too numerous, only to die of starvation and disease.

In our modern world we fight to keep death from our doorstep. Life expectancies are higher than anytime in history, and we now count human population growth in billions as the Earth gets smaller and smaller. We also try to keep from dying to our old ways, which prevents us from taking new paths and following the kind of knowledge and wisdom that American Indians have to teach us about being part of nature and living as one with the Earth and each other.

It is easy to forget that with every death we suffer, there comes both a loss and a gain. We lose the innocence and dependency of youth and gain the maturity and independence of adulthood. We lose unbridled freedom and experience liberation and deeper meaning through commitment and self-donation. We lose life itself and gain back once more our place in eternity. The second activity in this chapter explores death and loss, life and gain, as natural parts of living.

Questions

1. Why does the Old Woman say it is good for death to be final so that people will not come alive again after they die?

2. When the Old Woman's child dies, she tries to change things so death will not be final. What does the Old Man say? Why do you think he insists that death be final?

3. What would it be like if nobody or nothing ever died? Do you think people would like it that way? What would happen to all of the plants and animals on Earth?

4. What is overpopulation? What happens when too many animals or people try to live where there is not enough food, water or shelter to go around?

5. Where in the world are there too many people today?

6. Is death a good thing? A bad thing? How do you feel about death?

Activities
Enough Life Already!

ACTIVITY: Simulate a population explosion that exceeds the ability of the Earth's resources to support that population.

GOALS: Understand *carrying capacity*—that the resources on the Earth, or in any given habitat, are finite and can only support so many people and other living things.

AGE: Younger Children and Older Children

PROCEDURE: Tell the children they are going to be part of a population explosion. The boundaries of planet Earth's resources will be represented by some of the

Figure 22-1. The natural cycle of life and death is all around us. This tree has begun its journey back to the soil from which its seed first sprouted. Its remains are being broken down by fungi and will eventually nourish the seeds and roots of new plants.

children holding hands in a circle. These children will have signs hanging on them that represent the different parts of Earth's environment (as listed under "Materials"). You will need to use enough children holding hands to form the circle so that it is big enough to enclose the other children as they squeeze into the center, but small enough so that the circle cannot possibly fit everyone else inside. Explain that these resources can support only so much life; that they have a limited *carrying capacity*. If there are too many people, the Earth's limits will be exceeded and there will not be enough resources to go around—life support on the planet will collapse!

Have the "resources" hold hands securely in a circle and slowly keep adding people to the inside. Eventually the circle will fill and strain the arms of the "resources". Keep squeezing children in until the circle finally bursts. Be careful to have people watching on the outside to break the children's falls as the Earth collapses.

MATERIALS: String; cardboard and felt-tipped marking pens to make signs that represent different parts of the environment like trees, the sun, water (river, lake, ocean, rain), soil, crops, wind, animals and more as needed; lots of children.

Death and Life: Lost and Found

ACTIVITY: Create an image of two things that bear great meaning, one of which has been lost and one since gained. Share these images to discuss the things that they represent and the feelings that they evoke.

GOAL: Understand that death and loss, as well as life and gain, are all natural parts of life.

AGE: Younger Children and Older Children

PROCEDURE: Have each child draw a picture of or write a story about something or someone that she/he liked or loved very much but has lost. This could be a friend, parent or pet who moved away or died, a toy that was lost—whatever the child thinks of. Now have each child do the same thing for someone or something she or he cares deeply for, who (or which) has come into her or his life since that loss was experienced.

Sit in a circle and point out that death and life form a circle that is always taking and giving old and new things as we live our lives. Ask the children to share the pictures or stories of their losses and, after a few have shared, ask how the children feel hearing about the losses. You may want to open this sharing time with your own story. Do the same with the pictures and stories of their new-found person or thing, then share feelings again. Wrap up by sharing the fact that loss and death, as well as life and newness, are all part of life.

MATERIALS: Pencils, paper, crayons.

Extending the Experience

• Follow up the activities in this chapter with those in Chapters 15 and 16.

• Visit a cemetery and make gravestone rubbings. The stones' inscriptions sometimes tell something about the people buried there. Record names, ages and relatives off of the gravestones and try to construct a family tree. Ask the children what they think life was like long ago. How old did people live to be 50 years ago, 75 years ago, 100 years ago or more? What is the average life expectancy in North America today? What is this figure for people in less affluent regions of the world and for the poor segments of society in North America? (See the chart listing life expectancy figures that accompanies this activity.)

Now ask the children what has happened to the remains of the people buried in the cemetery. Lead into a study of how modern society prepares human remains for burial. How does this relate to the nutrient cycle of life and death?

Here are some life expectancy figures to use with this activity:

37 ± 3 years = life expectancy in general of Native North American peoples during late prehistoric times.[2]

35 years = life expectancy of Euroamericans (Europeans and their descendants in North America) during the late 1700s.[3]

63 years = life expectancy overall in the world, 1988.[4]

66 years = life expectancy in Mexico, 1988.[5]

75 years = average life expectancy for North Americans (Canada and the United States), 1988.[6]

Here are some additional 1988 life expectancy figures that are among the lowest in the world:[7]

52 years = Africa, overall average

Some African countries with especially low life expectancies, 1988:

Mali = 43 years
Guinea and Somalia = 41 years
Gambia = 36 years
Sierra Leone = 35 years

• Branch out into the study of the scarcity of energy, metals, wood and other natural resources at the local, regional, national and global levels. Study food and water supplies in those regions of the world where food, water and other resources are scarce. Listen to the news and read the newspapers for the current events that will guide you to up-to-date cases to study. Have the children put out a bulletin of their own to increase people's awareness of hunger and other global resource problems. Get them involved with fund-raising to donate money to relief agencies that work to alleviate hunger and other global problems. A good reference for information about world hunger and relief efforts is the periodical, *A Shift in the Wind.* Write or call the following office for copies:

The Hunger Project
1 Madison Avenue
New York, NY 10010
(212) 532-4255

The Hunger Project also offers an "Ending Hunger In-Service" workshop for teachers that is four to six hours long. This workshop helps teachers to incorporate the study of ending hunger into the curriculum.

Notes

1. See Chapter 16 for information and activities about the nutrient cycle, life and death in nature. See Chapter 15, *Friend for All Seasons* and *Season Suite,* for activities about change and the life and death cycle of plants.

2. William A. Haviland and Marjory W. Power, *The Original Vermonters: Native Inhabitants Past and Present* (Hanover, New Hampshire: University Press of New England, 1981), p. 181.

3. Ibid.

4. Population Reference Bureau, *World Population Data Sheet—1988* (Washington, D.C.: Population Reference Bureau, 1988). This publication is updated annually. To obtain a copy, write to: Population Reference Bureau, 777 14th St., N.W., Suite 800, Washington, D.C. 20005, or telephone (202) 639-8040.

5. Ibid.

6. Ibid.

7. Ibid.

UNITY OF EARTH

At first they thought that it was an animal, but as the shape drew closer they saw it was a woman.

CHAPTER 23

The White Buffalo Calf Woman
and the Sacred Pipe
(Lakota [Sioux]—Great Plains)

It was a time when there was little food left in the camp and the people were hungry. Two young men were sent out to scout for game. They went on foot, for this was a time long before the horses, the great Spirit Dogs, were given to the people. The two young men hunted a long time but had no luck. Finally they climbed to the top of a hill and looked to the west.

"What is that?" said one of the young men.

"I cannot tell, but it is coming toward us," said the other.

And so it was. At first they thought that it was an animal, but as the shape drew closer they saw it was a woman. She was dressed in white buffalo skin and carried something in her hands. She walked so lightly that it seemed as if she was not walking at all, but floating with her feet barely touching the Earth.

Then the first young man realized that she must be a Holy Person and his mind filled with good thoughts. But the second young man did not see her that way. He saw her only as a beautiful young woman and his mind filled with bad thoughts. She was now very close and he reached out to grab her. As soon as he did so, though, there was a sound of lightning and the young man was covered by a cloud. When it cleared away there was nothing left of the second young man but a skeleton.

Then the White Buffalo Calf Woman spoke. "Go to your people," she said, holding up the bundle in her hands so that the first young man could see it. "Tell your people that it is a good thing I am bringing. I am bringing a holy thing to your nation, a message from the Buffalo People. Put up a medicine lodge for me and make it ready. I will come there after four days have passed."

The first young man did as he was told. He went back to his people and gave them the message. Then the crier went through the camp and told all the people that something sacred was coming and that all things should be made ready. They built the medicine lodge and made an earth altar which faced the west.

Four days passed and then the people saw something coming toward them. When it came closer, they saw it was the White Buffalo Calf Woman. In her hands she carried the bundle and a bunch of sacred sage. The people welcomed her into the medicine lodge and gave her the seat of honor. Then she unwrapped the bundle to show them what was inside. It was the Sacred Pipe. As she held it out to them she told them what it meant.

"The bowl of the Pipe," she said, "is made of the red stone. It represents the flesh and blood of the Buffalo People and all other Peoples. The wooden stem of the Pipe represents all the trees and plants, all the things green and growing on this Earth. The smoke that passes through the Pipe represents the sacred wind, the breath that carries prayers up to Wakan Tanka, the Creator."

When she finished showing them the Pipe, she told the people how to hold it and how to offer it to Earth and Sky and the Four Sacred Directions. She told them many things to remember.

"The Sacred Pipe," said the White Buffalo Calf Woman, "will show you the Good Red Road. Follow it and it will take you in the right direction. Now," she said, "I am going to leave, but you will see me again."

Then she began to walk toward the setting sun. The people watched her as she went, and they saw her stop and roll once on the Earth. When she stood up she was a black buffalo. Then she went farther and rolled again on the Earth. This time when she stood up she was a brown buffalo. She went farther and rolled a third time and stood up. Now the people saw that she was a red buffalo. Again she walked farther and for a fourth and final time she rolled upon the Earth. This time she became a white buffalo calf and continued to walk until she disappeared over the horizon.

As soon as the White Buffalo Calf Woman was gone, herds of buffalo were seen all around the camp. The people were able to hunt them and they gave thanks with the Sacred Pipe for the blessings they had been given. As long as they followed the Good Red Road of the Sacred Pipe and remembered, as the White Buffalo Calf Woman taught them, that all things were as connected as parts of the Pipe, they lived happily and well.

Our last story brings together the parts of Earth. The White Buffalo Calf Woman gives the people the sacred pipe whose parts represent the animals, the plants and the breath that carry their prayers to the Creator. She shows the people how to offer the pipe to the Earth and Sky and the four sacred directions. These lessons teach the people respect; to live in ways that honor the interconnectedness of all things.

Discussion

The sacred pipe touches the heart of contemporary wisdom in ecology and environmental conservation. We teach of Spaceship Earth to show how we all travel together in a land that is beautiful and giving, yet finite and fragile. Over and over we hear of the "web of life," with threads that bind all together so that not one part of the environment can be altered without affecting the others.

American Indians give us the sacred pipe and the circle. These represent the unity of all things and the balance of the cycles that perpetuate life: cycles of life and death, nutrients, tides, stars, moons and seasons, water, gases, and of giving and receiving. We are reminded how long these circles have turned before we came into the world, both as individuals and as human beings collectively, and of how much power we possess as determiners who will decide whether these circles will still be turning for those whose song is yet to be sung.

The first activity in this chapter demonstrates how old the Earth is, how recently people have appeared on the Earth and what a dramatic impact we have had on the Earth in such a relatively short time. The children then experience the many gifts we receive from the Earth. Finally, the children thank the Earth for what it has given us, and they make a commitment to help the environment by doing something positive for the Earth in their own lives, to complete the circle of giving and receiving.

Questions

1. What are the parts of the White Buffalo Calf Woman's sacred pipe? What do these parts stand for?
2. What does she mean when she tells the people to take the right direction of the Good Red Road?
3. She shows the people how to offer the Pipe to six places: the Sky, Earth and Four Sacred Directions. What are these places? Why do you think these places are important?
4. What does it mean for the people to live, remembering that all things around them are connected like the parts of the Pipe?
5. How can we affect plants, animals, people and the

rest of the Earth by the things that we do? What can we do to take care of the Earth and keep the Earth strong and healthy for those children to come?

Activities
The Time of Our Lives

ACTIVITY: Walk a geologic time line to visualize the great age of the Earth and to discuss the immense impact people have had on the environment in the short time that we have walked the Earth. Discuss our ability to destroy the Earth with nuclear weapons.

GOALS: Visualize how short human history is relative to the Earth's geologic past. Understand what a powerful impact people have had on the Earth during the relatively short time that we have existed, and the potential destructive power of nuclear weapons.

AGE: Younger Children and Older Children

PROCEDURE: Mark along a trail, or in an open area, the distances shown in Figure 23-1 on page 190, which represent major events in the Earth's history. Do this by driving two sticks into the ground with a distance of 94 feet (28.7 meters) between them. Stretch the rope or string between these two sticks and tie it off at both ends, leaving the extra length of rope stretching beyond the stick that represents the present time. Drive the third stick into the ground about a few feet (one meter) beyond the "present time." Stretch the last length of rope up to this third stick and tie it off to represent time reaching into the future. Then tie the cloth strips onto the string or rope at the correct intervals.

As you walk this trail with the children, stop at each point and have children take turns reading the cards that describe the event marked at that spot. You may need to help young children with the reading. When you get near the end and are standing close to the point representing the present time, emphasize the brief amount of time people have been on the scene and yet how great the changes are that we have made in the world. As you stand at the place marking the present time, have the children look down the string pointing toward the future. Ask them what they think we will bring to future generations of people as a result of what we are now doing on the Earth. This point in the walk is a good time to mention that we now have enough physical power, through nuclear weapons, to undo the growth of our planet and all cultures in the span of minutes. And that despite this potential, even the smallest actions we take, when they are all added up, will have enormous impact on what happens to the

Earth and its inhabitants from now on.

The following activity, "Earth Circle of Life," should be conducted in the vicinity of the point marking the present time on this time trail. Explain to the children the connection between the past, our present actions (represented by the "Earth Circle of Life") and the future.

MATERIALS: Copy of Figure 23-1, hammer, string or rope 105 feet (32 meters) long, three 3-foot (.9-meter) sticks, eleven cloth strips for markers, long measuring tape, pictures for teaching aids, numbered index cards containing the information for each station along the time line.

Earth Circle of Life

ACTIVITY: (A) Stand in a circle to represent the Earth and the circles and cycles that are vital to sustain life. State the gifts given by each part of the Earth (sun, water, air, plants, etc.). (B) Thank the Earth for what it gives to us and promise to do something positive as a gift to life on Earth. Hold a ceremonial fire to symbolize the coming together of the gifts in the circle of giving and receiving between the Earth and people.

GOALS: Understand what each part of the Earth gives to people and other living things. Appreciate that people can thank the Earth, and that we can give back to it by taking care of it. Understand what we can do in our daily lives to be good stewards of the Earth.

AGE: Younger Children and Older Children

PROCEDURE: Beforehand: Make up the cards needed for the parts of the Earth for Procedure A, as described under "Materials."

PROCEDURE A: *Gifts from the Earth.* Bring all of the parts of the Earth together into a circle. Each small group of children, or individual child, will have a (some) card(s) with a symbol of a part of the Earth on one side (e.g. plants, water) and a brief statement of what that thing gives to people and other living things on the other side, as described in the "Materials" section. Explain that the circle of children symbolizes the Earth and the circles that keep life going: the nutrient cycle, life and death, and others described in the "Discussion" section of this chapter. Have the "sun" (a child carrying the yellow ball or other sun symbol) enter the center of the circle and tell what it gives to the people and other living things. The ball should be left in the center of the circle.

Now have each part of the Earth come into the center one at a time (that child or those children bearing the cards representing the parts of the Earth). The children will tell what each part of the Earth is and what

The Time of Our Lives
(time line)

The Past

1)   94 feet (28.7 meters)

all measurements are given in distances from Present Time

2)   73 feet (22.3 meters)

Scale: 1 inch = 4 million years, or 1 centimeter = 1.57 million years

1)   4.6 billion years ago:
—solar system is born
—Earth forms

2)   3.5 billion years ago:
—life begins on Earth

3)   405 million years ago:
—first life on land

4)   360 million years ago:
—first insects appear

5)   200 million years ago:
—dinosaurs appear

6)   136 million years ago:
—flowering plants appear

7)   65 million years ago:
—dinosaurs disappear

8)   300,000 years ago:
—oldest known remains of modern human beings (*Homo sapiens)* come from this time

9)   10,000 years ago:
—farming revolution begins
—most recent ice age ends

10) 2,000 years ago:
—birth of Christ
—beginning of modern calendar

11) 100 years ago:
—industrial revolution

3)   8.4 feet (2.6 meters)
4)   7.5 feet (2.3 meters)

5)   4.2 feet (1.3 meters)

6)   2.8 feet (.9 meter)
7)   1.4 feet (.4 meter)

Present Time

8)   .075 inches (.1905 centimeters)
9)   .0025 inches (.00635 centimeters)
10) .0005 inches (.00127 centimeters)
11) .000025 inches (.0000635 centimeters)

Future Time

Figure 23-1

its gifts are to people and other life on Earth. The cards will be put in the center near the sun and left there, and the children will return to the edge of the circle. Each child or group of children representing a part of the Earth will repeat this procedure until all have done so and all of the cards are in the center.

PROCEDURE B: *Gifts to the Earth.* Have each child sit in place in the circle and write down on a piece of paper one or more things she/he promises to do to take care of the Earth—such as to conserve water, use less electricity to save energy, help an endangered species or recycle her/his solid waste instead of throwing it away. Many other ideas are suggested throughout the chapters of this book. Also on this paper, have each child express thanks for the gifts that the Earth gives to her or him by writing something such as a poem, short letter or a short story or by drawing a picture.

Now, one at a time, each child will come into the center of the circle to say what she or he promises to do to take care of the Earth and to share the way that she or he has thanked the Earth on the paper. Then the child will drop the slip of paper into the fire ring and return to the circle. When everyone has done this, burn the index cards and papers containing the gifts both to and from the Earth. Spread the ashes over the ground. These ashes symbolize the children's and Earth's gifts to each other, which complete the circle of life, of giving and receiving.

MATERIALS: (A) yellow ball or other symbol of the sun; index cards representing parts of the Earth, with a picture on one side and a brief description of what that part gives to people and other living things on the other side. In large groups, some of these parts may be represented by several children. Or, in very small groups, each child may hold several index cards representing parts of the Earth. Here are some descriptions to include on these cards:

• sun—I(we) give light, heat and energy to make the plants grow. (The sun should be represented by a large yellow ball.)
• plants—I(we) use the sunlight and make food and oxygen for other living things.
• soil, rocks—I(we) feed the plants to make them grow (rocks, soil).
• air—I(we) give breath of life to the living things.
• water—I(we) quench the thirst and bring life to all plants and animals (rain, clouds, rivers, oceans, lakes, ponds and wetlands).
• seasons—I(we) — spring, summer, fall and winter — bring change each year: heat and cold, wet and dry, sleep and wakefulness, new life and old.
• animals—I(we) feed people and each other, help to

pollinate flowers and sow plant seeds, and bring movement and sounds to the Earth.
• stars and moon—I(we) light the night sky, guide the way and (moon) bring the tides.
• people—I(we) care for the Earth and hold all of the parts of the Earth in our hands.
• stories—I(we) bring the world to life in your imagination.
• life and death—I(we), life, bring living things where there were none before. I(we), death, make room for new life. We, life and death, keep the circle of life and death turning.
• circles—I(we) keep the life on Earth going and keep everything in a good balance.
(B) Fire ring or container for burning papers in, matches, pencils, one piece of paper for each child on which she/he will promise one or more thing(s) she/he will do to care for the Earth and express thanks for the gifts the Earth gives to us, one cardboard backing for each child to support the paper as she or he writes.

Extending the Experience

• Design a puppet show depicting the major periods of geologic history. Use a narrator to describe the changes in life conditions on Earth through time. Create dialogue for the plants, animals and humans as they appear in the course of Earth history.
• Rewrite the story of human history and how we have treated the environment through the present time. Focus on how people could have been better Earth stewards.

• Write a story for the *future* of the relationship between people and Earth. How will we treat the Earth? What will happen as a result? Write two contrasting versions of the story: one telling what will happen if we treat the Earth well, and one telling what will happen if we abuse the Earth.

• Create personal "Circles of Life" for each of the many resources commonly used, such as water, air, metals, glass, paper and food. Draw one circle for each resource on separate, large index cards and label them. Along each circle, describe or draw the resource, what it gives to people to use and how we can give back by wise stewardship practices, including: recycling resources such as paper, glass, metals and motor oil; conserving water, energy and other resources; and supporting environmental conservation legislation by writing letters to Congressional representatives. On the other side of each index card, keep a journal recording personal progress in following through with the plan of "giving back" to the Earth by completing that Circle of Life.

Thanking the Birds:
✦ Native American Upbringing ✦
and the Natural World

by Joseph Bruchac

One day thirty years ago, Swift Eagle, an Apache man, visited some friends on the Onondaga Indian Reservation in central New York. While he was out walking, he heard sounds of boys playing in the bushes.

"There's another one. Shoot it!" said one of the boys.

When he pushed through the brush to see what was happening, he found that they had been shooting small birds with a BB gun. They had already killed a chickadee, a robin and several blackbirds. The boys looked up at him, uncertain what he was going to do or say.

There are several things that a non-Indian bird lover might have done; given a stern lecture on the evil of killing birds; threatened to tell the boys' parents on them for doing something they had been told not to do; or even spanked them. Swift Eagle, however, did something else.

"Ah," he said, "I see you have been hunting. Pick up your game and come with me."

He led the boys to a place where they could make a fire and cook the birds. He made sure they said a thank-you to the spirits of the birds before eating them, and as they ate he told stories. It was important, he said, to be thankful to the birds for the gifts of their songs, their feathers and their bodies as food. The last thing he said to them they never forgot—for it was one of those boys who told me this story many years later: "You know, our Creator gave the gift of life to everything that is alive. Life is a very sacred thing. But our creator knows that we have to eat to stay alive. That is why it is permitted to hunt to feed ourselves and our people. So I understand that you boys must have been very, very hungry to kill those little birds."

I have always liked that story, for it illustrates several things. Although there was a wide range of customs, lifeways and languages—in pre-Columbian times more than four hundred different languages were spoken on the North American continent––many close similarities existed between virtually all of the Native American peoples. Thus ideas held by an Apache from the Southwest fitted into the lives and traditions of Onondagas in the Northeast.

One of these ideas, expressed in Swift Eagle's words to the boys, was the continent-wide belief that mankind depended on the natural world for survival, on the one hand, and had to respect it and remain in right relationship with it on the other. A friend of mine of Cherokee descent, Norman Russell, is a poet and botanist and author of a book entitled *Introduction to Plant Science: A Humanistic and Ecological Approach.* "Ecological balance," he said to me, "is nothing new for the Native American. It was their way of life."

Particularly Indian, too, is Swift Eagle's method of dealing with children who had done something incorrect, or out of balance. The Apache's gentleness calls to mind, for instance, what was said about children by Handsome Lake, the Seneca Iroquois visionary of the early 1800s. His body of teachings, which is called in English "The Good Message," was the basis of a revival of the spirit and strength of the Iroquois at a time when alcohol and loss of land seemed to be leading them toward destruction as a people. He is still regarded by the Iroquois as a prophet whose words were given him by the Creator, and "The Good Message" is still memorized and spoken in their longhouses in New York State and Canada. It covers many subjects and takes several days to recite. One of its sections deals with children. "Talk slowly and kindly to children," Handsome Lake says. "Never punish them unjustly."

His words are echoed by Indians of other nations. "Someone who strikes a child," a Kwakiutl woodcarver from the Pacific Northwest said, "has to be a great coward. Children are so much smaller than adults." "My father never struck me," my own Abenaki grandfather said. "Instead, he would just talk to me." Though it probably did happen from time to time, corporal punishment of children was the exception rather than the rule among American Indian people of the past, and this largely remains true today.

As the anecdote about Swift Eagle shows, children were taught the values of their culture through example and stories. Instead of scolding or lecturing them, Swift Eagle showed the boys how to build a fire and cook the game they had shot, giving the songbirds the same respect he would have given a rabbit or deer. He told stories that pointed out the value of those birds as living beings. The ritual activity of making the fire, thanking the spirits of the birds, hearing the stories and then eating the game they had killed taught the boys more than a hundred stern lectures would have done, and the lesson stayed with them all their lives.

Western education today tends to be didactic. Children are told—in books, lectures, film scripts and movies—*about* things, but rarely do them, experience them. Adults then test the children by having them answer questions about what they have "learned." There is good reason for this method, of course. The world our children must know about is too broad to allow them to learn everything through a hands-on approach. However, as many educators have observed, the result of such a method is too often learning that is more a conditioned reflex than a true understanding. Furthermore, the artificial divisions between fields of study—with natural science alone being divided into botany, zoology, geology, astronomy and hundreds of other areas—can lead to knowledge that is fragmented. It is like what you learn by dissecting a frog: you know the parts, but you cannot put them together to understand the animal. And, in cutting the frog apart, you have killed it.

Native American education, in contrast, has always been experiential and holistic. If you wish to know how to make baskets, you go to a basket maker and watch that person at work. If you are patient and watch long enough, eventually the basket maker may ask you to do something—to hold onto this coil of sweetgrass here, to help shave down that strip of ash. If you return the next day, and the next and the next, then one day you discover that you, too, know how to make a basket.

But making a basket is not all you will have learned. A basket maker knows which trees and other plants can be used and at which times of year they can be prepared. Thus you will have gained a knowledge of botany and of the rhythms of the seasons. When cutting a tree or uprooting a clump of sweetgrass, a basket maker gives thanks to that plant for sacrificing its life to help human beings. Tobacco is left in exchange, as a sacrifice. Thus basketmaking has a religious dimension. Stories also will have been learned—about the materials used in crafting the basket, about the significance of patterns and designs. Among the Pima people, the figures of the whirlwind or the man in the maze appear on baskets, and the stories connected to these figures are part of the basket maker's lore. There may even be songs. A Pomo basket maker once sang her basket song for me as she

worked, explaining that it had to be sung a certain number of times in just such a way. When the song ended, the basket was finished. Making a basket is not something easily learned out of a book. For American Indian basket makers (and, I'm sure, basket makers in other traditional cultures), it involves much more than simple handicraft.

Children, as any sensible teacher knows, respond to *doing* things. Activities are almost always the favorite part of a day for a child. Children also respond to stories. A good story, in fact, is very much like "doing something," for the events of the story come alive and the trials and accomplishments of the central character become the listener's own. The listener is more of a participant than a passive observer, as is the case with a television viewer.

Ray Fadden, an elder whose Mohawk name is Tehanetorens, knows the power of traditional Indian stories and has shown how they can be used in contemporary Western education. When Ray began teaching in the public schools in New York State four decades ago, many Native American people were turning away from their heritage. The old stories that taught people respect for nature were disappearing. Ray learned and retold those stories in his classes, and Indian and non-Indian students responded with enthusiasm. He became known as one of the foremost experts on the history of the Iroquois people, and recorded legends and traditions in beaded belts he made himself, drawing on the forms of the wampum record belts of past centuries. Eventually, without the help of any government or foundation funding, he built the Six Nations Museum in Onchiota, New York, at the northern edge of Adirondack Park.

The museum is built in the shape of a longhouse, its walls lined with display cases, its rafters hung with artifacts from the rich cultural heritage of the Iroquois. Many of the items in the museum, like the stories Ray tells, were given him by Iroquois people. Though he has retired from the public schools now, he keeps the museum open to the public through the warm months of the year, with the help of his artist son Kahionhes. He charges a modest admission fee, except for American Indian people, who are admitted free. It is his way of repaying them for the knowledge they have shared with him over the years.

On any given day during what he calls "the tourist season," he may be found at the museum reading one of his belts. It may be one that tells an old story, such as that of the brave hunters who followed the Great Bear up into the Skyland; or it may be a more recent tale of the damaging of the chain of life, which began with the destruction of the natural habitat and the extermination of natural species. Ray Fadden explains conservation as the Indian saw it, an ecologically sophisticated view of the interrelatedness of all things; a relationship that, as his stories indicate, was part of the Iroquois way for countless generations.

His stories are first and foremost for children. "You youngsters get in here and sit right down. I have a story that you need to hear." But anyone who sits down and listens quickly realizes that his stories are for young and old alike. "These stories are so strong that they were only to be told in the winter time when Mother Earth is asleep. If the stories are told during the summer, then the other creatures might hear you and neglect their work. That's how strong these stories are."

Ray lives what he teaches about responsibility for preserving the great chain of life. He has posted the land around the museum and maintains hundreds of feeding stations for the birds and other animals (feeding stations made necessary because acid rain and spraying for black flies have damaged the food chain in many parts of the Adirondacks so that it is hard for animals to find their natural food). The area serves as a sanctuary for many Adirondack animals, among then the huge black bears, which have a special relationship to Ray. In some of his stories, he tells how to show respect for bears. When the bears meet him in the woods, they lower their heads in greeting, and he does the same. (Though this may be hard to believe, I have seen it happen more than once.)

When Tehanetorens first taught in Indian schools in New York State, the idea of imbuing children with traditional Iroquois values or telling Indian stories was unthought-of or forbidden. Today, thanks to work like his, something closer to the old patterns of Indian teaching may be found within the walls of such institutions as the Onondaga Indian School in Nedrow, New York, in the heart of the Onondaga reservation.

A school run by the Onondaga community with the approval of the State Education Department, OIS uses Iroquois traditions in the school curriculum. The children's Indian heritage is even honored by the school calendar, which provides a vacation for students and staff during the time of the midwinter ceremonials, when the Dancing Stars (the Pleiades) are at the height of the winter sky. At the traditional thanksgiving to the maple trees, when the sap is gathered in March, the school holds a maple festival. The students tap the trees and gather the sap, and a sugarhouse is kept running out back, close to the school kitchen, to boil down the syrup. When it is time to dig wild onions, a group of students and teachers goes out into the fields around the school to harvest.

In the bilingual classroom supervised by Audrey Shenandoah, Onondaga students introduce themselves to a visitor by speaking their clan names and their own Indian names in Onondaga. Storytelling is one of the favorite activities here, for students from preschoolers to the upper grades. The walls and pillars of the basement room are decorated with paintings of clan animals—Wolf, Eel, Snipe, Bear and Deer—and the figures of Iroquois mythology.

Looking at those pictures, one sees that Native American traditions create from birth a sense of closeness to nature that most young people of European ancestry have never experienced. Among the Iroquois and most other Native American people throughout the continent, children are born into a clan. In the case of the Iroquois, you inherit your clan from your mother. Each clan is represented by an animal (among some other native people, natural forces such as Sky or Wind may take the place of a clan animal) and you identify with it. Just as in the majority culture astrology suggests that you are affected by your star sign (an enormously popular idea, no matter how often it is debunked or scoffed at), so too for Native Americans your clan seems to have some effect on your personality. I have often heard it said that members of the Bear Clan tend to be big and strong, that those who are "Wolves" are quick-moving and volatile, the "Turtles" are slow-moving and careful. Certain traditional stories are associated with different clans. A Mohawk story, for example, tells how the Bear Clan was given the secrets of medicine plants by the Creator, and throughout the continent there are "bear doctors." It is believed that bears suffer from many of the same sicknesses people do and that by watching what herbs a bear eats when it is sick you may learn to cure certain human illnesses.

Having a clan animal with which one is intimately connected is only one instance of how American Indian culture and stories create a sense of closeness to nature for native children. The forces of nature are personified in ways that I feel to be essentially nonromantic and usefully realistic. The four winds, for example, are associated with certain animals. The north wind is called the White Bear by some Indian nations. It is strong and cold and brings the snow. The east wind is called the Moose by the people of the northern maritimes. They see it walking out of the water with its great strength and shaking the moisture from its wide antlers. The south wind is the Gentle Fawn. It arrives bringing warmth, new flowers, green grass. The west wind is the Panther, striking with sudden force. Those names accurately describe the characteristics of those winds, are easy to remember, and make those forces, because they are better understood in the shapes of animals, less threatening.

Even the calendar is seen differently through the eyes of American Indian culture and stories. Instead of learning the names of the months of the year through the old rhyme, "Thirty days hath September..." American Indian children are still, through their elders and in schools such as the Onondaga Indian School, taught the thirteen moons. The time around November is for the Abenaki *Mzatonos Kisos*, "The Moon of Freezing," the time around October *Pebonkas Kisos*, "The Moon of Leaves Falling," around May *Kikas Kisos*, "Planting Moon." Each native people has its own names for the moon cycles, names that similarly reflect the condition of the natural world and also remind human beings of the activities they should be undertaking.

I can never think of the year without seeing in my mind the Turtle's back. In the stories of a good many Native American people, from California to Maine, the Earth was built on the back of the Great Turtle, who agreed to support the world. A St. Francis Abenaki elder and teacher of mine, Mdawilasis, once told me the stories connected with the Turtle's back.

"Count the number of squares of the Turtle's back," he said. "You'll see there are always thirteen. That is how many nations there were of our Abenaki people. Turtle remembers when others forget."

Then he went on to show me how the Turtle's back is also a calendar. There are thirteen squares for the thirteen moons. Around those large plates of the back on the Turtle are always twenty-eight smaller plates, for the number of days in every moon. "There are stories in everything around us," he said. "You just have to know how to look in order to see them."

The teachings that have been given to generations of Native American children in stories are ones that need to be understood by all of us. One of my favorite Abenaki stories is that of Gluscabi's game bag. It is a tale I have frequently told to students and used in workshops on storytelling and the Indian view of ecology.

Gluscabi is the transformer hero of stories told by the different Abenaki nations, from the Passamaquoddy of Maine to the St. Francis Abenaki of Vermont. In the story, Gluscabi goes hunting but is not successful. Angered, he seeks out his grandmother and convinces her to make him a magical game bag, which will stretch to fit anything placed within it. He then goes into the woods and puts the bag in the middle of a clearing. Then he begins to weep and moan. The animals come out and ask him what is wrong. "It is too awful," he says. "I cannot tell you." Finally, though, he does. "The world is going to be destroyed," he says. Now the animals become afraid. "What can we do?" they ask. "Ah," says Gluscabi, "You can hide in my game bag." Then all the animals in the world, even the great bears and the moose, climb into the game bag and Gluscabi ties it shut. When he takes them home, his grandmother sees the game bag is very full and asks, "What do you have there, Gluscabi?" "Nothing," he says. But she persists and he opens the game bag so she can see in. There are all the animals in the world looking up at her. "Now," Gluscabi says, "We no longer have to work to hunt. We can just reach into the game bag for food." But his grandmother shakes her head. "Animals cannot live in a game bag," she says. "And what about our children and our children's children? If we have all the animals now, what will they have to eat?" Then Gluscabi sees he was wrong. He goes back to the clearing, opens the game bag, and says, "All you animals, come out. The world was destroyed but I put it back together again." Then the animals come out and return into the forest.

Today, when the secrets of Gluscabi's magical bag, which can catch and destroy all of the animals of the world, are known all too well, it is important for such stories to be told. For ourselves and for our children's children.

⁘ Glossary and Pronunciation Key ⁘

to Native American Words and Names Appearing in This Book

The following rules are used for the phonetic description of how each word is pronounced:
1) A line appears over long vowels. Short vowels are unmarked. For instance, "date" would appear as dāt, while "bat" would appear as bat.
2) An accent mark (´) shows which syllable in each word or name is the one emphasized.
3) Syllables are broken with a hyphen (-).
4) Syllables are spelled out as they are pronounced. For instance, "Cherokee" appears as chair-oh-key.

Where appropriate, the culture from which each word or name comes is given in brackets [ ], followed by the meaning of that word or name, or an explanation of its significance as it appears in the text.

Abenaki (Ab´-er-na-kee or Ab´-eh-na-kee). people living at the sunrise, people of the dawn. A northeastern Algonquian group.

Adlivun (ahd-lih´-vun). [Inuit] land under the sea.

adobe (ah-do´-bey). [Spanish, from Arabic *atobe*] sun dried bricks.

Aja (Ah´-ha). [Inuit] name of Sedna's father in Chapter 11, *Sedna, The Woman Under the Sea.*

Algonquian (Al-gon´-kee-en). large diverse grouping of Indian peoples related by a common linguistic root. Algonquian Indians live in the Atlantic coastal regions from what we now call the Maritime provinces of Canada, to the southeastern United States, west to the central Provinces and down through the central states into Wyoming and Montana.

Ananse (Ah-nan´-se). [Twi, west Africa] spider trickster figure of Africa and West Indies.

Angakok (An-gah-kok). [Inuit] a shaman. *see* shaman.

Anishinabe (Ah-nish-ih-nah´-bey). correct name of people known as Ojibway or Chippewa. Means "The People."

Apache (Ah-patch´-ē). [Zuni Pueblo "ahpachu," meaning "The Enemy"] word used commonly today to refer to the people who call themselves Tineh (tih-ney)—"The People."

Awi Usdi (Ah´-wee Oos´-dee). [Cherokee] little deer.

Begochiddy (Bey´-go-chid-dee). [Navajo] Creator god.

Blackfoot. People of the Northwest plains and mountains who call themselves *siksika* (sik-sih´-ka), which means "black foot," referring to their black, dyed moccasins.

Cañon de Chelly (Kan-yun´ de Shāy). [Spanish] canyon in the Four Corners area of the southwestern United States with many ancient ruins.

Cayuga (Kah´-yu-gah). [Iroquois] one of the six nations of the Iroquois confederacy. "People of the Swampy Land."

Cherokee (Chair-oh-kēy´). corruption of a Lenni Lenape [Delaware] Indian name (Talligewi or Tsa la gi) for this very large southeastern tribe who called themselves "Ani Yunwiya" (Ah-nēe Yūhn-wi-yah)—"real people." One of the so-called (by whites) "Five Civilized Tribes."

Cheyenne (Shy´-ann). corruption of Lakota word "shyela," "those who speak a strange tongue." Refers to a people of the Northern Great Plains. Their own name for themselves is "Dzitsista" (Gee-tsi-stah), meaning "our people."

Chickasaw (Chick´-ah-saw). a people of the southeast, northern Alabama, northern Mississippi—Meaning of name appears to be lost; probably means "the people." One of so-called "Five Civilized Tribes."

Chippewa (Chip´-ah-wah). *see* Anishinabe.

Choctaw (Chock´-taw). a people of Mississippi and Alabama. One of so-called "Five Civilized Tribes."

Clan Mother. elder woman regarded as the head of a particular clan. Among matrilineal people such as the Iroquois, a Clan Mother has great power and is a major political force.

Colville (Kol´-vill). a native people of the Salish language family found in eastern Washington state.

Comanche (Ko-man´-che). corruption of Ute word, *komon´teia,* "one who wants to always fight me." A people of the southern Great Plains.

Creek (Krēek). name used for the people who call themselves "Muskogee" (Mus-ko-gee), probably because white traders found their villages along streams from the Atlantic coast of Georgia through central Alabama. One of the so-called "Five Civilized Tribes."

Crow (Krō). name usually applied to the native people of the Northern Great Plains who call themselves *Absaroke* (Ahb-sah-rokuh), which means "bird people," but could also mean "crow."

Dakota (Dah-kōʹ-tah), "Sioux." one of the seven main "council fires" of the Sioux people. "Dakota" is in the Santee Sioux dialect, means "allies," refers to the Sioux of eastern Plains, Minnesota. Sioux called themselves *Ocheti shakowin* (Oh-che-ti shah-kō-win), "the seven council fires."

Dine (Dih-nēyʹ), "Navajo." means "The People."

Eskimo (Esʹ-kih-mō). Cree word meaning "fish eaters," applied to the people who call themselves *Inuit*— "The People."

Ewe (Ehʹ-vey). a people of West Africa, in the nations of Ghana and Togo.

Gitchee Manitou (Gih-cheeʹ Manʹ-e-too). [Anishinabe] the Great Spirit.

Glooskap (Glooʹ-skap). trickster figure of northern Wabanaki peoples such as the MicMac of Nova Scotia.

Gluscabi (Gloosʹ-kah-bē). trickster hero of southern and midwestern Wabanaki such as the Penobscot of Maine. Gluscabi is "The Man Who Made Himself."

Great League "Iroquois." the alliance of peace forged among the formerly warring five nations of the Iroquois about 500 years or more ago by The Peacemakers and Hiawatha.

Hageota (hah-geyʹ-oh-da). [Iroquois] a storyteller.

Haida (hiʹ-dah). Pacific northwest Indian group of Queen Charlotte Islands, British Columbia, and the southern end of Prince of Wales Island, Alaska. Called Kaigani in Alaska. Known for their beautiful carvings, paintings and totem poles.

Haudenausaunee (Ho-dē-nō-showʹ-nē). [Iroquois] Iroquois name for themselves which means "People of the Longhouse."

Ha-wen-neyu (Hah-wen-neyʹ-oo). [Iroquois] The Creator.

Henh (hẽy *[nasalized]*). [Iroquois] expression used by storyteller to elicit response.

Hero Twins. Hopi, Navajo and Pueblo traditional stories have these two playful and powerful children as heroes who kill monsters.

Hiawatha (Hi-ah-wahʹ-tha). [Iroquois] corruption of Ayontwatha, which means "he who combs," the Mohawk who helped found The Great League.

Hogan (hoʹ-gun). [Navajo] traditional dwelling made of logs and earth used by the Navajo.

Hopi (Hoʹ-pee). contraction of *Hopitu*, "the peaceful ones," the names used for themselves by a town-dwelling native people of northeastern Arizona.

Inuit (Inʹ-you-it), "Eskimo." "the people," name used for themselves by the native peoples of the farthest Arctic regions, Iceland, Arctic Asia. Not regarded by themselves or Indians as American Indian.

Inung (In-ungʹ). Inuit name.

Iroquois (Earʹ-oh-kwah). corruption of an Algonquian word "Ireohkwa," meaning "real snakes." Applied commonly to the Six Nations, the Haudenausaunee.

Ishi (Eeʹ-shee). [Yahi or Yana] name of an early 20th century Native American Californian whose people were all killed and who spent his last years in a museum befriended and studied by Theodora Kroeber. "Ishi" means "man."

Ji-hi-ya (geeʹ-hi-yah). [Iroquois] vocables used in song.

kaamoji (kaa-mōʹ-gee). [Abenaki] an exclamation.

kachina (kah-cheeʹ-nah). [Hopi] sacred dancers or spirit people who bring rain, equated with ancestors and clouds.

Kahionhes (Gah-he-yōn-heys). [Mohawk (Iroquois)] name meaning "Long River."

Kalispel (Kahl-ih-spellʹ). a native people of northern Idaho. Name probably refers to the camas, an edible plant found there.

Kan-ya-ti-yo (Gah-nya-diʹ-yō). [Iroquois (Seneca)] name of a lake, Lake Ontario, meaning "beautiful lake."

Kiowa (Kiʹ-yo-wah). native people of Southern Great Plains (southwest Oklahoma). Name means "principal people."

kiva (kēʹ-vah). [Hopi] a chamber, usually underground, used for ceremonies.

ki yo wah ji neh, yo hey ho hey. [Seneca] vocables used in a canoe song—no translation can be made.

Klickitat (Klickʹ-ih-taht). a people found at the confluence of Klickitat and Columbia Rivers in the northwestern United States. Name means "beyond," referring to the fact they are beyond the Cascade mountains.

Kokopilau (Kō-kō-peeʹ-le). [Hopi] hump-backed flute player kachina.

Koluscap (Koh-lūsʹ-kap). [Wabanaki] variation of Glooscap, Gluscabi.

Kwakiutl (Kwah-kēʹ-yūt-ul). a people of the Pacific northwest, British Columbia coast.

Lakota (Lah-kōʹ-tah). *see* Dakota. "Sioux" native people of northern plains, Nebraska, Dakotas.

longhouse. large traditional dwelling of Iroquois people. Framework of saplings covered with elm bark with central fires and, to each side, compartments for families.

Loo-Wit (Lūʹ-wit). [Nisqually] Indian name for Mount Saint Helens.

Lummi (Lumʹ-mē). a Salish language-speaking people of Pacific northwest.

Maliseet (Mahl-ih-seetʹ). [Abenaki] An Abenaki people of northeastern Canada.

Manabozho (Man-ah-bōʹ-zo). [Algonquian] Algonquian trickster hero, "old man."

Masaw (Mah-saw). [Hopi] spirit of death.

medicine lodge. small lodge used for curing ceremonies among northeastern native peoples.

Medicine Man. general term used to refer to "Indian doctors" who effect cures with a blend of psychiatry and sound herbal remedies, as well as by use of spiritual means. Each Indian nation has its own word for this person.

Mesquakie (Mes-kwah´-kee). a native people of Iowa miscalled "Sac and Fox." "Red Earth People."

MicMac (Mihk´-mack). [Abenaki] a native people of northeastern Canada, Nova Scotia. Name means "our allies."

Mohawk (Mo´-hawk). Abenaki word "maquak," used to refer to the Iroquois who lived in area of Mohawk Valley in New York State and called themselves Ganeagaono (Flint People). Name means "cowards."

Multnomah (Mult-no´-mah). Chinookan language-speaking people of the Pacific northwest in Oregon next to the Columbia River.

Muskogee (Mus-ko´-jee). see Creek.

Naho (nah´-ho). [Iroquois] "I have spoken."

Navajo (Nah´-vah-ho). see Dine.

Nez Perce (Nehz Purse). a native people of northwest, Idaho, western Washington. Name means "pierced nose" in French, misunderstanding of word for themselves "choo-pin-it-pa-loo" (people of the mountain) for "chopunnish" (pierced noses).

Nisqually (Nis-kwal-lee´). Salish language-speaking people of Pacific northwest near Puget Sound.

nudatlogit (nu-daht-lo´-giht). [Abenaki (Penobscot)] "storyteller."

Odzihozo (Oh-jee´-ho-zo). [Western Abenaki] transformer hero. Name means "he gathers himself," or "The Man Who Made Himself."

Ojibway (Oh-jib´-wah). see Anishinabe.

oleohneh (oh-lee-oh´-ney). [Abenaki] "Thank you."

Oneida (Oh-ny´-dah). [Iroquois] one of the six Nations. Their name for themselves was "Onayatakono," "People of the Standing Stone."

Onondaga (On-un-dah´-gah). [Iroquois] the central-most of the 6 Nations, the "fire-keepers." Name for themselves is "Onundagaono," "People on the Hills."

Oot-kwah-tah (Ood-gwah´-dah). [Iroquois] the Pleiades, "The Seven Dancers."

Opis (Oh´-pihs). [Yurok] place name on California coast.

pahos (pah´-hos). [Hopi] prayer feathers.

Pai (Pi). a Yuman people of the Grand Canyon region.

Papago (pah´-pah-go). Southwest Indian group of southern Arizona. Nomadic horticulturalists. Prolific basket weavers. Two-thirds of the roughly 13,500 Papagos today live on reservations located mostly in Pima County, Arizona, with some living in Sonora state, Mexico.

Passamaquoddy (Pass-ah-mah-kwah´-de). people of eastern Maine. Means "at the plenty of pollack place."

Pawnee (Paw-nee´). a people of the northern Great Plains, Nebraska. Name may mean "horn" or "hunters." They call themselves "Chahiksichohiks"—"men of men."

Pennacook (Pen´-ah-kuhk). Abenaki people of New Hampshire. Means "down hill."

Penobscot (Pen-ahb´-skot). Abenaki people of central Maine. Means "the rocky place."

Pimas (Pe´-ma). a native people of southern Arizona who call themselves "O-o-dam," "The People." *Pima* means "no" in the language of the nearby Nevome Indians.

potlatch (pot´-latch). Chinook trade language word from Nootka word, "patshall," meaning "gift." A "giving-away" ceremony practiced among certain Pacific Northwest Salish native peoples.

Pueblo (Pweb´-lo). Spanish for town, refers to a number of "town-dwelling" native peoples along the Rio Grande in New Mexico who live in large adobe buildings like apartment complexes.

Sedna (Sed´-nah). [Inuit] name of woman who becomes the "goddess of the world below the sea," from Chapter 11, *Sedna, The Woman Under the Sea*.

Seminole (Sem´-ih-nol). a branch of the lower Creek peoples who united with the Yuchi, Oconee and other peoples in Florida to form a mixed nation in the 18th Century. The name means "runaways."

Seneca (Sen´-eh-ka). corruption of an Algonquian word "o-sin-in-ka," meaning "People of the Stone." Refers to the westernmost of the six Nations, "Keepers of the Western Door." The Iroquois who called themselves "Nundawaono," "People of the Great Hill."

Sequoia (Seh-kwoy´-yah). [Cherokee] name of the man who codified the Cherokee language into a syllabic script in the early 18th Century.

shaman (shah´-mun). an Asian term referring to one who speaks with ancestral spirits in order to heal or gain power. Often applied by Europeans to Native American medicine men.

Siksika (Seek-see´-ka). see Blackfoot. name of a Northern Plains—Northwest people, "black moccasins."

Sioux (Sū). *see* Dakota. corruption of an Anishinabe word meaning "snakes," which refers to those who call themselves "Dakota" or "Lakota" or "Nakota" or "Ocheti shakowin"—"The Seven Council Fires."

Sipapu (See-pah´-pu). [Hopi] the hole through which the people emerged into this world from the one below it. Every kiva has a sipapu in its floor.

Spirit Dogs. name which some of the Plains Indians gave to the horse when it appeared in the 17th or 18th Century. Their largest domestic animal prior to the horse had been the dog.

Sumig (Suh´-mig). [Yurok] place name on California coast.

Tabaldak (Ta-bal-dak´). [Abenaki] name for the Creator; means "The Owner."

Tehanetorens (Dey´-ha-ne-do-lens). [Mohawk (Iroquois)] name of Ray Fadden, an Iroquois Mohawk teacher; means "He is looking through the pine trees."

tipi (tee´-pee). [Siouan] Plains Indian dwelling, a cone-shaped house of skins over a frame of poles; means "dwelling."

Tlingit (Klin´-kit). a native people of the Pacific northwest.

totem (to´-tum). [Anishinabe] refers to the animal relatives regarded as ancestral to the lineage. Each person is born into a particular totem, inherited in many native cultures through the mother. Totem animals include Bear, Eagle, Deer, Turtle, Wolf, Snipe, Eel and many others. Common throughout North America.

tribe. from Latin "tribus." a term used by both Indians and non-Indians to refer to groups of Native Americans sharing common linguistic and cultural heritage. Some Native American people prefer to not speak of "tribe" but of *nation.*

Tsimshian (Shim´-she-un). a native people of the Pacific Northwest.

Tunka-shila (Toon-kah´-she-lah). [Lakota (Siouan)] refers to the Creator or one of the Great Benevolent Forces of nature, "Grandfather Rock."

Tuscarora (Tus-ka-ro´-rah). the sixth Nation of the Iroquois who were driven by the Europeans from the lands in North Carolina in the early 18th Century and resettled in western New York State; means "shirt-wearers."

Wabanaki Confederacy (Wa´-bah-na-kee). a loose union of a number of Abenaki nations circa 1750-1850 possibly echoing an earlier confederacy and influenced by the Iroquois League. Allied MicMac, Maliseet, Passamaquoddy, Penobscot and Abenaki. Wampum belts were introduced and triannual meetings held at Caughnawaga, Quebec.

Wakan Tanka (Wah-kon´ Ton´-kah). [Lakota (Siouan)] The Creator. "The Great Mystery."

Wampanoag (wom-pah-no´-ag). means "dawn people," sometimes called Pokanoket. Algonquian linguistic group of eastern woodlands which once occupied what are now Bristol County, Rhode Island and Bristol County, Massachusetts. Many were killed, along with the Narragansetts, by the colonists in "King Philip's War" in 1675 (King Philip was the colonists' name for Chief Metacomet, son of Massasoit). At least 500 Wampanoag live today on Martha's Vineyard, Nantucket and other places in the region.

Wigwam (wig´-wom). [Abenaki] probably from "wet-uom," which means "dwelling." Dome-shaped house made from bent sticks covered with bark, common to northeastern Abenaki peoples.

Wuchowsen (Woo-kow´-sun). [Abenaki] the wind bird.

Yahi. *see* Yana.

Yana or Yahi (Yah´-nah or Yah´-hee). *see* Ishi. A native people of California.

Yokuts (yo´-kuts). means "person." Among the most numerous of the California—West Coast Indian groups. Probably once numbered 10,000, including a population in the San Joaquin Valley; today they number less than 600.

Yurok (Yu´-rok). a native people of Northern California.

Zuni (Zoo´-ñee). [ñ = nasalized] a Pueblo people of New Mexico who call themselves "Ashiwi," "the flesh." Name comes from a Keresan Pueblo word whose meaning is unknown.

❖ Art and Photographic Credits ❖

All illustrations associated with the stories are by John Kahionhes Fadden.

Illustrations used in the "Activities" for each story are by Carol Wood, unless otherwise noted.

Fig. 2-1. Peter Hope, courtesy Vermont Institute of Natural Science

Fig. 2-2. Photo by Michael J. Caduto

Fig. 2-3. Cecil B. Hoisington, courtesy Vermont Institute of Natural Science

Fig. 2-4. Peter Hope, courtesy Vermont Institute of Natural Science

Fig. 3-1. Cecil B. Hoisington, courtesy Vermont Institute of Natural Science

Fig. 5-1. Peter Hope, courtesy Vermont Institute of Natural Science

Fig. 7-1. Peter Hope, courtesy Vermont Institute of Natural Science

Fig. 8-1. Adapted with permission from "Geosynclines, Mountains and Continent Building," by R.S. Dietz, *Scientific American*, 1972, (March) vol. 226, No. 3, pp. 30–38.

Fig. 10-1. Photo by Michael J. Caduto

Fig. 10-2. Peter Hope, courtesy Vermont Institute of Natural Science

Fig. 11-2. Cecil B. Hoisington, courtesy Vermont Institute of Natural Science

Fig. 12-1. Adapted with permission from Anthony Smith, *The Seasons*. London: Weidenfeld and Nicolson Publishing Co. Ltd., 1970, p. 54.

Fig. 12-2. Photo by Michael J. Caduto

Fig. 13-1. Courtesy National Aeronautics and Space Administration (NASA).

Fig. 13-3. Adapted from Smith 1970, p. 54.

Fig. 14-1. Courtesy Mount Wilson and Las Campanas Observatories, Carnegie Institution of Washington

Fig. 15-1. Adapted from Smith 1970, p. 14

Fig. 15-2. Peter Hope, courtesy Vermont Institute of Natural Science

Fig. 16-1. Peter Hope, courtesy Vermont Institute of Natural Science

Fig. 16-2. Ann Day Heinzerling

Fig. 16-3. Peter Stettenheim

Fig. 17-2. Lewis E. Carpenter, courtesy Audubon Society of Rhode Island

Fig. 18-2. Cecil B. Hoisington, courtesy Vermont Institute of Natural Science

Fig. 18-3. Adapted with permission from Friedrich G. Barth, and Allen & Unwin Ltd., London: *Insects and Flowers: The Biology of a Partnership*. Princeton, New Jersey,: Princeton University Press, 1985, p. 15.

Fig. 19-1. Don Blades, courtesy Vermont Institute of Natural Science.

Fig. 20-1. Peter Hope, courtesy Vermont Institute of Natural Science

Fig. 20-2. Courtesy Michael J. Caduto

Fig. 21-1. Courtesy Vermont Institute of Natural Science

Fig. 21-2. Michael Warren

Fig. 21-3. Adapted with permission from Verne E. Davison, *Attracting Birds: From the Great Plains to the Atlantic*. New York: Harper and Row Publishers, Inc. © 1966 Verne E. Davison.

Fig. 22-1. Ann Day Heinzerling

Fig. 23-2. Courtesy Joseph Bruchac

Map adapted from *Indians of North America*, courtesy National Geographic Society. Cartography by Stacy Morin, Country Roads, Inc., Orrington, Maine.© Copyright 1989, Michael J. Caduto.

⋄ Index of Activities ⋄
Arranged by Subject

Using this Index

1) Look in the "Index of Activities by Subject" beginning on this page and find the subject(s) you want to teach. The broad subject headings are listed prior to the detailed subject index.
2) Find the number(s) given in the index to the right of the subject you want to teach. These numbers identify the appropriate activities in the chronological list found on this page. The page number for each activity is given to the right of that activity in this list. The suggested learning level for each activity is given to the left of the page number: (Y) indicates younger children (roughly ages 5 to 8 years), and (O) indicates older children (roughly ages 9-12 years).

LIST OF ACTIVITIES AND THIER LOCATION IN THE TEXT
The numbers given to the left of the name of each activity correspond with the numbers listed in this index. Page numbers are listed to the right of each activity.

INDEX OF ACTIVITIES BY SUBJECT
Broad Subject Headings in this Index

DETAILED SUBJECT INDEX

✤ Notes ✤

✤ Notes ✤

✚ Notes ✚

✤ Notes ✤

Keepers of the Earth

began the tradition . . .

Extraordinary teaching tools
to introduce children to the natural world

By Michael J. Caduto and Joseph Bruchac